To my family, who have always loved me the most.
To the Posse, the bravest bunch of women on the planet.

Contents

Introduction

Why Write Poetry? I've Got Dishes and Laundry to Do!

For each of us as women, there is a deep place within,
where hidden and growing our true spirit rises. . . .
Within these deep places, each one holds an incredible reserve of
    creativity and power,
of unexamined and unrecorded emotion and feeling.

—Audre Lorde

First things first: If you are thinking of making your fortune or getting on the *Oprah Winfrey Show,* writing poetry is not the way to do it. And even if you think poetry can get you there, this book won't. If you think this is your ticket to fame or notoriety of any kind, your time is better spent on those dishes and laundry. Seriously: How many *published* poets do you personally know? Poets who have actually been *paid?* When was the last time *you* paid money for poetry? It's not gonna happen. Getting published is not the purpose of this book.

With that said, I firmly believe you should write poetry, even though you will probably win the lottery before being published, and have a better chance of being the next American Idol than of being the next Maya Angelou. (Note: Emily Dickinson was dead before she was famous.) To mold words into a poem is a grand and glorious accomplishment, even if no one in the world sees it but you. A poem is a little book that has just the right amount of words, a perfect little world, a grasp on something that can't be touched. It is beautiful and necessary. The reason that you should write poetry is simply because you want a more creative, expressive, and authentic life. And, quite honestly, the world could use more poetry, even if it's just your own little world.

But how many of us have time to ponder how fall leaves change from yellow to gold? Or the utter perfection of a newborn baby's pinky toe? When was the last time you actually saw a rainbow? When was the last time that your leaving-wet-towels-on-the-floor husband inspired flowery words? Thankfully you don't have to have time for endless contemplation, nor does your life have to be perfect. Poetry is life as it is happening, not as you think it should be. You don't need anything other than what is really happening to you. Right now. However, what you do need is an unwavering belief that you are worth spending a little time on, time completely to yourself, time that you can spend however you damn well please, even on something as frivolous as writing poetry.

You don't have to write perfect poetry, and that is not even remotely the goal here. The idea is to use poetry as a means, a means to a more creative, expressive, and authentic life. There is no right or wrong, good or bad. You can do it. Don't let any of the "forms" you saw in the table of contents intimidate you.

Why all the form? you might be wondering. *Why can't I just write free verse?* We can all slap together words and phrases and call it a poem, and you know what? Then it is. But, my thought is if you're going to do something and devote some time to it, you might as well challenge yourself and attempt something more. In addition, poetry, and writing in form in particular, can be extremely beneficial to your life; writing poetry can help you let go of what's holding you down, experience gratitude for the life you were given, explore what this person of you is all about, and let you fly as high as your creative spirit will take you. And there are certain forms that work better for different purposes.

For example, a sonnet can help you work through an emotional situation; a haiku can help you appreciate and stay in the present moment; and the villanelle can help you find your own voice.

I will introduce you to some of the different forms and types of poetry. I will explain some things you need to know, like iambic pentameter, but you will not hear some of the more complicated terms of poetry, like *synecdoche* or *hemistich* (it's just not necessary for our purposes here). Writing in form is a way to focus your mind and deal with something specific. It takes discipline and as a result is incredibly rewarding.

For each kind of poetry, you will find examples from "famous" women poets (just because you haven't heard of her doesn't mean she's not famous) as well as—and this is the best part!—examples from women just like you: women with careers; women who work at home; young women; not-so-young women; married, single, and everything in between women; women with kids; women expecting new kids; and women with no kids. The incredible women you will meet in this book make up the original Poet

Posse. We are simply a group of women who decided to try to live more poetic lives. And we are accepting new members, so I hope you'll consider joining.

You don't have to have a degree in English or even have ever liked English class. The Poet Posse is comprised of everyday women with everyday lives. We are far from perfect. I, for one, spend too much money on black sweaters and jeans I can't wear to work; I have been known to bribe my toddler with candy and videos just to get ten minutes of quiet; I sometimes spend more time in my workday reading msn.com gossip or updating my zappos.com wish list than actual work; and I more often than not love my husband and hate his guts all in the same hour. I have never published a poem in my life, but have used poetry to help me get through postpartum depression, separation after ten years of marriage, and just to help me laugh at and gain perspective on how mundane and insane my life can be all in the same day. It has also come in handy as I negotiate how to fit spirituality in my life at the different stages of my life.

I drink more Diet Coke than water; I don't wash my makeup off every night; and I have not kept a New Year's resolution to date. I don't pretend to be a great poet, or even a good one. I came across a term while researching for this book: *poetaster*. It means "a bad or trashy poet, especially one with literary pretensions which exceed his or her talents."

Fine, that's me. I've been called worse. Someone else's negative labels only make you more interesting at cocktail parties. I have spent an entire Saturday afternoon looking for the perfect pair of black pants and I have spent an entire Saturday afternoon trying to perfect a sestina. I didn't accomplish either goal, but I certainly know which pursuit I felt better about.

What will you get from all this? My hope is once you read about poetry, read some examples from published poets, and then see what women just like you write, you'll want to try it on your own. Once you start to write poetry, you will begin to recognize the possibility for poetry all around you. If you can see the poetic in everyday life, then you can experience your life in a more poetic way, encouraging perspective, appreciation, and a sense of humor. There is beauty in children, even when they are messy and argumentative. There is beauty in your home, even when it is full of dirty laundry. There is beauty in your surroundings, even when you are stuck in smog-filled traffic. There is beauty in you, even if you haven't had a pedicure in six months. All you need to do is practice writing it, and then it'll be easier for you to see, live, and know.

There are a couple of ways to read this book. Of course, one option is to blast your way through it, intending the entire time to write a super great poem and then, when finished, toss it aside, never to attempt or think about it again. And that's okay. I get credit for one copy sold anyway. However, I would suggest another method. Rather than read it all at one time, slow down: try to read a chapter every two weeks, or even a chapter a month, while going about your everyday life: work, family, traffic, reading best-seller fiction before bedtime. Let that chapter sink in and see if you can recognize the possibilities all around you, in your life as you are living it. Give yourself enough time with each chapter, with each kind of poetry, to let your life speak to you through that particular kind of poem.

When reading the sestina chapter, you might suddenly remember a detail of your wedding that you had long forgotten; when reading about the haiku, you may actually notice the wildflowers blooming in the weeds on the side of the highway; when reading the ode chapter you might decide to write about that fabulous blue dress you saw while shopping instead of adding yet another meaningless charge to your already over-loaded credit card; and when reading the list chapter you might indeed find inspiration in the contents of your children's over-flowing toy box.

You don't even have to start at chapter one and faithfully fol-low the chapters in their correct order. The numerical order is completely arbitrary. If you want to remember someone you've just lost, start with the sestina. If you feel like you've gotten lost somehow in the journey from the laundry room to the bedroom, then start with the villanelle. If you've fallen in love for what seems like the first time, by all means, start with chapter one and the sonnet.

Then, when finished, you can refer back to chapters in the event that something happens that makes you seek out a partic-ular form or type of poetry. Whatever your approach, the intent of this book is to give you another tool to help guide you through some tough times, give you a creative outlet, as well as a way to not only *see* but *live* your life in a more poetic way.

There is such a wealth of beautiful, inspirational poetry out there; I have tried to mention recognizable names in poetry, as well as more modern examples of each type. At the time I was writ-ing this, I was able to find all of these poems online. As the Internet turns over faster than denim at the Gap, I did not include actual websites (also as they may be showing these poems ille-gally), but you should be able to find these examples easily either online or at the library. If you still have a *Norton Anthology of Whatever* lying around from your college days, you may be in luck for many of them. Please try to make the effort to find at least one of these poems per chapter.

You will also find "soundtracks" for each chapter. Music and poetry are almost indistinguishable to me. Poetry is not separate from life; it is life at its most expressive and interacts with everything around you—just like music. Maybe poetry is music without instruments and music is poetry with instruments. I often find music an inspiration to write. So, I included some songs that I hope will get you in the mood to write, or at the very least, tickle your creative funny bone or jog a stubborn memory. Some of these lists are from me, some are from the Posse. If nothing else, you have the beginnings of some new lists for your iPod.

Both for the examples of poetry and for the soundtracks, I've included only poetry written by women and only songs sung by women. I believe that women's voices are shared, that when you honestly pursue something, you can find another woman out there who can empathize. I think women's voices are talented and beautiful and are often overlooked for a more booming voice. Just allow me my rah-rah, yeah women moment, here. It's my book.

Each chapter is centered around a theme, a way to let that particular kind of poetry enhance your life. Maybe this means working through something difficult, appreciating something you take for granted, or simply finding something creative and productive to do with some hard-won free time. These ideas are simply guidelines, ways that the Posse and I have found these types of poetry helpful in our lives. This book means whatever you want it to mean, and you will get out of it exactly what you put into it.

Warning: Once this poet within is released, I can't be held responsible for the consequences. It is entirely possible that you will experience more joy, have better sex, develop a keener sense of humor, or even (gasp!) keep a damn fine journal. At the very least, knowing the difference between a sestina and a villanelle, you'll impress your high school English teacher at your next high school reunion.

Poetry is the most demanding of the written arts. I am here to help you get started writing. But mastering the art is up to you. You probably never will, but you'll enjoy the pursuit. And if you acquire the perfect pair of black pants along the way, please let me know where you got them.

The Posse Lineup

Beverly: mid-fifties, married, full-time job teaching at the college level, three grown children (Missouri/Pennsylvania)

Jen: early thirties, married, full-time job as project manager for a government agency, one toddler, one baby (Virginia/California)

Kellie: mid-thirties, single/never married, full-time job working for the government, no kids (Virginia)

Erin: mid-thirties, married, full-time job as regional sales manager for a mortgage company, one toddler, a baby on the way (Kansas)

Nikki: mid-twenties, single/engaged, college student/full-time job in hospital administration, one toddler, one baby (Kansas)

Angie: early thirties, divorced/remarried, part-time job writing educational grants/stay-at-home mom, three kids (Oklahoma)

Thelma: early eighties, single/divorced, two grown children (Texas)

Debbie: early thirties, married, stay-at-home mom, one toddler, a baby on the way (Texas)

Lori: late thirties, married, part-time job as an attorney, three kids (Missouri)

Katie: late fifties, single/divorced, VP of finance and customer service for a worldwide medical transcription company, no kids (Kansas)

Kris: mid thirties, married, full-time job as editor/also a published author, one toddler, a baby on the way (Kansas)

Heather: late thirties, married, stay-at-home mom, two toddlers (Missouri)

Michelle: mid-forties, married, full-time job in publishing, one toddler (Missouri)

Shannon: early thirties, single/never married, part-time job as waitperson in an upscale restaurant, no kids (Oregon)

Wendy: (author) mid-thirties, married, full-time job as editor, one toddler (Kansas)

The Poet Posse wasn't another group to add to an already full social schedule. It wasn't a scribbled-in commitment on the first Monday of every month. We mainly corresponded, laughed, and shared via email. Scattered all over the country, most of us have never even met face to face.

We took this poetic journey over the course of a year. In that year, two had babies, and two became pregnant. Between us, we have fourteen children and three of us have no children. We went through separations, divorces, and new relationships. The youngest of us was twenty-four when we began, the oldest eighty-something. We know infertility, addiction, obsession, disappointment, and loss. We came to know joy, strength, humor, acceptance, and freedom. We learned things about ourselves we didn't know when we started and learned enough about the world we stumble through every day to make our steps a little more deliberate. We are funny, irreverent, honest, and not ever complete. Consider joining the Posse; you'll fit right in.

Chapter One

Work through an Emotional Situation: The Sonnet

To have in general but little feeling, seems to be the only security against feeling too much on any particular occasion.

—George Eliot

Even before I knew exactly what the sonnet was, I was attempting sonnets. My first, quite embarrassing attempts at poetry resembled the sonnet, if accidentally. I can first remember writing poetry in high school. When I was in the ninth grade, I had a huge crush on this boy Scott. Well, I don't know if you could officially call it a crush, as the sentiments were reciprocated—the problem being that these feelings were also reciprocated with his *girlfriend*. We snuck around for a while because in a small town (I lived in Poteau, Oklahoma, population 8,103 at the time) that seems the appropriate thing to do, instead of coming out with it all. It also fueled my typical teenage desire for as much unnecessary drama as possible.

I wrote poem after poem about my terrible—though clearly self-inflicted—situation. There was a lot of rhyming—love/dove/above, joy/coy/boy, lies/goodbyes/cries. They varied between sounding like jump-rope chants and love-song-nursery-rhymes, and every one was *very* intense. None is as world-weary as a fifteen year-old-girl in love.

I somehow convinced my friend Mindy, who had a class with Scott, to "accidentally" drop one of my more passionate masterpieces and "encourage" him to pick it up. I honestly thought that he would then know the *depth* of my feelings, which, of course, would render him powerless to my poetic charms, compelling him to immediately leave his blonde, beautiful, actually very nice girlfriend. This foolproof plan worked up until the knowing the "depth of my feelings" part, unless of course that depth was wildly humorous, as I think he might still be laughing.

Though my cheeks still turn a little pink at the thought of my early attempts, I learned at an early age how poetry can help you express your emotions—and also that sometimes poetry really should be for the sole benefit of the writer.

Eventually, I left Scott and Poteau and moved with my family to Germany—one dramatic ending I never saw coming. It was in the American high school there where my English teacher Ms. Larson introduced me to the sonnet. Ms. Larson was the cool teacher. She was petite and gorgeous; she wore her teased, impeccably styled hair in a banana clip (she may be the only woman in the world who could still get away with wearing one) and dressed in matching vest/pants combos. She taught her class precariously perched on the corner of her desk, one foot swinging to some inaudible beat. I still can't hear a John Donne poem without hearing the tap-tap-tap of a heel on a wooden desk.

It was here where I was informed—quiet rudely in my opinion—that poetry didn't have to rhyme (the nerve! the challenge! impossible!), but that if it did, it was one of the most challenging things to write. I learned exactly what a sonnet was, the mechanics of writing one. I also learned the pleasure of composing them. I gravitated not only toward the rhyming but also the emotional intensity. I now had a name for my poetry and rules to follow (which, like a child, has always made me feel safe and productive)—so I felt like a *real* poet, a legitimate *writer* for sure.

Moving from a small, Oklahoma town—with a strong, small-town twang that is *not* the same as a sweet, Southern drawl—to literally a foreign country—where, never mind the accents, I couldn't understand the language itself and truly didn't understand boys wearing eyeliner—was hard and lonely. I wrote a lot of poetry, and since I now knew what a sonnet technically was, I wrote quite often in that form. I simply loved the way rhymes sound (always have and still do) and certainly had a lot of adolescent emotional intensity to work with. Though perhaps I could not have verbalized it at the time, I reaped the benefits of using poetry and poetic form in particular to sort out my feelings. I retreated to the sonnet again and again to pour out my emotions.

Fast-forward nearly fifteen years. I'm ten-years married with one beautiful son, living in a perfectly acceptable house (even though the garage door opener never worked properly) with flowers in the front yard and plenty of tall, old trees in the back. I was thriving in a perfectly respectable career, where I was well respected and got to leave before five every evening (even if said *career* didn't really pay any better than a plain old *job*). Other than the garage door opener snafu and what I perceived as normal in-my-thirties-just-had-a-baby-and-might-want-more-out-of-my-life stuff (power, prestige, Manolos—but not at the expense of being the perfect mom, mind you), life was good—or so I thought. Ten years into our marriage, my husband and I decided to separate.

It seemed like a sudden shock then, but of course now I see it was a culmination of about four years of growing apart. This was an intensely difficult time. It defies description—it's one of those things that sounds like a cliché when trying to define in words. Perhaps most difficult, it wasn't because my husband was this bad guy doing all these terrible things to me, or vice versa. We didn't fight (out loud) or hate each other and there wasn't that one thing that I could point to and say with some amount of res-olution, *Ah, yes, it was when that happened.*

It was kind of like . . . well, I will drive my car for a thou-sand miles or more with the MAINT REQD light on. It's a terrible habit, totally laziness on my part, but to me it doesn't mean some-thing's *broken*, it just means it's time for an oil change, or maybe the 40,000 mile tune-up. It's nothing serious, because that is when the CHECK ENGINE light comes on. It can wait. So I drive around, confident that I will still get where I need to go, even though I *should* get the situation checked out. Eventually it all breaks down. It was kind of like that.

I felt that everything I believed in—family, loyalty, commit-ment, soul-mate defining love—was suddenly deemed illusionary. I didn't know what to do—how really to carry on. I found myself questioning everything. I mean, if my marriage could fall apart, what else had I been so wrong about? I had to rethink and rede-termine everything I thought was important—essentially redefine myself. (What if I was no longer a wife? A part of a couple? A traditional family? What was I?)

So, instinctively, I turned once again to poetry. I was older, supposedly more mature, but my feelings were no less intense than at fifteen—indeed, I had much more at stake, my family—so I turned once again to the same form that helped me through a shattered heart and intense loneliness before. I sought the sonnet out like an old, forgotten, comfortable friend.

The act of writing sonnets (or even just attempting to write) was calming, gave me a huge sense of release—and left me feeling empowered. Once I wrote down my feelings, I owned them, and then I felt I owned a little more of me. After some years of marriage and having a baby, sometimes that feeling is hard to come by. Writing sonnets forced me to narrow down what I wanted to say, forcing me to figure out how I felt (even if only at that moment). At first, I was absorbed by my hurt, so my sonnets were full of blame and self-pity, but the more I wrote, the more I was able to concentrate on all the other things I felt, how I was *affected*, without all the external blame—and eventually without the internal blame.

I still write them, and sonnet-by-sonnet, I know I can make it through whatever emotional chaos gets thrown my way.

But Why a Sonnet?

One feels very *poetic* even contemplating writing a sonnet. It has such a high society, getting all decked out in an amazing, slinky black dress and barely-there strappy shoes *just to make an appearance* feel. I mean, this isn't a *limerick;* it's a *sonnet.* I'm not even sure you can drink cheap beer when writing a sonnet.

A tried and true, emotional poetic form, the sonnet truly can help you work through an emotionally difficult situation. As the poet Sonia Sanchez once said, "When I have had to deal with formal pain, I have written in the sonnet." I honestly don't write very many "light" sonnets. It is a form that has consistently helped me with some heavy, emotional stuff. To sit down and write these poems was to breathe me in and breathe me out in words. The process gave me validity, expression, and direction and kept resentment, sadness, guilt, and regret from living inside my heart and devouring it from the inside out.

The writer Lee Smith once said, "I never know what I think until I read what I've written. And I refuse to lead an unexamined life. No matter how painful it is, I intend to know what's going on. The writing itself is a source of strength for me, a way to make it through the night." Though ideal for working through affairs of the heart—which certainly doesn't have to be the result of a heartbreak, but could be due to infertility, loss of or estrangement from a loved one, or simply wondering where the heck love is—the sonnet is helpful in any situation where you have so many conflicting emotions, it's hard to tell exactly what you're feeling.

I felt like I was in a kind of a daylong darkness for a while, with all that was going on in my personal life. It felt like my entire way of living life was out of whack (too bad there aren't chiropractors for life), but writing poetry, writing my sonnets, felt like the occasional firefly lighting up a hot, dark summer night. It gave me a small light to follow, a small gleam of direction.

This is the one of those fireflies. I wrote it right after my husband and I separated. Before this, I probably hadn't written a traditional sonnet in about ten years. Yet, my old familiar comfort was waiting for me in the blank pages of my journal like a cup of hot chocolate in my mom's kitchen.

I wanted to feel some degree of *okayness* with it all, but I was so all over the place. Was I glad? sad? And, oh, how there was anger! Then, the very next second, a sense of cloudless freedom emerged, quickly followed by engulfing sadness that gave way to hope while I wasn't looking. I needed structure, a definite path to follow to figure at least some of it out. We were in counseling— believe me, there was counseling—but I wanted something that was just for *me,* not necessarily for *us.* So I turned to the sonnet. It was productive to sort through my messy emotions, experiencing (or reexperiencing) them, and then put form to what I could. It felt like I was at least attempting to clean things up a little.

"I NO LONGER HEAR YOU"

I no longer hear the sound of footsteps
Walking hopefully down the church aisle
I hear whispers, slamming doors, going steps,
Empty room spaces—but no denial.

I no longer hear sweet college laughter
Beer jokes and pot giggles, innocent fun—
Just mocking happily ever after
In liquor-soaked "you were always the one."

I no longer hear the rustle of sheets
As you roll over to say I love you
I no longer hear myself in defeat
Say over and over I forgive you

I no longer hear you, but there is sound:
Hope, regret, though silent to most, abound.

—Wendy

It's been a while, but I can read it and remember exactly how I felt at that moment. I may not *want* to remember, but I know I *need* to. In the midst of all the sadness, disappointment, and confusion, I indeed did have hope. That feeling was buried deep beneath a lot of other things, and writing helped me bring it more to the surface. Seriously, I didn't figure out my marriage in just this one poem, but I tell you, writing this sonnet and more than a few others, I figured out a little more about me, which in the end is what helped the most.

It was challenging for the Posse to write honestly and straight, knowing that it could end up in a book for every browser at Barnes & Noble to read. Poetry done right can be painfully personal, and while the process is enormously beneficial to the writer, often the words are not meant for the eyes of others. So, this next poem is anonymous at the writer's request. It was the only way it could be written, as well as the only way it can be shared.

She was experiencing martial issues specific to her and turned to the sonnet to try to figure some of it out. "This poem is about my relationship with my husband," she says. "It's about doing what I have to do to keep things on an even keel between us. I feel like he is always waiting for me to do something 'wrong,' so I find myself not able to do or say exactly what I feel because it's not worth the fight it causes."

She and her husband have been married for almost ten years and have been through most of the "biggies" in marriage: separation, babies, and the breakdown of trust. She's tried every way she knows to be a good "wife," yet feels it's never enough. She had a range of emotions she didn't know what to do with. She loves her husband, believes in their marriage, yet also yearns to be understood, appreciated, and at the very least listened to. She began to feel that no matter how loud—or silent—the fights got, she was no longer heard.

She had never written poetry prior to this, but sat down with her feelings—after a morning of trying unsuccessfully to express them to her husband—to write a poem. The five feelings that best describe her state of mind when beginning the poem were, "down, disheartened, mentally-tired, disappointed, and resigned." But, even if her husband wouldn't hear her, she was determined to speak.

I WAKE UP DETACHED

I wake up detached again in our bed
I can feel him breathing, while loneliness
Opens my day—"it's all in your head"
He says again as I gasp for breath.

My sacrifices I keep to myself
As the days fade together into blue
I say nothing lest I threaten his wealth
Of self-control, goodness, and wisdom true.

Day dissolves into night—invisibly
I do what must be done. There are no words
I slip silently through the hours so he
Does not feel me and we continue blurred.

Daily I prepare for what's coming next
For a world who sees just what it expects.

—Anonymous

"I liked writing in sonnet form because to truly convey what I was feeling, I had to be very selective and make sure the word I chose reflected the exact emotion I was feeling," she says. "Honestly I was a bit surprised by what I ended up with. I knew I was feeling down about my relationship, but writing this helped me put a finger on what exactly my issues with him were."

Though writing a sonnet did not suddenly make her marriage perfect, it did give her quite a lot. The five feelings that best described her state of mind after writing the sonnet were, "powerful, angry, courageous, proud, and optimistic." "Before this exercise," she says, "I would not have thought it could be as helpful as it really was. It helped me see that I have some control over what is going on and I felt a bit more powerful after writing it."

The next example comes from Kellie. She used the sonnet to deal with a personal struggle. Single, never married, and in her mid-thirties, Kellie's questioning the paths she's chosen because, honestly, she never thought she'd still be *single, never married, in her mid-thirties*. As she says, "When I was younger I envisioned being in love, getting married, having a family . . . just so much more by this time in my life." It's tough for Kellie—indeed anyone—to reconcile the life she wants to the life she currently has.

Kellie maintains a strong daily faith in God and strives to be grateful for all that she does have, especially the simple pleasures in life (even turning shopping for a dictionary into a four-hour event). She is not blind to her blessings. Yet, meeting a special someone, falling in love, and having a family is something Kellie *wants* and always envisioned as being a part of her life. "As I get older," she says, "I think more about a family, and I tend to focus on it—or the lack thereof. I have to accept the fact I may never fall in love or have a family and that is sometimes hard."

"I know I can get a job and earn a pay check, but do I have what it takes to be a wife and/or mother?" Kellie wonders. It is a difficult thing to accept because deep down, she truly believes she's got what it takes. The fact that these things have not yet happened to her has left her in emotional chaos, caught somewhere between striving to appreciate what she has, yet yearning for things she doesn't have. As she says, "I sometimes feel as if I took a wrong turn in life somewhere. 'Seasons Change' expresses the turmoil that exists within my spirit at times."

SEASONS CHANGE

As the seasons change, my spirit is tried,
Same ole empty promises, lies, and good-byes,
I stand alone each day questioning why I've been denied,
While the rain covers my tears, my heart slowly dies.

As the seasons change, my mind labors without rest,
Contemplating and agonizing over my past mistakes,
I struggle with love unconditional, but I do my very best,
Time is unforgiving, recording every step he or she takes.

As the seasons change, my dreams succumb to doubt,
While wrestling with reason and grasping at hope,
I'm realizing the gifts are those we journey with and not without,
Making it easier to forgive, laugh, and cope.

So, as the seasons change presenting opportunities anew,
Keep despair at bay, move forward, and take pride in what you do.
—Kellie

Kellie says, "I wrote this poem for myself as a self help, in a way. I wanted to go beneath the surface of my emotions and really explore my true feelings." She had some conflicting feelings to work through—gratitude countered by yearning, discontent countered by hope. Writing a sonnet helped. She says, "I learned that I have to deal with disappointment and keep on living because my situation is nowhere near 'bad.' Lonely and bad are two different things in my mind."

But why the sonnet? you may be asking. *Can't I just write a poem with no form?* Of course you can, but the process of writing a sonnet is conducive to working through something emotional. You only have fourteen lines, which must follow a certain pattern, to say what you want to say. You must go through your emotions and all their layers to get to what is really important, to what really fits in those fourteen lines. You have to think and rethink to find your words that fit. This intensive process helps you work through each individual emotion, instead of being overwhelmed by it all. It's kind of like laundry: looking at a huge pile of dirty clothes can discourage anyone. But when you sort through it, separating colors and temperatures, it seems more manageable.

Writing a sonnet also forces you to write down what you are feeling in a thoughtful, introspective way. When you have your sonnet as proof, as a tangible reflection of how you are coping, you own the situation a little more. I like to say, "When you write it, you own it." Writing a sonnet is both cathartic and empowering. It's not easy. But working through something big never is.

So What Exactly Makes a Sonnet?

Unless you were busy flirting that day, junior year, in high school English, I'm sure you have at least a vague idea of what a sonnet is—you may have even had to write one. It may sound a little intimidating, conjuring up visions of women in seventeenth-century corsets and names like Elizabeth Barrett Browning, but think of it as the Prada of poetry, the brand name, a classic, one that never goes out of style.

There are three basic things you need to know: Sonnets are comprised of fourteen lines, employ rhyme and meter, and are usually focused on one subject. There are two different kinds of sonnets: the Italian sonnet and the English sonnet. I write in the English form, so that is the form I will show you. Do look up the Italian form if you're interested; each is equally acceptable. The English version is simply my preference.

The fourteen lines in the English sonnet are often divided into three stanzas of four lines each (the four line stanza is called a *quatrain*) with the last two lines set as a *couplet*.

The traditional rhyme is: ABAB CDCD EFEF GG.

The sonnet employs the meter of iambic pentameter, which sounds fancy and difficult, but honestly isn't. It simply means each line of the poem consists of five iambic feet, or ten total syllables, and five stresses. The stresses kind of stress me out too, but it really isn't that tough. The stress pattern for iambic is unstressed, stressed, five times, equaling the ten syllables.

As if all the iambic pentameter stuff weren't enough, the sonnet gets bit more involved: Different parts of the sonnet are intended for different action. (Kind of like a department store: each of the departments functions differently—i.e. women's clothes, accessories, fine jewelry, shoes—but it is still one big store.)

The subject is revealed in the first quatrain, is further explained (complicated or developed, whatever the intent) in the second quatrain, and then further still in the third quatrain. Just one of the challenges is the third quatrain: It is difficult to continually develop the subject, so the third quatrain tends to be the most challenging.

There is also something called a *turn*. This is a noticeable shift in how the speaker views her subject. Often very slight, this is simply a change in direction or mood. Around the beginning of the thirteenth line—or at the end of your final quatrain or beginning of the couplet—is where the turn should take place.

It sounds like a lot to consider, but think of putting the different parts of the sonnet together like putting together a really great outfit. It takes all the parts—you can't skip the shoe or accessory department—to make a great, smart outfit.

Tips on Form
- Though traditional sonnets follow a specific rhyme scheme, writers often mix it up; in fact, modern sonnets are often written with no rhyme at all.
- There are three main elements to the sonnet: rhyme/meter, single subject, and length of fourteen lines. Try to stick with at least two of the three if you truly aim to write a sonnet.
- Want to hear some great, inventive rhyming? Listen to Missy Elliot or Lil Kim. Listen to the radio. You'd be surprised how much music rhymes, whether hip-hop, country, rock, or alternative.
- Ask a kid for rhymes; I guarantee he/she will give you things you never thought of. My son gave me squish/wish, Darth Vader/hater, and bug/hug.
- You will probably find a thesaurus helpful. Whether the old-fashioned kind or the one on your computer, it might help you find a different word when the one you want has too many/too few syllables or doesn't fit the rhyme scheme.

Posse Pointer

Katie—her sonnet is featured in a later chapter—had a secret for sticking to the form without losing her train of thought and without misplacing what she intended to say. She used her background in accounting. She used Excel and marked off the syllables and lines in a spreadsheet. "Then," she says, "I did not get worried or tied up with the form, I could just 'see' where I was and what I needed."

For Further Reading

It's easy to find examples of the sonnet—it's a form that's been around for more than eight hundred years. On the Internet, you can find examples from Ella Wheeler Wilcox or Elizabeth Barrett Browning. In fact, Browning's *Sonnets from the Portuguese* is one of the most widely known collections of love lyrics in English and generally considered to be her best work.

The first woman to win the Pulitzer Prize for Poetry, Edna St. Vincent Millay is considered to be a modern master of the sonnet. Try to find "I Will Put Chaos into Fourteen Lines"—she is writing about a sonnet, in sonnet form, and it is just perfectly beautiful—or "Love Is Not All."

One of the best ways to get better at writing sonnets is to read more sonnets. You'll get a better feel for how the form works, and you might even find inspiration for a sonnet of your own. Here are some modern sonnets to check out:

- "The Sonnet-Ballad" by Gwendolyn Brooks
- "Sonnet" by Alice Dunbar-Nelson

- "After the Bomb Tests I" by Jane Cooper
- "The New Colossus" by Emma Lazarus is a sonnet, the very same poem that can be read on the base of the Statue of Liberty.

Maybe we can't claim the brilliance of Millay or Browning, but we all go through the ups and downs of love and life and we *are* capable of creating poetry from those experiences.

What Should I Write About?

The sonnet is historically an emotional form of poetry. Maybe it's because it offers a conclusion, the couplet at the end, a chance to figure it all out. It's almost as if we could, through one fourteen-line poem, make sense of our feelings and gain at least a small amount of clarity, the rest of our world might make a little more sense too. Whether writing about love, loss, loneliness, or change, the sonnet can help you work through something emotional you are grappling with.

Here is another sonnet I wrote. It was almost as beneficial as seeing a therapist to sit down with all my unruly emotions poking me from the inside, and attempt to soothe the fray through writing. (I actually found writing poetry, the sonnet in particular, to be an invaluable companion to counseling, whether it was marriage or one-on-one.) This next sonnet is based on an entry I came across when I found an old college journal while cleaning out my lingerie drawer.

I have kept journals in varying degrees of intensity since high school. Sometimes I write faithfully and intently every day for six months, only to discard the journal and not pick up another until months later. Page after page of this new journal is filled with notes, ideas, pictures, receipts, and half-finished poetry, not a single, complete sentence—until it too is eventually tossed aside, as another mood overtakes me. As a result, I have about ten or so half-full journals lying around. I never lose them, but I never remember where I put them either.

When I found this journal—hardback like a real, serious *book*, a blue and silver swirly pattern, like a peacock's tail, on its cover and handmade ivory, unlined pages sticking out jagged from the side—hidden under a pile of wool socks and winter tights, I almost ignored it. I recognized it immediately and knew it undoubtedly contained some intensely embarrassing writing. But, I couldn't resist the temptation to look, like when you see a wreck on the side of the highway or when some distinguished man in a business suit has left his fly open. So I looked. (I always look.)

I thumbed through and stumbled across an entry that left me laughing out-loud. It was a very woe-is-me college moment: bad dates, boys not calling, I deserve so much more etc., etc., etc.—I had a serious bang-cutting incident as well—basically your all-around terrible time that is a miracle you ever *survived*. How *indignant*, *appalled*, and *critical* I was with the world, that terrible world that was plaguing me with such *difficulties*. It was one of those rare, great moments where I could practically *feel* the seriousness and intensity yet also completely appreciate how utterly ridiculous it was now, having lived through it and beyond. The best part was that I identified with that feeling *exactly* as I stood there, fifteen years removed from the time it was written.

I was alone and cleaning out my lingerie drawer on a Friday night because I was separated from my husband. There was not a small amount of self-pity and finger-swagging at the world going on. It appeared my dramatic flair and propensity for feeling sorry for myself was as strong in my thirties as it was in my twenties. It's easy to blame the world, because then we can't possibly be held responsible for doing anything about it. I sat down and wrote this sonnet, inspired by the entry I found and how those feelings still exist.

"FUCK YOU, LOVE"

Fuck you, Love, arriving here unannounced
like a guest too early for a party—
hair's a wreck, makeup's a mess so I pounce
not seeing what I wanted wrapped subtly

Fuck you, Love, leaving here so abruptly
like when everyone decides to drink red
leaving the white. Unexpected by me,
it's a nasty red hangover in bed.

Fuck you, Love, slowly and painfully dying
It's exhausting having to push you out—
the last guest to leave. the host spent, sighing
Just go! better to wonder than to doubt.

Why can't you ever fucking get it right?
Because in the end, I'm the one who's fucked.

—Wendy

I had a nice, cathartic laugh at myself, both because of the drama of the entry and also because it seemed I hadn't evolved much since college. The journal entry was also funny to me because it's actually not how I feel most of the time at all and is so *not* me—I think I've used the "F" word in public all of five times, and I can remember exactly what I was wearing each time. But that is one of the great things about poetry: you can adopt a voice that is not your own at all. (I actually do believe in love, Jack-and-Diane love, Hubbell-and-Katie love, Ross-and-Rachel love, Gatsby-and-Daisy love. My parents got married when they were sixteen and are *still married* for gosh sakes.) With poetry, you can scream at the top of your lungs, have a wonderfully obvious, obnoxious, childish outburst, and no one has to know about it but you; you can turn the page and move on.

You'll notice the last line isn't rhymed. It's a departure, but it felt right for this particular poem. (Of course, in the end, it's always *us* who doesn't get it right.) This poem was just plain fun to write. It helped put a lot of my way-over-the-top drama in perspective. It helped me see that what I *feel* isn't always an accurate take on what is really happening. It helped me see that low feelings pass and feeling sorry for myself doesn't help them go any quicker—but that writing about them just might.

Sonnet Soundtrack

Though sonnets can be written about any subject, it is essentially an emotional form. Sonnets were traditionally about love—"How do I love thee? Let me count the ways" is from Elizabeth Barrett Browning and is one of the most widely quoted lines from a poem of all time—and the sonnet is the form that I've always retreated to when I really feel like a pint of Ben & Jerry's but don't want the calories. In that tradition, here are my top five love songs:

1. "Nothing Compares 2 U" Sinead O'Connor
2. "Here with Me" Dido
3. "Hold on to Me" Courtney Love
4. "Miss You" Lisa Loeb
5. "Get Here" by Oleta Adams

A lot of bad things happen—separation, divorce, death, life-altering accidents, sickness—and it has to be part of the yin and yang of life that poetry exists to help us with these things. We can take even some of the *really* bad things and make something beautiful and meaningful from them. Even more, we can learn about and experience our true selves in the process.

Angie chose to deal with one of the most difficult happenings of her life: the death of her mother-in-law, someone she loved dearly and respected greatly. Angie chose to write about Darlene's death because Angie didn't have an opportunity to explore or let out the range of feelings that go along with the death of a family member at the time of her death. Darlene's death was unexpected, rapid, and particularly difficult to watch. Darlene was a ten-year cancer survivor, but when diagnosed a second time, she died just four months later.

Angie recalls, "Her death was so disturbing. She literally starved to death as her organs failed one by one. Her skin was grey and thin and she could barely speak the last month." Angie remembers when they finally decided on hospice care: "I feel like that was the day she let go and began to die. It took almost six weeks after that for her body to deteriorate to the fifty pounds of skin and bones that was left, and in the last days she was unable to speak and unrecognizable." After Darlene's death, there was a kind of self-imposed silence, as the family didn't talk about it, express their feelings, or show them to each other. "When Darlene died," Angie says, "no one really talked about anything. Not sadness, pain, missing her, or grief. *Nothing.* So I pretty much respected that and kept it to myself also."

Understandable, certainly. Everyone deals with loss and death in their own way. Angie wrote this sonnet, not only as a tribute to Darlene, but also to give herself an outlet for all the things she was feeling that she was keeping to herself out of respect for the rest of the family.

SONNET FOR MY MOTHER-IN-LAW

Silent demon crawling in like black night
Sneaking up on the weak and unaware
Ravaging the bodies as they will fight
Never prejudice in the pain you share

Growing and spreading like a wildfire
A flame the healers unable to cure
Consuming the body with unbearable desire
to draw the last breath and join Heaven's choir

The shell of your victim laying in wait
For the wrath afflicted in nearing end
Withered to nothing; awaiting her fate
The Light stretches out His merciful hand

The body is ash but her soul is free
The pain no more . . . just an angel to be

—Angie

Darlene's death was painful on so many levels—as Angie says, "The pain of watching a loved one die, the true pain she felt in the process, the pain left by her not being here." Writing this poem helped Angie let some of her pain go so it didn't weigh her down as much anymore. "Just to get it on paper," as Angie said, helped. Once it's "out there," it's not so much "in here."

Angie showed the poem to her husband and he appreciated that Angie loved his mother so much that she carried much of Darlene's pain around with her. He's okay with Angie letting it go too. They still don't talk about Darlene and her death much, but this one poem helped Angie verbalize and recognize her own grief, sadness, loss, and anger.

Though the poem deals with the many levels of pain when a loved one dies such a horrible, disturbing death, the last two lines are uplifting, almost an acceptance that Darlene's death was a blessing, an end to her physical pain. Angie figured out that in addition to her feelings of sadness, grief, and anger there was also relief that her suffering was over and thankfulness that God had taken her. When Angie got to the end of the poem, she acknowledged that Darlene was in a much better place. As a result, Angie was able to get to a much better place herself.

"Sonnet For My Mother-in-Law" is an excellent example of not only how to sort through conflicting emotions and give yourself an outlet for them, but also a good example of how poetry can give you something beautiful out of something terribly sad and ugly.

Spanning the gamut of emotional subjects, Jen chose to write her sonnet about the exact opposite subject of Angie's poem—birth, specifically, the impending birth of her second baby boy. Jen had a lot of conflicting emotions regarding being pregnant, the expansion of her family, and the realities of being a mother to two. In her words, "I'm freaking over having another baby. What was I *thinking*?!"

"What am I going to do?" she wondered, "I don't like babies. They cry too much. I am not looking forward to the next three months or so—I might go crazy. And there's Ricky [her three year old], who really is good most of the time, but who continually has to challenge my authority and go against everything I say. He just plain doesn't like to listen to me. What if this one is the same way?" It's an overwhelming, confusing time to be sure, because, of course, she's also excited about giving Ricky a brother, loving another life, and experiencing the joys of motherhood.

She wonders when the baby moves if he'll be good at soccer like his dad; she remembers Ricky as a baby and wonders if he will have the same unusual, beautiful grey eyes; she takes her pre-natal vitamin (even though it makes her nauseous) and hopes that he'll be strong, tall, and smart. It's not lost on her that she has the privilege of watching another child smile his first honest smile, take his first brave steps, and tell his first funny joke.

Ah, and then there's life as it is. She laments, "My house is a pit. I cannot remember when I cleaned the bathrooms last, but it's at least been two weeks. Yuck. It makes me tired just thinking about it." Two kids certainly don't make the house any cleaner. Jen tackled her own mess of emotions in her sonnet.

SECOND BABY

An expanding belly that grows and grows.
Mood swings that come in the day and the night.
How long since I wore my cute, skinny clothes.
Nine months of waiting, no end in my sight.

Round angel face and a cute little nose.
Our family of three is complete with four.
Five tiny fingers and five tiny toes.
Our house is filled with love forever more.
Family must leave, we are on our own.
Eternal sleepless nights and endless days.
Will we be able to survive alone?
We stumble around in a sleepless daze.

Can I love him as much as my first son?
Is there room in my heart for everyone?

—Jen

I wouldn't get you this far and tell you that after completing this sonnet, Jen is now happy and content as can be, filled with an unrivaled love and intense, unbridled anticipation for her new bundle of joy—or that her bathrooms are suddenly sparkling clean. She's still pretty scattered. Yet, she did get a handle on some stuff and writing this sonnet did help. Taking an unusually quiet, drizzly afternoon to write helped Jen sort through her conflicting emotions by forcing her to write them down and figure out exactly what she wanted to say. Jen says, "I tried to organize my thoughts into how I was feeling about it all—and what I could finally admit on paper is that I'm scared to death."

Sure, it's still scary, but as Jen admits, "It's okay to acknowledge that it's going to be hard and stressful because it's also going to be loving and fulfilling." It's normal to feel doubt as a mother when you can't imagine loving another child like you do your first. It's normal to freak out over dirty bathrooms. And it's normal to be scared to death over something as life-changing and life-affirming as bringing another child into the world. As Jen realized, naming the fear that you feel takes away a bit of its punch.

I have used the sonnet to deal with a difficult separation; another Posse member her own marital problems; Kellie used it to deal with feelings of discontent; Angie painful loss; and Jen feelings of panic and confusion. The sonnet is suited for any situation that is filled—indeed overflowing—with emotion.

Even if your sonnet is not technically perfect (clearly I consider myself *above* iambic pentameter), I guarantee you'll learn something about how you're feeling if you give the sonnet a serious try and if you are genuinely open to learning something about yourself—but beware: sometimes what you learn may be startling. You have to be open to hearing your truth, which can be difficult to hear. Then, perhaps even more challenging, you have to be willing to act upon that truth.

Tips on Subject

- It is often overwhelming and defeating to try to write about big, general things. Try to concentrate on one particular instance, or one particular feeling. Instead of a breakup in general, perhaps just the moment you knew it was definitely over, and even better, the moment when you were *glad*.
- Honesty is key. You have to say what you really feel and not what you think you should feel or what you think others want to hear. This is why you are writing for *you*—and not the *you* others see in the office, around campus, or even at Bunco the first Tuesday night of every month—the private you. You won't get anything out of it if you don't choose to be honest. Your feelings—whatever they are—are valid and important for no other reason than that they are *yours*.

- Making another person the focus of your sonnet is perfectly acceptable. But remember this is for you, not for that other person. It is a lot easier to write about other people than yourself. It's kind of like compliments: often it's easier to give them than to receive them.
- It's okay if it's a process. Write about what comes easily first and work yourself up to the big stuff.

Give It a Try

Writing a sonnet affords you the opportunity to work through something difficult and emotional that you might be dealing with: separation, divorce, a breakup, infertility, loneliness, depression, anxiety of pregnancy (whether with your first or third), death, or the uncertainty of the future. Of course, in most situations there is not just one emotion, but a dozen or so conflicting, confusing sensations. You may need to write more than one sonnet to really get at the root of something.

There are many different ways to go about getting started writing your sonnet. What works best for me is to just sit down and do it, just get it all out in sonnet form, no matter how imperfect or far from what I intended the first draft is. I sometimes start with notes or an outline of what I want to accomplish, but most of the time I simply sit down and plow through until I come up with *something*. Then I go through *much* editing and rewriting. The rewrites are often more about opening up myself a little more each time to honesty than about the words so much. Sometimes I find inspiration in an actual event (like the physical act of someone leaving), sometimes I find inspiration in my journal (like my old college entry), or sometimes I find inspiration in some feeling I have in the pit of my stomach, a gnawing that just won't go away until pen is set to paper.

If you want to practice before you tackle something emotionally big, or want to get the hang of the form first, here are some ideas to get you started on a love sonnet:

1. Go ahead. Write a ridiculously frivolous love poem like you are fifteen again and in love for the first time. It feels good to remember that feeling. And it may help you remember what it was like if you've been with your significant other for a number of years. It's fun to be silly in love.

2. If you want to write about love in more realistic terms, think of a significant other. Try to write down a few sentences of what you think of him/her first thing in the morning. Then write down a few thoughts in the middle of the afternoon. Then write down a few thoughts right before bed. You may have the makings for your three quatrains right there. Writing it down first, not in sonnet form, may help you be more yourself, without forcing it too much. (This person doesn't have to be a lover in the traditional sense. He/she can be your child, best friend, mother, sister, etc.)

3. Write a sonnet to Love. What would you say? What would you ask for?

These are fun exercises to try to help you get you started writing sonnets, even for a little practice. But if you really want to reap the benefits of a sonnet, tackle something big. If there is a situation you are grappling with, not sure how you really feel about it all, give yourself permission to make how and what you feel a priority. Try not to give in to frustration. Sonnets take practice, like any hobby where you actually create something (knitting, sewing, scrapbooking, painting, composing, etc.), but the end result is worth it.

A Poetic Pause: Lightning Sonnets

Bunko is so *common*. Monopoly? please, no one really wants to be The Donald. Pictionary? what is this 1982? Here is a hip game that is perfect for a girl's night in. It's called Lightning Sonnets. The end result is a sonnet composed by the group.

First, assign a moderator for each round. Then, put a selection of subjects written on plain paper, folded so they can't be seen, in a bowl. The subjects can be anything. If you are gathering with a group of girlfriends, you can choose things like shopping, men, friendship, bubble bath, vibrators, whatever. For a baby shower, you could consider babies, diapers, sleeplessness, joy, etc. Place the subjects in a bowl and have someone choose. This is the title and focus for the sonnet.

Now, each person will take a turn writing a line, trying as much as possible to stick with the pattern of ten syllables in iambic pentameter. There should be a place where the person can be alone with a bit of quiet—maybe a bathroom—and the really tricky part is that the writer only gets three minutes. (Hence the name *Lightning* Sonnets.) The moderator is in charge of the timer.

The moderator is also in charge of keeping the lines organized, in the right order, but the next player can only see the preceding line and the word that he/she must rhyme with. The player with the beginning of a stanza has to start from scratch.

Ideally, you'd have fifteen players (one moderator, then fourteen for the fourteen lines), but it's fine if some players have to take double turns or sit out a round. When the last person is finished, the moderator puts the lines together in the order they were written and gives a formal reading. As formal as he or she can muster, since usually the poem makes no sense whatsoever and is hysterical.

Chapter Two

Make Sense of Memory: The Sestina

The work of art, which I do not make, none other will ever make it.

—Simone Weil

The sestina represents my first adult relationship with poetry. I wrote my first sestina—my first grown-up poem—in college during a summer course. Writing a sestina was an assignment, and I sat up all night writing that poem—I had, of course, procrastinated until the night before. When I was finished, I knew, *knew* for some reason, that it was a darn good piece of work. And it wasn't sleep-deprived delirium; even to this day, if my professor were to walk up to me on the street and say otherwise, I wouldn't believe him for a minute because I felt good about it, I was so *proud* of it. I walked out of that class certain in my ability as a writer, certain in my skill as a poet, certain in my worth. It was a fleeting feeling, but for that moment, I felt like I could do anything. It might sound like pure hyperbole, but that's the way I remember it, and it's one of my favorite memories.

One of my not-so favorite memories? I had the same professor the next semester for a Shakespeare class. After the final, said professor followed me out of the class and stopped me in the deserted, hallowed hallway of Gittinger Hall. There is a particular feeling in the air—the palpable presence of a thousand deep breaths—that is unrepeatable no matter where life takes you, of a university hallway right after an early-morning final. All I wanted to do was get the heck out of there, perform my ceremonious throwing away of my notes, breathe in the fresh air of freedom, and celebrate the end of the horror that was that class with a before-noon drink with my friends. But all that had to wait. The professor called after me, and when I turned slowly around (I had to finish my eye roll before facing him), he told me how he had enjoyed having me in his class (which is dubious, considering I hardly ever showed up) and then said, and I quote because I will never forget this, "I will miss seeing you most days, especially your striking red fingernails." *Creepy.* And way more creepy than my fascination with acrylic red nails.

Thankfully, neither Creepy Professor Guy nor the hell that was Shakespeare class kept me from writing poetry. Like many an English major before me, there was a time when I was determined to be not only a writer, but A Poet. This was shortly after getting my first "real job" in publishing. When I learned of an opportunity with a publishing company through the most random way possible—I ran into my brother's eighth-grade girlfriend at Talbots and she worked for the company—I considered it fate and jumped on it. Well, not long after starting as Production Editor in the Calendar Department, my idealism quickly turned to realism, and

I learned that this particular job was not going to catapult me to literary stardom. Though I dreamt up many a plot and character lineup while sitting by the copier, it was not exactly what I had in mind.

However, I couldn't shake the urge. Since I had always enjoyed poetry, I researched poetry contests on the Internet. I relied on my previous success with the sestina and entered four or five of these contests with a collection of sestinas divided into two parts: Summer Sestinas and Winter Sestinas. Sometimes covering a walk through a snowy, deserted plaza and sometimes a recollection of a favorite childhood summer memory, it was a random sampling of the people, places, and events of my life. I was truly convinced that I would win one of these contests and that would be the beginning of my Poetic Life. Six months, one portfolio of twenty sestinas, and $50 later, I was still unknown. *Shocking.* I resigned myself to being a Normal Person and not A Poet.

A few years ago, I found those sestinas, tucked away in a brown leather satchel my husband gave me our last Christmas in college. The shoulder strap broke, so I stashed it broken, though still full of life, in the back of my closet, where it stayed, unopened and undiscovered, for years. Sure, I had seen it here and there as I rummaged for my black suede knee-high boots (not *leather* or *ankle* boots) or for the white cotton shirt with the three-quarters sleeves (not *sleeveless, long-sleeved,* or *short-sleeved),* but it never occurred to me until one empty Saturday night that found me cleaning out my closet. I saw it as I had a million times before, but this time I decided to see what was there.

I caught my breath and felt oddly emotional when I saw my sestinas. This collection of poetry instantly transported me to a much sweeter, much more innocent time. It was a time when I still had grand, poetic dreams and more importantly, still thought them possible. I was twenty-four at the time they were written and I almost felt twenty-four again, sitting Indian-style on the floor, surrounded by old shoes, clothes, and meaningless bills. I had forgotten how I lovingly photocopied each poem, afraid for a moment that when the copier sucked it in, it wouldn't give it back. I had forgotten how much of me was in that collection of twenty-three pages perfectly spaced and stapled professionally in the upper left hand corner.

As proud as I was and still am of that collection, I felt a heavy sense of disappointment in myself. Sure, I still write poetry; I often find poems unexpectedly in my purse or sometimes even crammed into pockets (for some reason I am always particularly charmed by the ones I find in my heaviest winter coat), but I stashed away my dream along with those old poems. I felt a sense of loss for that delicious certainty I had as a young woman. Where was she?

It occurred to me that suddenly full Saturday night that winning a poetry contest or receiving any type of validation or recognition for writing poetry is not necessary to live a Poetic Life. My closet is still a mess and quite often I can never find what I want, but I found a lot that night. I found A Poet.

Why a Sestina?

I'm not sure I would have ever heard of a sestina if not for that one summer class, but I've been under its spell ever since. I've spent many a rainy Sunday afternoon or totally broke Saturday night writing sestinas. The sestina appeals to me because it has a specific form that is easy to follow but allows quite a bit of leeway within those boundaries. It's kind of like what a good parent tries to do. Or kind of like deciding what to wear to a black-tie event: you can be creative but there are conventions.

Perhaps because I started writing sestinas at a time when I became so much of what I was eventually going to be—my college years—when so many strong memories are made, because I come across an old sestina every once in a while that reminds me so specifically of someone I had forgotten that I Google them the first chance I get, and maybe also because I still have those moments when I think *this might be significant; five or ten years from now I want to remember this* so I aim for the sestina, this is a form that is tied to memory for me. It's a way to appreciate, record, and remember the people, places, and events of my life. As the writer Elizabeth Bowen once said, "The charm, one might say the genius, of memory is that it is choosy, chancy, and temperamental: It rejects the edifying cathedral and indelibly photographs the small boy outside, chewing a hunk of melon in the dust."

It is incredibly important to record our memories. Memory, after all, is our lives: either we are remembering or making memories. The bad memories we use as lessons, as hard-won experience. The good memories we use to puff ourselves up or to help us through a tough patch. When writing about the significant people, places, and events of our lives, we acknowledge our memories—all of them—and accept them as a part of who we are. Writing about the important, people, places, and events of your life, helps define your life—*in your own words.*

Memory invariably leaves holes; it would be impossible to remember *everything*. If you get in the practice of recording the people, places, and events in your life, your life will be fuller, with fewer holes. You may have long forgotten that boy chewing a hunk of melon in the dust, but the sestina offers you a chance to remember.

To make sense of memory goes beyond the mere recording of it. To make sense of memory means that we claim what is ours, what has been ours, and what we hope will always be ours. You own where you've been and take responsibility for where you're going. The people in your life (even the not-so-nice ones) are there for a purpose that you decide. The places in your life show you where you've been so you can be sure of where you're going. The important events help you remember the things that have made you who you are. The sestina offers you a chance to not only remember your life but also to make sense of it along the way.

I am typically a pretty optimistic person. Though poetry has helped me get through some really tough times, it has also helped me celebrate the truly great times—especially the ones I didn't know were great until they were gone. I like to write about my good times. It makes it impossible to truly forget, and I get to remember it from my perspective. And even better, I like to read things when it's clear that when writing it, I loved life—specifically *my* life.

I wrote this sestina my last summer in college. This is one of those instances when I didn't know an event was significant at the time, but I am so glad I recorded it because it has become almost too big to fit into a single time frame since. It was one of those perfect Fourths of July: steaming hot as only an Oklahoma summer night can be, teetering on the brink of unbearable, spent drinking cheap, barely cold beer. We were all still would-bes, too young for could-have-beens. This poem brings back not just this one Independence Day, but also that whole summer, the summer before we graduated from college. It was a good one. I didn't appreciate it nearly as much as I should have at the time. It was the last real summer of my youth, a summer before marriage and mortgages, car payments and kids, when everything that was, was just one night. A time when I still had the chance to be everything I wanted to be. Whenever I read it, it reminds me what I wanted to be (it's so easy to forget!). Most of all, it reminds me to *just be*.

4TH OF JULY

the clouds: puffs of gray chiffon on a black velvet night
the diamond studded fabric covering my being
aged oak trees acted as tall pillars holding up the sky
as the breeze blows timidly, afraid to disturb or alter a single moment,
allowing the summer night to swallow me
with outstretched arms melting me into her world.

i lay my head back and watch the clouds glide over the world,
watch them move the whole night
in swirls and sensations like ripples through me.
the utter ecstasy of just being
floods the moment,
as the moon guides the clouds across the sky.

i feel small and wonderfully insignificant under the black sky
watching large leafy fingers loom overhead holding the world
stopping and prolonging at will each perfect moment
into a collection of secrets held by the night—
not to be divulged to just any being,
teasing and beckoning me

the first explosion of light shocks me
as it rips open the sky

exposing its being:
letting the diamonds slip out and sprinkle the awaiting world,
before blackness reclaims the night
but—of course—only for one moment

only for one beautiful anticipation filled moment
that seizes and captures me
until released by the night
and her erupting sister sky
as gem sized flashes blanket the breathless world
lingering, awing every breathing being

my entire being
is absorbed into this very moment
of a bright, flashing, magnetic world,
wrapping her black leafy fingers around me
and telling me secrets: the sky
tells me that I belong to the bright night.

being me
is easy this moment under the sky
when the world is light at night.

—Wendy

I would have without a doubt forgotten this one magical night, if not for this poem. We didn't take any pictures, nothing earth-shifting happened. Yet it was a memorable night. When reading this, I'm reminded that I don't always know the good times until they're gone. This poem reminds me that I have to be constantly on the look out for the Time of My Life, because I really don't know when those times may occur. Whether on a random Fourth of July or just another Tuesday night, I might as well face each moment like it has the potential to be the Time of My Life. I like thinking that my seemingly ordinary, boring days are simply unwritten sestinas.

Sestina Soundtrack

The sestina has a tradition steeped in music. The sestina originated in twelfth-century France, invented and performed by troubadours. Troubadours were court poets and competed with one another to produce the wittiest, most elaborate, and most difficult styles. Their poems were always accompanied by music.

It might get your creative juices flowing to make up a sestina soundtrack of your own. If you have a particular memory you want to write about—especially if it's a good one (your wedding, your senior year in high school, your first kiss, your first house, and so on)—it might help to listen to songs that remind you of that time. I was first introduced to the sestina in college, and here are my top five favorite college songs, which remind me of the best of those times (and yes, I realize I'm dating myself):

1. "I'm the Only One" Melissa Etheridge
2. "All I Wanna Do" Sheryl Crow
3. "What's Up?" 4 Non Blondes.
4. "My Lovin' (You're Never Gonna Get It)" En Vogue
5. "Groove Is in the Heart" DeeLight

Thelma chose to write about a memory from when she was seven years old. The occasion was the fair, a time of year she anticipated all year long. She looked forward to the rides, the cotton candy, the music, and the gathering of all her cousins. Because she lived on a farm, the fair was a rare time filled with gaiety and crowds. But her favorite part—the thing she loved most each year—was the carousel ride. It's a special memory: one of a thousand collected over the years of her life but also one that stands out more than the rest.

This memory is special to Thelma because it was something she got to experience with her father. As Thelma says, "One thing I think that made this ride memorable was that my Dad was on the carousel, and there are not too many fun things I remember he did with me. He was always working, with so many chores to do. He was not one to openly express his feelings and, as I think back, it's things like this that let me know he cared about us."

THE CAROUSEL RIDE

I have a very large storehouse I take with me wherever I go,
I know you raise your brow and give me that look,
That says, "it just isn't so."
Within it are stored many memories I've collected through the years,
Many of these bring joy I find,
But many of them bring tears.

For now let's forget the tears,
And to another room we'll go,
So many things there we can find,
Here's a memory I really treasure, let's take another look,
In it I find a lesson I have learned throughout the years,
And that is why I value it so.

This was a day I had looked forward to so,
Let's see why the joy turned to tears,
We lived on a farm and this only happened once a year,
Mom and Dad would cease their labor and off to the Fair we'd go,
I was so excited and everywhere I looked,
To see if the Carousel I could find.

I was so happy as the ride Dad did find,
My heart was pounding so,
I was in awe of the decorated horses and took a closer look,
The ride began then my shoe came off and quickly flowed the tears,
But the music played on and up again the horse did go,
This is what I've remembered all through the years.

That joy and disappointment have gone hand in hand as I've
    walked through the years,
In this room are many joys I've found,
As time, like the Carousel, so fast did go,
The thrill of graduation, love and marriage, our sons we treasured so,
Although sometimes I'd wonder as I wiped away their tears,
Would they ever grow up so some peace I could find, if I looked?

Now let's go to the corner they say makes us strong and take
    another look,
I see happiness crumbled like the marriage of thirty years,
The bond between us grew weaker, then broke, leaving many tears,
Yes, the kids had grown up and an empty house was all I could find,
Quiet and loneliness engulfed me so,
But just like the Carousel, the music played again and up and
    down life goes.

So happiness comes, sometimes goes, but if we'll stop and take
a look,
It can be found again through the years because there's much to
make it so.
Then at the end of this ride, we'll find there's been much more
joy than tears.

—Thelma

As is evident in her poem, this carousel ride has come to mean much more than a childhood trip to the fair. The memory is special to Thelma because this carousel ride has come to represent her view of life—how it's full of ups and downs and, the more ups and downs, the fuller one's life. This particular memory has come to hold a greater significance than she could ever have guessed at the time.

At eighty-plus, Thelma has her fair share of memories, of ups and downs. Writing this poem helped her not only remember a special moment with her dad but also reflect on how she feels about memory in general. To Thelma, our memories, both good and bad, fill a storehouse for each of us. We choose which memories to revisit—in which area of our storehouse we spend the most time. Thelma prefers to acknowledge the bad times but remember the good ones.

Whether good or bad, memory is a gift. Writing it down in sestina form makes it a gift we can keep reopening. As Thelma says, "As I remember, I pay tribute to my parents for all they sacrificed for me, to my siblings (seven of them) for all the fun and fights we had, and to my two sons, who have been, and still are, my pride and joy. They have blessed me with two daughters-in-law whom I treasure and added to my storehouse of memories, six grandchildren, [and] five (and number six on the way) great-grandchildren. Thank you, God, for filling the corners of my storehouse with so many blessings."

I asked her if it was easy for her to keep this positive attitude about memory. She answered honestly, "No, the positive view-point is not one I find easy or always manage to have in every circumstance. I have nearly succumbed to some [other viewpoint] along the way. This is more hindsight than foresight, and as I look back at the situations that were bad and see how they eventually worked out, though maybe not my way, it gives me hope that so will things in the future." That's Thelma for you: a woman in her eighties writing about the past and thinking about the future.

You might be asking yourself, *Why take the time and effort to write a poem about memory? Can't I just take some pictures?* Putting this extra effort into making sense of a memory (whether person, place, or event), you make it uniquely yours and, indeed, make sense of it—put it into context, appreciate it, accept it as part of your life as it is, and maybe even acknowledge its influence in the memories you are currently making.

A photograph of a memory is priceless, for sure, but the photograph is only what is on the surface. Writing a poem is like writing down what you *see* in the photograph. What was the weather like that day? Why isn't your mother in the picture? Why is your brother frowning? How genuine is your smile? Not everything in a particular memory may fit in your sestina—you have to decide what is truly important; you basically have no choice but to make sense of it. By doing so—by making peace with it, recognizing it as a shaping moment in your life, or simply showing gratitude for a particular person or place—you also give yourself a tangible remembrance you can revisit as often as you like. It is even possible that you may not get the sense of it until you come across your poem months, or even years, later.

The sestina is a tool to help you make sense of memory either by putting negative memories in their place or by pouring out gratitude for the good in your life—that which is and that which has been. When we make sense of the past, often the present begins to make a little more sense, too. And when we aim to appreciate the present, often the future is full of even better memories.

So What Exactly Makes a Sestina?

Even though Kris says that the term *sestina* reminds her of a south-of-the border dance, complete with ruffled skirts and mad feet in thick black heels, it actually goes back to twelfth-century France. And even though Debbie says it seems more complicated than a calculus equation, it really is not that hard to write. I've just always felt so *legitimate,* yet *creative,* when writing one—kind of like wearing racy underwear underneath a business suit.

The sestina is a poem that has six stanzas with six lines apiece, completed by a final seventh stanza that has three lines. A six-line stanza is called a *sestet;* the three-line stanza is called an *envoy* or *tercet.* The lines can be any length, with no rhyme involved. The rule, what gives it a *form* other than the length requirements, is that the final word of each stanza is repeated throughout the poem in a specified pattern. For all the trivia fans out there, this recurrent pattern of end-words is known as a "lexical repetition." Like this (the letters stand for the end words):

Stanza 1: ABCDEF
Stanza 2: FAEBDC
Stanza 3: CFDABE
Stanza 4: ECBFAD

Stanza 5: DEACFB

Stanza 6: BDFECA

Stanza 7: ABCDEF (Remember, this last stanza is only three lines instead of six; each line has two end-words per line. Though any order of end words is acceptable in this final tercet, this is the traditional order.)

The letters in the stanza lines stand for the end word, so you can see how the last word in each stanza acts as the end-word for the first line of the next stanza. The pattern continues until the end words have all appeared in each position in each stanza. The final stanza—the envoy—uses the six end words: two in each line, one in the middle, and one at the end.

The sestina is a poetic form that relies on six repetitive words. The repetitive nature of this poetic form encourages, forces *you* to decide the focus of the poem—you get to decide what is repeated throughout. This works well with writing about the people, places, and events of your life. There are usually sparks, hues, and flashes that are repeated throughout recollection; it rarely flows through your mind like a perfect narrative. You get to decide what is memorable about the experience, and sometimes the poem shows you when you yourself were not even aware of it. A sestina makes what you are writing about uniquely *you*. It helps you determine what you want to remember, what was special about the subject, or what the memory (person, place, or event) means to you.

Tips on Form

- Whatever your method, choose your six words carefully. You'll be spending the entire poem with them. Especially during your first attempts, pick words that are easy to work with. Consider using conjunctions like *and* or demonstrative words like *that*, which are easy to use in a variety of different ways.
- Think of words that have multiple meanings (for example, words that can be nouns or verbs, like love and hate; or blue, which can be both a color and a state of mind); they'll be easier to use. Again, you'll be spending the entire poem with them.
- Though a sestina is traditionally unrhymed, it's okay if you choose words that do rhyme. It could add interest or lend the poem a lighter tone.
- It's okay to use homonyms—words that sound alike but are spelled differently—like red/read, to/too/two, so/sew, and weak/week. The end words can also be modified—like "run" to "ran" or "live" to "life"—to give the initial word greater dimension.
- So, how does one come up with these all-important six words? Every writer has her own methods, and I'm sure that, with enough practice, you'll come up with yours. Most of the time I decide what I want to write about first and then write the first stanza. I rewrite it until I'm happy with it, and then I use those six end words. Other writers find it helpful to come up with six meaningful words concerning the subject by taking the time to seriously reflect; others write down the first six words that come to mind when first thinking of the subject. Some find it helpful to write a prose paragraph and then extract from it six significant words. You'll find a method that works for you.

Posse Pointer
As soon as Erin decided on her six end-words, she kept these words, labeled ABCDEF, where she could see them. She also kept the "formula" for the six long stanzas and last shorter stanza in sight. This way, she didn't lose her train of thought trying to remember what word to use next. I have to do the same thing each time I sit down to write a sestina.

For Further Reading

Reading sestinas written by experienced poets can help you get a feel for how to work with the form and how to repeat six words without sounding repetitive. Bernadette Mayer, an important and respected modern-day poet, has written two beautiful sestinas "The Aeschylus" and "People Who Like Aeschylus" that you can probably find on the Internet.

There has been movement by many poets to bring traditional poetic form back to modern poetry, so there are examples if you really want to find them. Try Googling "sestina examples" "sestina" or "sestina poetry." Here are a few examples of sestinas written by modern women poets:

- "Sestina" and "A Miracle for Breakfast" by Elizabeth Bishop
- "A Green Place" by Honor Moore (My favorite. Do try to find and read this one.)
- "Hall of Souls" by Deborah Digges
- "Untoward Occurrence at Embassy Poetry Reading" and "Toward Autumn" by Marilyn Hacker

What Should I Write About?

The sestina is an excellent form for remembering the people, places, and events in your life. Its length and repetitive words lends itself well to telling a story, recalling a conversation, or remembering something you only see in flashes, in scenes. Angie chose to remember a favorite time from when her children were young: naptime. After I read Thelma's poem, I wrote one about the most recent trip I took with my son to the State Fair. I wish I had written a sestina 9/11/01. *How* you remember will be as obvious as *what* you remember in the kind of sestina you write.

Kris chose the sestina to write about an influential person in her life—her grandmother—who passed away. Kris says, "My grandmother is a perfect example that it doesn't matter how much education you have (she only went through the eighth grade) or how great of a career you have (she worked as a telephone operator until she married my grandpa). What really matters is the way you live your life and treat other people." Kris remembers how many people came to her funeral. Everyone from the boy who bagged her groceries at the grocery store to the nurse who helped care for her at the end of her life was there, seeking out family members so they could tell stories of her sweetness and kindness. It seemed everyone had a story.

To write her own story in the form of a sestina, Kris thought about her grandmother; and it was her grandmother's hands that stood out in her memory. Kris remembers a time when her grandmother was able to keep a poinsettia alive not only for months after Christmas, but *years*. Her grandmother's hands fascinated Kris. As she says, "My grandmother was a very hard worker. My grandfather had been a bread-oven mechanic, and they had four wonderful sons, so money was tight; but Grandma was very good at budgeting/saving. The reason I remember her hands so well is because they were so smooth and perfect, like her, and I always found this ironic considering all of the hard work she did with them (cooking, cleaning, gardening, laundry, raising four sons, etc.)."

MY GRANDMOTHER'S HANDS

My grandmother's hands
Are smooth, a contrast to the well-earned lines on her kind face
And perfect, like her soul
They have tended gardens with love,
Cooked meals, and
Made a home

They raised four sons in this home,
They are golden brown from the sun, these hands
The same color as her eyes, so like my father's, so like mine, and
So like my daughter's, my daughter, whom she will never know
*   face to face*
And yet I think she does, as I feel surrounded by her love
And I feel her soul

Such a pure soul
Where one is always home
And there is always love
Once so strong, now fragile are these hands
They smooth back wisps of her gray hair from her face
I remember a time when I was a child and the music began and

She clapped while I danced and
Sang from my soul
I look up into her loving face
And I am home
She reaches out her hands
And I am filled with love

These hands have swaddled babies with love,
Changed their diapers, burped them, and
Fed them, these hands
They have blessed more than one little soul
And kept them safe at home
And brought a smile to that little face

Gently she touches my face
I feel her love
I am home
She takes me in her arms and
Strokes my hair and soothes my soul
Such beautiful hands

I look up at her face, her kind face, and
I feel the love pouring from her soul
I am home in her hands

—Kris

After writing the poem, Kris said she could read it and see her grandmother's hands more vividly than if she were looking at a photograph, because she was able to remember the loving things she did with her hands. She plans to make it available to her daughter, who didn't get the chance to know and love her great-grandmother. Though writing it made Kris aware of the loss in her life, it also lifted her spirits to know that she remembered so many important things about her grandmother so many years after her death. Kris likes the idea of remembering a loved one through a poem. She says, "I think it's a great way to preserve your memories of them and possibly provide a tribute to them—words are forever. Good or bad, they can't be taken back." I love this poem. It made me stop and think of my own grandmother, which is always a nice thing.

Like Kris, I like to use the sestina to write about people. I have three best friends in my life (not including my mom and my sister): my childhood best friend, my college best friend, and my adult best friend. My childhood best friend is like a $5 bill you find unexpectedly in your coat pocket when you're broke and starving. We can go months without speaking and yet, when we do, it seems to be at the exact moment I need her most. My best adult friend is a person who helps me be better. Whether it's about my choice of mortgage loan, potty-training methods, or my shoes, she always makes me feel like I'm better than I am—probably better than I ever will be. But my college best friend is the only one who has lived with me as both a child and an adult in the span of our friendship. I met her when I was eighteen and was closer to her than to any other human until I was twenty-three. She was there when I became most of what I am going to be, and she encouraged me every day (and still does) to be all that and a bag of chips. I go weeks without calling and don't tell her nearly often enough how much she means to me, but our friendship simply always *is*.

MY FRIEND

Her hair is not brown because she is my friend—
it is the caramel chestnut brown of a song
belted out with all the freedom of a convertible in summer,
the perfect center of a Gerber daisy—more striking than all other
    hues—
a strong and vibrant circle,
the richness of a worn leather cover of a favorite book.

Her conversations are not simply words, but an open book,
filled with whispers, adventures, and the flammable gossip of a
    true friend.
We join hands in a tight circle
holding in with fierceness the honesty of our song.
She speaks in shades of orangeyellowredtangerinecanaryfire—all
    the brilliant hues
and promises of an exploding sunset in summer.

Her voice does not just sound, but sings like summer
with the unexpected surprises of a haiku book,
or hot rain with its secrets and steamy hues,
the voice of my friend
(most admirably never afraid to sing her song)
blesses as the sun tans all in her circle.

Her eyes are not green, but a pond, a circle—
deep, dark, and mysterious in the July heat of summer—
a smiling, laughing, croaking green song—
a poem about trees that could fill an entire book.

A deeper shade of what it is to be a friend,
she is sparks and shocks that defy definition in hues.

Her smile isn't in hints of red or pink—but a combination of hues,
a deepness that brings to mind red wine shared in a secret sister-
*   hood circle*
and the new pink that can only be recommended by a trusted friend.
A blend of shades like the perfect rose garden in an unbearable
*   summer,*
this smile is as elegant as a classic book
found with luck at a striped-canopied local bookstore for a song.

My reflection is not stuttering verses but a sailing song,
not black or white but comfortable gray in subtle hues.
Common themes link our lives (even when reading from a dif-
*   ferent book.)*
The strongest dot in a circle
and as miraculous as the first star on a dark summer
night, I am as the way I see my friend.

I sing songs in a different circle,
and write in a book of poems and working summers,
but, indeed, the hue of my hair is not just black because she is
*   my friend.*

—Wendy

In a grown-up life in a full, bustling city with coworkers, acquaintances, other mothers, neighbors, aerobics buddies, and family who enter and exit my life with ever-increasing frequency, I sometimes forget about the people who have always been there for me, even though physically they may not be near me. Reading this poem helped me remember how some friendships, thankfully, don't seem to decay with age as our bodies do. It feels reassuring to know that some people are who they are even when they change, because true friendship allows growth and experience. As people come and go, I need to remember the people who stay. I do each time I read that poem.

While Kris, Thelma, and I use the sestina to write about "good" memories, dealing with memory and writing poetry about memories can be enormously beneficial in dealing with the not so pleasant past. We all have past events that, whether in our control or not, we have trouble reconciling. I came across the sestina "First Time: 1950" by Honor Moore while reading *A Formal Feeling Comes* by Annie Finch.

In this book, Moore recalls trying to write about a painful event from her past: molestation at the age of five. After several attempts in her adulthood to get the story out in verse, Moore finally found an outlet in the sestina. She says, "I began to write, raw in my childhood memory, and the poem came, taking dramatic, sequential shape in the sestina form. Its restraint became the walls of the room; the recurrence of end words a verbal equivalent for the relentlessness of the molester's intentions. Embraced in its sure architecture, the violated child, silenced for thirty years, is free to tell her story." Like Moore, you might find the sestina is the right form for you to get out a painful memory. And like Moore, you might find that it takes several attempts to truly set it free.

In Erin's sestina she attempts to reconcile memories of the past to help with a major life decision. In this poem, Erin asks herself if she's ready, willing, and able to have another baby. This is a difficult decision not only because of the obvious, but also because Erin's memories of her first baby aren't all that pleasant. He was textbook colicky. He cried every single night for a three- to four-hour block. There was nothing Erin could do except try to get far enough away to not lose her sanity. But there isn't a house that large, as most mothers know. Erin remembers, "I literally thought I would lose my mind and thought I must be doing something dreadfully wrong as a mother for my child to sob uncontrollably every single night. It took me two years to get over that deal."

Add to the mix that he is now at an age where Erin can experience a little more freedom and autonomy; she's worked hard to get where she is in a career that is important to her; and, no matter how many celebrities are having babies well into their forties, she's in her late thirties and feels like *it's now or never*—and it adds up to a tough decision. As Erin says, "This is something I have been agonizing over for about a year now."

Whether to have another baby or not is a difficult decision for anyone. Erin has to truthfully ask herself, as she says, "Do I want to experience those things again? Is it worth it?" She also admits, "I am terrified of making a decision I will regret." How does one acknowledge the past without letting it cloud decisions about the future? How does one learn from the past to make better decisions about the future? How does one make sense of it all? Here is Erin's poem:

DO I DARE?

Do i dare travel down that road again?
So rocky, tiring, winding . . . joyful.
You're in my thoughts, my dreams.
I can almost see your face sometimes

If i am long enough still.
What keeps me from taking a step?

Ah, that first step,
"that'll get ya" they say again.
Those voices, i wish they would be still.
"it's my purpose!" so triumphant and joyous
I yell back at them sometimes,
Though unconvinced, as you permeate my dreams.

Those familiar dreams—
They're back. A first step,
A warm snuggle, soft crying sometimes.
Can i do this again?
What if it's too hard, i worry—and not joyful?
Then i take a breath and the earth is still.

I look at my world and still
Wonder—can i fulfill all my dreams?
Sweet freedom, so joyous—
I cling to it yet as i step
Into my role again,
So torn sometimes.

I quietly ponder sometimes
Fulfillment and purpose and what am i missing, still
There's that voice in my heart again:
"realize your dreams.
Don't be afraid—take that step.
You'll be surprised at what you'll find. Such joy."

Along with that joy
Comes the heartache sometimes.
Beware that break in the step—
It's with me still.
Should i push away the dreams
And move on again?

I listen. Listen again. Your sweet songs are so joyful.
I imagine those tiny kisses sometimes and sweet baby dreams.
I am afraid of what's to come, still I know it's the right step.

—Erin

Honestly remembering and finding the right words for her sestina helped Erin acknowledge all the things that were so hard about having a baby—and also all the things that she loved. It helped her be honest about both and put both the good and the bad into perspective. Writing helped her realize that what happened in the past doesn't necessarily dictate what will happen in the future. She says, "I feel free to make the decision on whether to have another one—the decision is *not* made for me. I felt very *free* after writing my poem." So what is Erin going to do? Is she going to have another baby? Well, she's five months along, and anxious to have new memories of her new baby.

There are several different ways to make sense of memory through a sestina. Writing a sestina about something painful in your past—such as an abusive childhood—may help you experience some self-prescribed healing; writing a sestina about something important that is happening right now—like a graduation, wedding, or birth—will give you a uniquely special something to look back on as you remember the day; and writing a sestina about someone significant in your life helps you either express gratitude for their presence and positive influence in your life *or* lets you lift yourself above whatever hurtful thing this person put you through. As Erin demonstrates, it can even help you put the past in perspective to better deal with the future.

Memory is a tricky gift: it lets us remember the happy times yet also reminds us of the not-so-happy times. It is not completely reliable, but it's all we've got, because time doesn't stop. Your memory is one of the only things in this life that is uniquely yours, and it is something that no one can take from you. But, although it can't be taken away, it can, unfortunately, slip away. Why not start respecting and preserving your most precious and defining memories now?

Tips on Subject
- Go through old photos to help older memories come to the surface. It's okay if what you remember isn't *exactly* what happened.
- Whether a good memory or a bad memory, you must be honest. You must give your version of events validity; this is for you. No one else. Aim to *truly* remember, even if it's painful or feels unfair.
- If you have a significant event coming up—a wedding, a girls' weekend, a vacation, a birthday—consider writing one sestina in anticipation of the event and then another after the event has happened. It makes for a great pair of sestinas, and the differences between the two versions of the same event will be as telling about the event as the two sestinas will be themselves.
- You do want to choose a subject you are enthusiastic about. Sestinas are long poems—especially for beginners. It will be easier to keep your momentum and follow through to completion if you feel passionate about your subject.

- If you get stuck, take Moore's example and put it away for a while. Try another subject. Return later and see if your words flow more freely.

Give It a Try

Writing about the people, places, and events of your life helps you determine their specific place in your life. This could mean letting resentment go or celebrating someone's indispensable encouragement and support. This could mean remembering where you've been so that you can be surer of where you're going, or it could mean documenting where you are because you never want to walk again the long road to get there. This could mean conquering a painful event from your past or remembering an iconic accomplishment. Whatever your intent, making sense of memory by writing a sestina ultimately helps you make better sense of *you*.

If you need a little more help, here are three exercises to help you get started writing a sestina:

1. The sestina is based on sixes, so work with that. If your son or daughter is turning six, use each year as a stanza, or perhaps devote a stanza to each birthday party. If you are celebrating your sixth wedding anniversary, write a stanza for each year.
2. Use your house as your subject. You can focus on the house itself—on the outside structure, the yard, the garden. Or you can focus on the colors, design, and feel of the house. Or you can concentrate on one single room. Perhaps describe your favorite spot in the house. A quirky take would be to describe an odd room, like the bathroom or the guest room closet.

Another option is to write about your favorite memory associated with the house, if you've lived there for some time.

3. Think of a significant woman in your life. Perhaps your grandmother, mother, or aunt, or maybe a teacher who was particularly encouraging. Pay tribute to her influence. Acknowledge how she helped you become the woman you are.

Though a sestina's form is forgiving, it is still difficult to maneuver around six words you're stuck with, and it can be equally challenging to manipulate those same six words over and over. Try to stick with it. You'll have a unique view of your memory when finished. Ultimately, the poem will most likely tell as much about you as your memory does.

A Poetic Pause: Twenty-four Exposures, Twenty-four Topics

It's hard to be constantly full of ideas to write about. By the end of your poetic experience with this book, you might—believe it or not—actually find yourself with some spare time that you really want to fill writing a poem. But what if you're all settled in . . . and then blank? Here's an idea that should yield you about twenty-four ideas to pull out in case of blankness.

Get a disposable camera. Yes, I mean the cheap kind you can get at any drugstore. No, a digital camera won't accomplish the same thing, because you can immediately see your picture and have the power of deletion. (If only life worked like a digital camera.) Okay, you could use a 35mm or some other fancy model, but because the idea is to carry it around for a few days or a week, a disposable makes the most sense. Now carry this camera around and take pictures of *whatever* for about a week—the more random the subject the better. Take a picture of a blade of grass, your dream house across town, or the dead tree at the end of the street. Point the camera out the window at a stoplight. Take a picture of people coming in and out of the mall on a busy Saturday. Take a picture of your baby sleeping, your toddler coloring, your teenager sulking. Take a picture from your office window. Photograph your unmade bed, your dirty dishes, what's inside your refrigerator—whatever strikes your fancy. Now get your pictures developed.

When you get them back, I think you'll have twenty-four good subjects you can pull out from time to time if you can't think of anything to write about.

Chapter Three

Examine Your Life: The List Poem

God made me a businesswoman and I made myself a poet.
—Amy Lowell

I love lists. Rarely will you find me at the grocery store without one. If you do, it's probably because I'm not feeling well or because I was forced to go to the store for "just milk and bread." In the latter case, if I don't have a list, I guarantee you I'll come home with white chocolate–covered Oreos and a new shade of lipstick. I carry lists not just because I like to be organized, because I want to be sure I don't spend too much, or because I don't want to forget something important, such as canned mandarin oranges—though those are good reasons—no, really, I just like to make lists. I love to sit down and list things—anything.

I always have a running list of books I want to read. I like to list the remodeling I would do on my house with all the time and money in the world. I like to name the cars I would buy everyone if I won the lottery. One of my favorite ways to ring in a new season is to sit down with my current *InStyle* and list all the new things I need—okay, *want*. Of course, I never actually go out and *buy* everything on that list (the denim knee-high boots I thought I needed in fall 1999 is one good reason not to), but I feel excited about the new season and hopeful about things to come just making the list. It's about *possibilities*. I just might have an occasion in the upcoming season to wear a metallic-silver, fifties-style party dress. Something that exciting *just might happen.*

My newest list obsession is play-lists for my iPod. I can spend hours making different ones. A few of my current favorites are: "If I Had a Convertible," "Get Pumped!," "Rainy Tuesdays," "Happy Days," "Days That Started Out Happy but Need a Little Help," "The Color of the Day," "Girl Power," and the one I'm currently working on of my favorite '80s songs: "Big Hair, Bigger Dreams."

If you are a list-lover like I am, there is no euphoria like the holidays. These are the best list-writing times and practically demand particular, shiny notebooks just for the occasion. Christmas has so many great opportunities: gifts for everyone in the family—not including stocking contents, which have their own list—goodies and treats to make (or, in my case, *buy)*, holiday cards to send, parties to attend, decorations still needed for the house, liquor to buy for Christmas Eve, and so on; and then there is the after-Christmas fun: items to return, things to look for on sale, things I wanted but didn't get, things to donate to the Salvation Army, and additions to my on-going list of the worst gifts I have ever received.

But the culmination of the entire list-making year ends in the List of All Lists. This is the time for the Mother of all Lists, the List Mack-Daddy: The List of New Year's Resolutions. You might remember me saying I haven't kept a New Year's Resolution to date. It's true. But that never stops me from making that list. I don't lose hope or enthusiasm until around January 9. I have the clear and resolute intentions to lose five pounds, be the sexiest wife on the block, read all the Pulitzer Prize–winning books, get a kick-ass promotion and a raise that actually matters, cultivate in myself the goodwill of Mother Teresa and the diplomacy of Condoleezza Rice, *and* be the best mom ever. It all seems so *possible*.

I even like reading old lists. It gives me a sense of what was important to me at the time. I could compile a book of lists and it would be a more accurate life story than an expertly written, perfectly developed novel. My Saturday afternoon Target shopping list is more telling of what was important to me, filling the details of my life, than a journal entry from that same day.

My mom was putting my son to bed one night recently and let him choose his night-night story. He picked out a *Frog and Toad* book with a few different stories. My mom said, "Oh, let's read 'The List.' It always reminds me of your mommy." Now, I don't need a list to tell me to run after my list if my list blows away, but I won't deny that I find an immense amount of comfort and control in lists, even if they're never completely checked off. I'm *attempting* to improve, organize, and move things in a positive direction, and just attempting to makes me feel productive. I'm also dreaming, wishing, and pushing the limits of my life.

What a great thing for all us list-lovers out there—the list poem! Even if you aren't as obsessed with lists as I am, it's an easy form to learn and to start with. The list poem helps you appreciate the seemingly mundane, Monday-through-Thursday details of your life. Moreover, it offers you the opportunity to really examine your life and all its glorious minutiae. You gain insight into the life you're leading and may even expose what's missing. It can open up your life to the person who really needs to know it—*you.*

Why a List Poem?

The list poem is one of my favorite forms to write in because you don't need any special talent for metaphors, rhyming, or any other poetic devices, and you don't need a huge, momentous, or even difficult experience as your subject. All you need is your life, your things, your surroundings—everything your eye can see. Of course there's *always* more than what we see. The list poem is a chance to get to that *more.*

It's easy to coast through our days, weeks, months, years—then, all of a sudden, we've coasted through life without ever taking the time to examine what our life was all about. It's the details of our lives—where we lived, what we enjoyed, why we don't like green, the view from the kitchen window of our very first house, and the receipts of our purchases—that make up our lives. It's not so much the big moments like graduation, weddings, birth, or death as it is the days in between that make up the bulk of life. Those are the days we need to examine, the days that contain the things that go on all the time. If we miss all that, we miss *all that.* As Diane Ackerman once said, "I don't want to get to the end of my life and find that I have just lived the length of it. I want to have lived the width of it as well." The list poem can open up the sides of your life so that you can examine—and live—it all.

Virginia Woolf is one of my favorite writers. She says in *A Room of One's Own* that "to write a work of genius is almost always a feat of prodigious difficulty. Everything is against the likelihood that it will come from the writer's mind whole and entire. Generally material circumstances are against it. Dogs will bark; people will interrupt; money must be made; health will break down."

I will probably never write a work of genius—true—but, maybe, just maybe, genius can be found *in* dogs barking, people interrupting, money being made, and (even more probably) health breaking down. Trust me, I am *not* disputing Virginia Woolf; I'm merely offering a different view. Perhaps one's genius is found in the midst of these "material circumstances." And even if genius is *not* found in these everyday facts of life in its happenings, the *pursuit* of it in the midst of these things will make life a little more poetic anyway. Surely there is room to appreciate and record the intermissions of life as well as its events.

So, I say, let dogs bark and people interrupt. Make money and keep healthy—*live*. I think the genius of life is found in its details: in that I see the same white cat strolling across my neighbor's too-green summer lawn, leaving a little "gift" every evening between six and six-thirty; in my son's latest playground adventure; or in the contents of my medicine cabinet. Insights into your life or the world around you often come, paradoxically, from considering the little things that surround you all the time.

I was lugging my purse—which is about the size of a small carry-on yet weighs as much as a full-sized suitcase—into the elevator that takes me to my car in my office's parking garage. I was tired and weighed down, thinking, *Why do I carry all of this around with me?* As the elevator plunged below the ground, it all of a sudden seemed more like judgment on my life than on my choice of purse and its contents. When I got home that evening, I sat down and wrote down every single thing in my purse (even the old stuff, the embarrassing stuff, and even the stuff I ended up throwing away—*everything)* and then I spent the next few days rereading, revisiting, and revising that list with the intent of writing a list poem. Here is the result:

MY PURSE

one white sock, no mate
    how curious to find one small generic white sock
wallet, only has diet coke coins
    bought at one of those fake designer shops so I
    supported terrorists but I didn't know until watching
    the 5 o'clock news and all I got was torn stitching so
    my credit cards are always falling out though the
    label is stitched on really quite well
new day financial letter, open
    rates have never been this low apparently I'm pre-
    approved so I feel approved oh the things I've done to
    achieve that status
midwest christian counseling center bill, unopened
    on principle stupid dr. Alexander with his bad shoes
    and encouraging eyes letting J play him like that
cell phone, red
    only rings when I'm driving
sunglasses, knock-off black jackie-o
    how he and I laughed and laughed trying on sunglasses
    on the street that day
magazine rip-out, my dream missoni wedges
    so high and so dangerously red fantasy shoes for my
    if-only life

oh, look: the state fair stub

> *our little tradition please don't ever get too old I
> promise I'll always let you eat the last bite of
> funnel cake and ride the scariest rides and in that
> order*

a lipstick compartment, 3 lip liners 1 lip brush 2 lip
pencils 7 lip glosses 4 lipsticks 1 tinted chapstick

> *Cosmo says the way your lipstick is worn down tells
> what kind of person you are well none of mine are worn
> down enough to be telling*

4 x 6, mom and dad smiling arm-in-arm in their new kitchen

> *don't know why I keep in here instead of the photo
> album it overwhelms me so of course I look at it every
> day*

coupon, $10 off nine west flats

> *which I'll never wear no matter how sparkly my 5'5"
> claim would be a bit suspicious*

another coupon, free panty victoria's secret

> *damn expired three days ago*

little pink notebook, with three butterflies

> *handy when I just have to write down what I think of
> the new stoplight at 47th and Belleview the latest
> reason why I need that blue dress or remember
> chocolate milk*

receipt holder, a letter-size envelope I took from work

> *bursting open precariously held together with a strip
> of scotch tape the oldest two Christmases ago J's
> watch the newest Saturday black pencil skirt I haven't
> worn yet*

post-it, to pick up the dry cleaning
   crap forgot
room, for more
   how curious to find one's life fits in a bag no matter
   size or style
   right the sock mcdonald's requires socks for the play
   area still don't know where the other one could be
   better keep it just in case

—Wendy

This poem tells every loud, obnoxious, painful, and embarrassing thing about me at this point in my life. I don't know whether to be proud that I wrote a poem that tells so much or depressed that this is what it tells. Regardless, this poem tells you almost every important thing about me, my likes, dislikes, even my loves. I could see what was too heavy to carry, and it had nothing to do with the size of my purse. I could write pages and pages in a journal and this one poem would reveal infinitely more about my life—indeed about *me*. It's amazing what you find out about yourself when you go through something you carry around every day, hardly giving a second thought to what you cram in it, and then look through what you find for some type of truth. It's truth you'll find if you are really looking. I also lightened my load. Seriously, who needs to carry around all that stuff?

Lori also chose to write about a part of her life that she deals with every day, something that affects each and every decision that she makes, that colors her view of the world— what some say *really* makes the world go 'round—yet would never have thought of writing a poem about before: *money*. Money is one of the details of our lives, one that, if truthfully examined, can tell a lot about how we live our lives. As Gloria Steinem once said, "We can tell our values by looking at our checkbook stubs."

Money has always been an influential factor in Lori's life. "My parents were always in debt," she remembers. "We weren't poor, but there was constant strife about not having enough money. I felt tremendously insecure about it." To have more financial security in her own life, Lori sought a lucrative career—law—and attained a top-notch education—Harvard and the University of Virginia Law School. She's a successful, well-respected attorney who has been with the same law firm for more than ten years. "Yet," she admits, "no matter how much I make, debt just hangs over me like a dark cloud. How could that be?"

Lori made the brave choice of dissecting something that not only makes up a huge part of her life and its direction but is also something that has been taking her in a direction she wants to change. As Lori says, "You challenged me to write a list poem to examine *my life*. Well, I'm never one to shun a challenge and I know I've had a perpetual problem with debt, so this was my chance to face up to it."

MONEY AND ME

I earn
a good salary. I always wanted to be "somebody," a professional.
*   So I wouldn't have to struggle like my parents;*
so I could have whatever I want.

I support
three kids. They go to private school. I want my kids to have a
*   better education than I had;*

a husband. My father was always "on the verge of" being laid-off. Eventually, he retired after thirty years with the same company. My husband lost his job after less than a year. But then again, I always wanted to support—
myself.

I save
for my children's higher education;
for my retirement. I had my kids "late" in life, so these events could coincide. Any expert would say I save—
far too little.

I spend
on renovating an old house with good bones. We've redone the kitchen, bathrooms, woodwork, floors, closets, walls, even the landscaping. Now I'm ready to move. I want a bigger house;
on curtains, pillows, and rugs. I wanted everything to match, not like the hodge-podge of hand-me-downs my mother lived with for so long. But the truth is, I'm in an endless cycle of debt. Because I spend—
more than I make. Just like my parents.

I want
to set a better example for my kids;
to get out of the debt spiral. I want—
freedom.

I'm cutting up my credit cards.

—Lori

Lori learned a great deal about how seemingly small actions can add up to a big problem—as she puts it: "Where does my money go? How am I prioritizing and why?"—through the process of writing her list poem. She figured out that as much as she's tried to avoid it, she's following in her parents' footsteps. "Writing the list poem made me realize that I've been repeating the same habits as my parents," she says. "I've been spending money to feel secure, to feel like I had 'enough.' Ironically, by spending too much I have been perpetuating the same insecurity of my childhood."

Because she's supporting three kids of her own, it's a cycle she wants to stop. "Financial security, of course, comes not from what material things we possess but from saving and spending wisely. Although that point may be obvious, it was lost in my daily life," Lori says. For her kids' future as well as for her own, she made a decision. "My list poem," Lori states, "is my call to stay focused on what matters."

So did she cut them up? Well, she did cut one into tiny little shards and has stopped using the other.

A mechanic can't fix a car engine without looking at all its parts. That's what the list poem can do: help you look at all the parts.

So What Exactly Makes a List Poem?

A list poem is deceptive. It is deceptively simple and simply deceptive. (Just like women—that's why you're going to be so great at this one.) It is just what it sounds like: a list of things. But a list poem challenges you to analyze what the list says about you. It's a great opportunity to act as a reporter; it is perfect for the who, what, why, where, when, and how of your life. Dare to ask yourself things like *where am I? what am I doing?* and *how did I get here?*

A list poem has no mandated rhyme, meter, or line length. There are really only three things to try to remember when writing a list poem:

First, in addition to "listing" something, you are trying to *tell* something as well, to point something out, saying, "look at this in a way that's beyond the surface" or "think about this in a different way." Your latest iPod list of breakup songs—though truly inspired—is not in itself a list poem. But I'm sure you could use that list with some imagination; maybe you could arrange the titles so that they tell the story of the affair. There should be some thought, some innovation involved. Something in your list poem should be surprising, unexpected, or perhaps startlingly honest. What you *tell* is up to you. The list poem has authenticity because it is derived from your personal experience.

Second, you should have a beginning and an end, like any other type of poem. This is the main thing that makes it poetic and not simply a list. It also helps wrap it up. The lists of our lives could go on and on and on, but that's just boring. Providing an end also gives you an opportunity to learn something from the list.

And third, your list poem should feel/sound/look like a list. This doesn't necessarily mean that each line has to start with the same word or exactly the same way, but your poem should have a consistent style and give the impression of a list.

List poems are often humorous or treat the subject matter unexpectedly. The lines are often fragmented, like a train of thought, just like a real list—I bet you have never used a full sentence when writing your grocery list. Sounds pretty simple so far, doesn't it? There truly are no more instructions than that. What makes a list poem challenging is making it something more than a list—opening yourself up in such an honest, self-reflective way that your poem reveals something about you. Of course, that's also what makes it so beneficial to write.

So, you might be wondering, *why can't I just make lists? Why think poem?* I make a lot of lists that never turn into poems, and most of my lists wouldn't make good poems. So, by all means, continue the list making. (I'd have to go to List Makers Anonymous to stop, but fortunately it's not listed.) However, looking at something you see every day, contemplating something you think about every day, or retraveling the road you travel every day—all with the intent of writing a poem—will give you insight, new perspective, and (possibly) new knowledge. You'll see something you never saw before, think more clearly than you thought before, and travel more in tune with your surroundings than you did before. Using the details of your life to write a poem is an enlightening way to record your life, examine its direction, and consider its meaning. So take the time to analyze some part of your routine, thoughts, surroundings, life—*you.*

Tips on Form
- It isn't necessary that each of your lines begin exactly the same way. It does help your poem come across as a list poem, but you can be flexible. Think of it as a conversation with yourself.
- You don't have to rhyme or use any particular meter or rhythm; and your line lengths can be whatever you choose—but it is certainly advisable to *try* some poetic devices such as simile, metaphor, and intense description.
- Often the trick is to throw in something completely unexpected to help your poem sound like verse and not *just* a list.
- A list poem, like any list, has a tendency to ramble on, so give it an ending. A lot of times, the end is when the unexpected happens.

Edit. Chances are your first attempt will feel more like a list than a poem. This is one form that will benefit from revision. You can add in more magic each time you revisit it. You might also find that you end up taking things out. Not everything on your list will find a permanent place in your poem.

Think about the choices, big and small, that you make daily; some of your automatic responses to life's questions; or what it is you fear most. Consider why your favorite color is pink, why you hate orange food, or why you cry over long-distance phone commercials. Appreciate the individual flowers in your garden, not just its view as a whole. Aim to examine your life through its details—what you carry around in your purse or where your money goes. An examined life is a life that you own, that you take full responsibility for living.

Posse Pointer

Both Jen and Lori benefited from sharing their list poems. Jen had the tendency to get too "wordy." Sharing her poem with a trusted friend gave her the feedback she needed to cut it down to what was essential. Not only did it make for a better poem, but she also learned a lot more in the process. Lori shared her poem with me. As a result, we discovered yet another thing we have in common, and we have been able to offer each other support, encouragement, and advice concerning a challenge we both face.

For Further Reading

The list poem is one of the oldest forms—The Bible's Song of Solomon is a list poem in which the speaker lists the many attributes of his love, and the book of Genesis can be seen as a list poem providing the branches of Adam's family tree. Yet it is also a form that has come back into favor in modern times. It feels modern because of its freedom from rhyme and meter and because of its varied, almost erratic line length.

Lucille Clifton's poem *Wishes for Sons* is a great list poem that I was able to find on the Internet. You can also find it in her book *Blessing the Boats*. She was the first author to have two books chosen as finalists for the Pulitzer Prize. She has also raised six children: an amazing poet—and woman—indeed.

Here are a few other examples of list poems.

- "Why I Hate Martin Frobischer" by Phyllis Moore. This is my absolute favorite and one of my favorite poems of all time.
- "Goodnight Moon" by Margaret Wise Brown. Yes, the children's book. The contents are actually a lovely list poem.
- "Index of First Lines" by Annie Dillard. This is from her book *Mornings Like This,* which is a collection of found poems. Basically, she takes the first lines of poems from *The Penguin Book of Contemporary Irish Poetry* and *Poets from the North of Ireland* and arranges them into a poem—a list of first lines.
- *When I Count to Three* by Lauri Bohanan. Every mother in the world will get it.

What Should I Write About?

A list poem is a wonderful way to record your life in an honest, introspective way, an excellent opportunity to peek around hidden corners and round up the dust bunnies. You can use this form to write about any aspect or detail of your life—your surroundings, your family, your loves, your hates, your secrets, your fears—absolutely anything. Anything at all. Thelma wrote a delightful poem, "Things I Like About the Golden Years"; Kris wrote about what she loves most about each season; Angie listed some of the influential women in her life; and Katie revisited something she wrote for her father's funeral.

The possibilities for subjects are literally limitless. Use the things that you do, think, see, and encounter everyday, as inspiration. Record sights, sounds, and smells or reasons, intuitions, and excuses—in addition to your wants, dislikes, and preferences. You can't ask for a more accommodating or inclusive poetic form.

Nearly every Posse member who is a mother and attempted this type of poem wrote about her children. Debbie was inspired by Lucille Clifton's poem and wrote her own "What I Wish for My Son." Erin wrote "Why I Adore Cale," and Heather wrote a beautiful poem about both her toddler daughter and her new baby. Michelle was inspired to write about her daughter because of the conversations they have every day on the way home from school, talking about what made her daughter mad, sad, and glad that day.

"It has become such a part of our day," Michelle says, "that oftentimes she will jump in the car and say, 'do you know what made me sad today?' and proceed to tell me a story. Most days I don't have to even ask." Michelle had been thinking of what to write her list poem about when, one day, after school, she was suddenly struck by the importance of these daily conversations. Michelle realized it probably wasn't always going to be so easy. "I know I need to pay attention now because this is probably practice for the bigger stuff later—not that someone calling her poopie head is not huge now," Michelle says. "So we talk through poopie head and cheating now in hopes that we can talk openly about drugs and sex later."

THINGS THAT MAKE LUCY MAD, SAD, GLAD

She gets mad when
She loses at Uno, her newest favorite game.
Being told NO!
Not being able to do a cartwheel, jump rope, or tie her shoes (all
*   things she has almost mastered but not quite yet).*
I pick her up late from school, even if it is only five minutes and
*   she isn't old enough to tell time yet.*

She is sad when
Gus, or she thinks that's his name, runs from her.
Pop Pop and Grand Mom leave after a visit
The Cheetah girls break up for about ten minutes in their latest
*   movie.*
She gets scolded and she thinks I'm mad at her.

She is glad when
She thinks no one knows she is trying to cheat at her new favorite
*   game.*
The moon is full and bright and her Pop Pop calls to make sure
*   she has seen it.*
Hearing Elvis on the radio.
Riding the Tilt-a-whirl.
Vanilla milk from Starbucks.
Writing Scooby Doo, after watching way too many episodes of
*   Scooby Doo.*
Wrestling with her Dad.
Playing kissie monster with me.

—Michelle

As mothers, our interactions with our children, our responses to being a mother, or even the idiosyncrasies of our children are facts of life that we don't often explore. Either there is simply not enough time—something we often take for granted—or it's a matter of the little things in life getting overlooked for the bigger things. Sometimes it's just plain scary to look at our children closely and see ourselves. Yet this facet of our lives deserves to be explored; being a mother changes who you are, how you think, and what you hope. As Michelle says, "I know what makes Lucy mad, sad, glad while she is four—I just hope and pray I do when she is fourteen."

The list poem is a wonderful form for recording what it is to be a mother by "listing" your kids. You can start out simply and easily and list what you love about them. You can write about their sounds and smells. You can take Debbie's approach and consider what you hope for their lives. Or you can write like Michelle and consider the personality of your child—maybe some part of your routine with them. Whatever your approach, writing about your kids will open up the Mother side of you and ultimately teach you as much about yourself as it does about your children.

Imagine if you found the poems of your mother. You might find "Morning Thoughts," "Why I Hate Chocolate," or "Reasons to Marry Ed." Maybe you always knew she liked to get up at 5 a.m. but never really knew why. Maybe you never knew she didn't like chocolate after baking your favorite double chocolate cookies every Christmas Eve. And maybe she actually married Joe. Her life would open up to you in a way it never could in conversation. Imagine what an incredible find that would be.

I'm not suggesting that you write with the intent of sharing, but think of this form as a way to record your life: your thoughts, your feelings, what you like and what you don't, what you carry around, where your money goes—any *detail*. Writing a poem about these things requires that you examine them in a way simply making a list or writing in your journal does not. Poetry is a gift; it's something that is difficult to write dishonestly; it is a form of personal writing that encourages—practically demands—depth, insight, and feeling. The list poem is perfect for the details of your life—the things we often overlook that end up making up days, weeks, months, years, and our entire lives.

Jen and her family made a big move to San Diego from the East Coast, and Jen hasn't been exactly happy. Moving around has always been a detail of Jen's life—she's not only lived many different places but has also traveled extensively—so it was curious to her that she was so unhappy. She considered herself a pretty adaptable person before this. She decided to tackle the movement of her life—the source of her current discontent—to try to find some insight into how to be happy where she is.

WHERE I'VE BEEN IS WHERE I AM

Flipping through the photo album of my life,
flooded with memories, defining moments.
Maybe not the grandest of occasions,
but ones that have shaped where I am.

At 10, family vacation to Silver Dollar City . . .
oh, the joys of photographing awkward pre-teen years (mom
*   still proudly displays that awful picture in which only she*
*   looks good);*
I learned that growing up isn't always beautiful.

At 14, move to Germany . . .
new friends, new country, new me (we all gained 20 pounds from
*   mom's daily after-school treats; thank goodness she went back*
*   to work);*
I learned how to accept things that are different.

At 15, Spring Break trip to Yugoslavia . . .
Sisterly bonding, carefree fun, spending all our money on the
*   tanning bed so everyone would think the weather was nice*
*   (it wasn't);*
I learned how to fake it when necessary.

At 16, trip to Euro Disney . . .
first school trip after that special boy moved away, the heart-
*   break of being alone;*
I learned to be "me" instead of "we."

At 17, Senior Spring Break trip to Spain . . .
my first trip without parental control, drinking, dancing, and tan-
*   ning with friends;*
I learned to trust myself to embrace freedom.

At 18, back to the States for College . . .
tears at the airport, wanting to grow up but not wanting to
    leave home;
I learned what it meant to be brave.

At 19, moving to New Jersey . . .
running away from bad decisions and loneliness, rushing back to
    a first love, easier than feeling alone;
I learned how to escape.

At 21, moving to Virginia after college graduation . . .
struggling with being a "grown-up," too proud to ask for help,
    working two jobs and still not being able to turn on the heat
    in winter;
I learned what it was to be on my own.

At 25, honeymoon in Cancun . . .
so in love with the rest of our lives ahead of us;
I learned how to dream.

At 29, baby's first plane ride to Oma and Opa's . . .
new mother jitters, the fear that he'd cry the whole trip, relaxing
    when the plane landed and he had slept the entire time;
I learned it's never easy being a mom.

At 31, moving to San Diego . . .
the sadness of leaving friends, trying to find again who I am and
    where I fit in, if I fit in;
I learned I have to keep learning how to be "me."

How will these blank pages be filled? Where else life will take me?
I've learned where I've been is always where I am.

—Jen

Going through a mental photo album, Jen realized that although some of her life's movement involved friction, she had learned something valuable and irreplaceable with each repositioning. She also realized that it generally wasn't the big things that her mind photographed; it was the little instances that stayed with her and taught her the most. She became conscious that each move contributed something—that she's kept something important from each place, whether it seemed significant at the time or not. The details—the truth—of who she is made up of all the places she's been. "Now I'm open to learning something from my life in San Diego—from my daily life here in all its current misery," Jen admits, "and I'm actually excited and encouraged to learn what that might be."

One night not long ago, I was lying in bed with my son, reading him a story. I closed the book, looked over at him, and absorbed him snuggling up against my arm. I thought to myself, *I love this moment.* And, all of a sudden, an entire poem came to me. I was inundated with memories of the many momentous, defining, life-changing events that have happened in my house, but I was also flooded with daily occurrences such as stories, smiles, and late-night snuggles that go unrecorded. And I let it come. I got up, went to my own room, and just let the images, memories, and flashes flow in and out of my mind. The next morning, I got up early, sat down at my computer, and wrote this poem.

IN THIS HOUSE

I have given birth and I have died

I have laughed big fat tears and I have cried

I have danced swaying with an infant, bouncing with a baby,
    boogeying with a toddler, and rockin' out with a kid

I have collapsed with sadness

I have loved and lost and I have lost and loved

I have painted crimson, sunflower yellow, and baby boy blue

I have seen red

I have trudged down two flights of seven stairs weighted down
    with laundry, guilt, study, fear, a sick kid, love

I have walked back up liberated by pride, belief, determination,
    courage, skill, resolve

I have pretended and I have been true

I have complained it is too small for three and again that it is too
    big for two

I have walked in with groceries and I have walked out with books

I have yelled and scolded, demanded, chided, and hollered

I have sung and whispered, giggled, teased, and kissed

I have been lonely and I have stood alone

I have cleaned out closets and I have filled the space where the
    chair used to be

I have shared truths, coffee, confidences, and more wine than a
    heart can hold

I have been destroyed when lives were unraveled and in my
    favorite green chair secrets told

I have wrapped and unwrapped presents

I have received generosity and I have survived disappointment

I have cooked and I have burned

*I have worried about money and I have shown off my new red
    boots*
I have hurt and I have healed
I have slept like a baby, for the baby, and with a baby
*I have listened to the night birds in their nest outside my
    window*
I have wished, dreamed, wanted, and yearned
I have written, worked, pursued, and learned
In this house in this house in this house I have I have I have.

—Wendy

It was one of the most enlightening writing experiences I've ever
had. It opened my eyes. I saw the *sides* of my life. I've always com-
plained inwardly about my house, though I've never really let on
to anyone else. I tell most people I think it's "cute," or I elaborate
on the benefits of having large, mature trees to shade the backyard.
We bought it as a "starter house" and yet, six years later, we're still
here. Most of my friends have bigger, much fancier houses—you
know, the ones with big closets (even in the guest rooms), enormous
bathrooms with separate baths and showers, and immaculate land-
scaping without a single errant weed. I've honestly been even a lit-
tle *embarrassed* about my house, especially lately. I have people
over, but not my friends with the bigger houses. As I sat and listed
all the things that have happened in this house, it seemed almost a
miracle that this house—or any house, really—could *house* so
much. I felt lucky and oddly safe. This structure—this *detail*—that
I enter and exit every day without an ounce of appreciation has
given me so much. My small house has a huge presence. I have
really *lived* here—more so than in any other place to date.

Somehow I know that I eventually will move on. I'll remember this is where I brought my son home from the hospital, where I wrote my first book, and where I learned I could live by myself. But I also want to remember the late-night pancakes with my son in our yellow kitchen, the holly I planted that thrived despite the lack of full sun, and the dark, deliciously quiet mornings I sat writing at my computer. I will remember this house as the place where I started to examine my life and appreciate its details.

Tips on Subject

- Try to look at your chosen subject differently than what first comes to mind. If you first think of "why," consider sights, sounds, or smells instead, for a fresher, more magical perspective.
- Remember, honesty feels good—and no one has to see it but you.
- Not every poem has to be deep and full of layers. Sometimes a chocolate chip cookie hits the spot just as much as a seven-layer chocolate cake. I remember reading an account of an exchange between a reader and Pulitzer Prize–winning author Eudora Welty. The reader asked her why all her stories had something significantly green in them, probably expecting a complicated answer full of symbolism. Welty simply answered, "Because green is my favorite color."
- For literally an entire book of list ideas, try *List Your Self* by Ilene Segalove and Bob Velick. Many of them would make great poems.

List Poem Soundtrack

Here is a list of Michelle's favorite songs. "My favorite songs are as diverse as the feelings they conjure," she says.

1. "Chucky's in Love" by Rickie Lee Jones. This song reminds me of one summer when I worked at the pool. It rained almost every day, so my friend Cassie and I would sit inside and listen to this song. We must have heard it a thousand times. I still love this song and my friend Cassie.
2. "Nothing Compares 2 U" by Sinead O'Connor. I can never hear this song without it almost ripping my heart out, just like someone I used to know. Enough said.
3. "Power of Love" by Marsha Ball. We played this song at our wedding. It still makes my husband cry when he hears it. Well, I hope it is the song—and not the actual wedding—that makes him cry.
4. "At Last" by Etta James. The song I wanted to play at our wedding! But I'm glad I let him choose.
5. "We Are Family" by Sister Sledge. We play this at all our family weddings, and all the women dance together.

Try making your own list; it may not spark a poem, but it will at least give you the beginnings of a new playlist for your iPod.

Give It a Try

Don't let your life go unrecorded and unexamined. List poems are one of the best forms for documenting your life—and not just the huge, momentous occasions like giving birth, getting married or divorced, or finally making partner, but also the small details that really make up our lives: the contents of your diaper bag, why you chose sunflowers over roses, what you were buying at

Wal-Mart the day your divorce was finalized, or how the street moved that first Monday morning on your way to work.

Writing a list poem gives you the chance to see what is really there and not what you pretend is there; it also helps you see what you pretend isn't there. So, whether writing about your kids, the pages of your photo album, what is in your purse, or where your money goes, it can be an informative, expansive experience. Go ahead: take a *good* look.

If you are one of those people who need a concrete assignment, here are three exercises to help you get started:

1. List what you hope the world is like in twenty years. Not only will it tell you twenty years from now a lot about yourself twenty years before then, but it will also say a lot about how you may want to start changing your life now.
2. List the contents of your favorite room in your house, but try to make it magical. This also works for your office or, if you travel a lot, a hotel room. This can help you see the ordinary things, the things you see every day, in a new light, perhaps appreciating them a little more.
3. List the contents of your kitchen junk drawer. Just what is all that stuff you're harboring in there?

It is easy and rather comfortable to travel down our roads on cruise control. But we will never truly live our lives if we do. Regret is the result of an unexamined life. You gotta occasionally risk it, put the pedal to the metal, get out the pen, and write—and see where you end up. The list poem is a way for you to take inventory of your life. It can be a checkup on what you're doing and where you're going.

Once you get into writing list poems, you'll find they're more challenging than they sound. But they are also rewarding, in that they allow you to see your life differently. Not only can poetry help interpret your life—it can influence it as well. Who knows? You may come up with a resolution for next year's list. It may even be the one you do keep.

A Poetic Pause: Poetry and Journaling

Writing poetry and keeping a journal are like the best of girl-friends. They help each other be better.

Poetry can add a dimension to your journal, a way to use your free-flowing thoughts, a way to sort and make sense of all the things you feel and experience. It also helps you remember your days in a beautiful, song-like way, instead of as the drudgery an ordinary day can sometimes sound like.

The poet Adrienne Rich began dating her poems to under-score their existence within a context. She rejected the idea that poetry existed separately from the poet's life. A poem could put a certain situation, experience, or time in context, sometimes more powerfully and recognizably than page after page of writing. I sometimes use a haiku as the "date" of my journal page instead of using actual numbers. If you keep a journal, I encourage you to make poetry an active part of your journaling.

Just like the best friendships, the relationship is reciprocal. Journaling can be just as beneficial to your poetry. When you feel like writing a poem, especially if you have something you need to work out, reading over journal entries dealing with that situation may help you find the words. Writing the poem will help you put them in order.

In addition, when you need to take notes—like when day-dreaming your ghazal, making a list of rhymes, making an actual list for a list poem, or recording impressions for a sestina—your journal is the perfect resource. I adore coming across lists of rhymes. It seems so innocent and uncontaminated, no matter what it was that I was actually writing about.

I often find inspiration for a poem in my journal, whether from an actual entry, a jotted scene description, or an old receipt stuffed between the pages. If you regularly write poetry but don't keep a journal, I encourage you to consider starting one. You don't have to write in it every day or channel your thirteen-year-old self for a "Dear Diary" feel; it's your book, and you can compose it any way you like or simply use it like an idea book for your poetry.

One of my favorite journal entries is from a journal I have long since tossed aside. It is a picture of my son tormenting our dog, accompanied by a list poem. When he was four, he liked to try to force our dog to sit on top of a beanbag that he pushed down the stairs. He reasoned that it was like a ride for the dog. Clearly, this ride was only enjoyable to one of the parties involved. With the delay of my digital camera, I barely caught him at the edge of the frame, a blur chasing the dog. To some it would seem like a "bad" picture, but it is *so* my son. He can't be bothered to slow down for much. I wrote a list poem called "The Sounds of a Four-Year-Old Boy." I have the picture and the poem paired together in my journal. I could write an entire book about my son and how much I love him (and why), and it would not tell as much as that single page. I could also craft an entire scrapbook of his fourth year, and it would not show as much as that single picture with that poem.

Chapter Four

Let Your Mind Wander: The Ghazal

I have dreamed in my life, dreams that have stayed with me ever after and changed my ideas; they have gone through and through me, like wine through water, and altered the color of my mind.

—Emily Brontë

The ghazal (pronounced "guzzle," but with a *gh* instead of hard *g*) is the reason you are reading this book.

Since the third grade when I wrote my award-winning (admittedly third place) short story of how leprechauns saved the fairies in the woods behind my house, I've wanted to be a writer. This side of me would come out when I had one too many glasses of wine and would go on about what I was *going* to write, or when my husband and I were sitting up late at night talking *what ifs*— but I never did. It seemed too hard. I would say I didn't have the skills and oh, if only I could go back to school. In reality, of course, I didn't want to take responsibility for a dream, for a goal, for my life—for possible failure.

It was when I started to write sonnets that I found myself not only writing something I enjoyed but also something that gave me back as much, or more, than what I had put into writing it. Add to the mix upheaval in my personal life and a bit of job dissatisfaction, and I became suddenly, acutely aware that I *was* responsible for my life, goals, and dreams—whether I liked it or not. So I decided to write a book.

I decided to write a book I would love, a book I completely believed in, a book that would hopefully help a few other women just like me. I also, in my own little way, wanted to try to improve the world. I sincerely believe that more poetry in the world will make the world a better place. You can call it naïveté; I call it hope.

To write poetry in form gives me structure when the rest of my world seems to be raging out of control; it gives me balance when it seems like spilled milk is enough to send me over the edge; it gives me purpose when turning on my local news makes me aware of the senseless, incomprehensible turmoil that is everywhere; and it helps me tap into my creativity when it seems the most imaginative thing I encounter is whether to wash lights or darks. I decided to write a book on poetic form because it is something I wholeheartedly believe in and can provide personal testimony about. It can help women live fuller, more in-tune lives and, with a larger presence with more widespread practice and respect, would make the world one I would be prouder to live in.

So I started on the Internet, looking for poetic forms other than the ones I remembered from college courses. As I was Googling and Yahooing, I came across a form I had never heard of, the ghazal, which is an Arabic word that means "talking to women."

I stopped and thought, *Well, this is one I've got to try.* Then I wondered if anyone else would be interested in trying, too. I wondered if other women would be interested in writing poetry in form and with benefit. I also considered that other women might find poetry as helpful as I do in keeping their lives balanced, creative, expressive, cleansing, uplifting, and, ultimately, more authentic.

"Talking to women." The phrase haunted me. Then I thought, well, why should my book contain poems from women who already know how to write, who already know how poetry can fluff up the pillows of one's life? Perhaps readers will get more from seeing how women just like them do it—because, of course they can: I *knew* that. And here we are. Thanks to Yahoo!, Google, and one rather obscure form of poetry, the Poet Posse was born.

However, after my initial brush with the ghazal, I busied myself writing my proposal. I researched forms that were more familiar to me and began to experiment with those; I didn't think about the ghazal again for months. When I got around to creating a table of contents for my *official* book proposal, I remembered "talking to women"; so I added it to the table of contents and went on my merry little way.

One Saturday morning, I pulled out my computer to work, and it wouldn't turn on. At all. No power, no juice, nothing. I won't sugarcoat this: I *freaked* out. I knew I could get the tech guys to look at it Monday morning, but until then I was going to lose *an entire weekend.* Then I remembered that, just the day before, I had picked up two ghazal books from the library. What was my excuse? None. So I begrudgingly took the books out, figured out the form, and hunkered down. I'll be honest with you. I didn't know if I could pull it off. But I didn't give myself a choice, and I put pen to paper.

That Saturday morning was amazing. I'm hooked. The ghazal and I, we've just become acquainted; we're still getting to know each other. We're just now flirting a bit, but I feel a full-fledged, torrid affair coming on.

Why a Ghazal?

The ghazal was developed in Persia in the tenth century. It is arguably the oldest poetic form in popular use today—and by popular use, I mean worldwide; this is a form that isn't as mainstream in America as, say, the sonnet or even imports like the haiku—not yet, anyway. Steeped in middle-Eastern traditions and imagery, and not quite mainstream in America, the ghazal is the most exotic form of poetry you'll find in this book. Stumbling across it felt like realizing that what I thought was hand-me-down costume jewelry is actually real, expecting cubic zirconium and getting diamonds.

The best thing about the ghazal—and what makes it unique and difficult for some to grasp—is that its strung-together couplets are not supposed to be related. You are not meant to carry a theme all the way through. Seriously: no title, no deep, obscure point, and no intentional direction. The scheme (rhyme and refrain, which you'll learn a little later) is determined in the first couplet, and then subject matter, tone, style—anything and everything—can change from couplet to couplet.

You can be comic, tragic, romantic, religious, and/or political, all in the same poem. The only commonality is a rhyme and refrain. It is like a string of poems instead of one long poem. The ghazal lets the poem come to you instead of you having to chase it down. It's like lying back on an unseasonably warm late-fall day and cloud-watching. What comes comes. Hence the ghazal is perfect for daydreaming, letting your mind wander and following it wherever it takes you.

But there is a prerequisite: you have to recognize and accept the importance and benefit of taking time to sit and let your mind wander. As Gloria Steinem once said, "Without leaps of imagination, or dreaming, we lose the excitement of possibilities. Dreaming, after all, is a form of planning."

Dreaming is not a waste of time, especially for women. We often spend so much time taking care of everyone else—husbands, children, older parents, crazy siblings—or taking on huge responsibilities at work that what *we* need, want, and dream gets lost in the shuffle. We owe it to ourselves (and to our families) to take the time to let our minds wander and to see what occurs to us— what is important, what is essential—and what it is that is in our minds. This is what happens when you daydream, and it is what happens when you write a ghazal.

I have two favorite places to daydream. I like to close my office door and stare out the window; the view is of the hotel across the street. I can also see Main Street, which is an interesting street in any town or city. A lot occurs to me there.

I also like to sit on my living room couch on Sunday mornings, my only company a cup of coffee, looking out the window. The view is of a big rosebud tree—it really needs to be removed, because it's too close to the house and much of it is already dead; but it just keeps sprouting beautiful purple buds each spring. Even more occurs to me there.

I have been taking the time, lately, to try to write ghazals during these precious moments of peace, and doing so has been enormously enlightening. It makes these times seem that much more luxurious and indulgent. I am always surprised at what I write.

It's almost unintentional, like my subconscious takes over. What is really on my mind becomes clear, and often it isn't at all what I would have guessed.

One afternoon, I was sitting in my office preparing to go to lunch. I was planning to skip out to Macy's to buy a blue dress I had been eyeing. I was feeling not a small amount of pre-buyer's remorse, because there was no way I could justify *needing* this dress and I honestly didn't have the money to spend on it. Oh, but I *wanted* it.

It was a wrap dress, the perfect style to hide an imperfect stomach yet show just the right amount of leg. It was office-appropriate and yet perfect for Saturday-evening dinners out. The blue was one of my best colors—a deep, royal blue, rich and jewel-toned. This color just *does* it for me. It makes my eyes look bluer, and my hair blacker, and, I don't know why, but I swear it makes my ass look perkier, even when it's just a sweater. It's *my* color. I was once hit on in the canned goods aisle when wearing this color. But, really: I didn't need it, and I couldn't afford it.

I was playing around with the ghazal in my spare time, so I thought to myself: *Okay, sit here and write one ghazal, and, as a reward, you can go buy that dress.* So I dutifully sat and worked on a ghazal. Sure, at first, visions of blue dresses and all that this one dress was going to do to improve my life were on my mind (I was sure not only that it would lead to great sex but also to a promotion, to jumps ahead on the wait-list at restaurants, *and* to free drinks when out with my girlfriends), but it wasn't really long at all—maybe fifteen minutes of writing—until my mind had moved on to different things. I couldn't, after all, spend more than a couplet on just that blue dress.

BLUE

Blue blue blue. early summer ocean blue.
not mine, better than me blue. Now I'm blue.

Rain rain rain. His sweet little voice informs
it's God crying—well, who knew? Now that's blue.

No no no, aquamarine, steel, or slate.
There it all is: right on cue, he says blue.

Why why why? We almost had it all—or
at least most. Was it all you and your blues?

Yes yes yes! when she looked with man-made eyes.
I could see it in you too—glad for blue.

Sigh sigh sigh. An eye roll. I've been that way
you say—Wendy's perfect hue: royal blue.

—Wendy

I never did get the dress.

So I decided to try an experiment with the ghazal. I determined that every time I got the urge to buy something—and 99.9 percent of the time, these "somethings" are shoes and apparel—I didn't need or couldn't afford, I would try to write a ghazal first. For an entire *month,* this is what I did. It might sound easy to you. But shopping is one of my major bad habits. I shop on the Internet when I'm bored at work but should be working; I go to Target over lunch for ibuprofen to relieve the headache I feel *coming* on and return with a Rolling Stones T-shirt, a denim skirt, and a movie from 1989; I will go to the Gap for new jeans for my son and add on a pair for myself when I already have ten pairs in my closet. I spend money I don't always have, and I spend time that I find I have in an increasingly short supply.

So for *one whole month* I sat down with the ghazal and daydreamed instead of needlessly, wastefully shopping. The result? I spent $265 less that month. I wasn't perfect; I still had the occasional slip, succumbing to my dark side. I bought red boots in early September when it was still 95 degrees outside, so that the store "wouldn't run out of my size," but I was honestly able to redirect my mind with poetry the majority of the time. And the best part was that I didn't feel regret in the things I didn't buy—not at all. Who knew that daydreaming a little more often would leave me more in my Citibank account?

There was a time for Angie, too, when she greatly needed and, even more greatly, appreciated the chance to daydream, letting her mind wander free from its current situation. Today she says, "Daydreaming was the key to keeping my sanity." One of her best friends has a disease called Sarcoids, and very few doctors in their area knew how to treat it. So Angie and her friend traveled from Oklahoma to the National Institute of Health in Washington D.C. to seek treatment.

As Angie says, "She is very sick and it just breaks my heart to see her like this." Biopsies, tests, and late-night hospital halls left Angie with the need to escape—but she couldn't go anywhere.

She decided to use this time to write a ghazal. Once she decided on her repeated word and her rhyme—both of which were simple and stuck with "ing" endings—she made a list of rhyming words and just started writing. She worked on it the week they were in D.C., carrying her journal to the hospital and adding verses as they occurred to her. "It was nice and relaxing—tension-lifting, even—to just dream of different things to write about," she says.

LIFE

Class ring, name on notebook, who loves who
High school crush, cheating hearts, breaking up

Slamming door, locked tight, pillow on the couch
Silent sulking, sorry later, making up

White dress, three tier cake, roses in hand
Walk the aisle, vows, the kiss, messing up

Waves rushing, foaming caps, stroll over the sand
Penthouse view, castle dreams, living it up

Wrapped tight, nursery cap, cradle by the bed
Eyes blink, moments gone, baby growing up

A dozen years, starting new, change is nearing
God's blessing, strong will, life's loose ends tying up

—Angie

Angie found writing a ghazal intriguing because she was surprised at the direction the poem (and her daydreaming) went. Spending her days with a friend and uncertain of her friend's future made Angie more sensitive to the happenings of her life—both what was to come and what had already come. Not surprisingly, her spare thoughts were consumed by thoughts of her own life: If she were to become suddenly sick, what would she be most proud of? What would she regret?

When Angie first started her ghazal, she was remembering her wedding to her husband—one of the happiest, proudest times of her life to date. But the more she wrote and thought, her first wedding—a mistake, and not the most rewarding moment for her—came to mind as well. When Angie finished her poem, she realized, "The poem laid out different areas of my life and was just a look back at where I have been." She uncovered an appreciation she was hardly aware of, even for the so-called mistakes of her life. The whole process made her realize, "I don't believe in regrets; it all just makes you who you are today and [who you] will be in the future."

Taking time to daydream during a stressful, difficult time when faced with a friend's uncertain health helped Angie appreciate her own life: past, present, and future.

Allowing yourself time to daydream—whether because you need a moment to get away from it all and regroup, or because you have lost the ability to see dragons and hippopotamuses in the clouds, or because you want to reconnect with yourself and your true dreams, or because you need to redirect yourself from a bad habit—is time well spent. And the ghazal is the perfect form to use when daydreaming. It is structured enough to command your mental attention yet free enough to let your mind slip from its leash. Go ahead: let your mind wander—who knows where you'll end up?

What Exactly Makes a Ghazal?

I had never heard of the ghazal before doing a little poking around on the Internet, so don't feel out-of-the loop if you haven't either.

I could quite possibly have gone my entire life without exposure to it, but, thankfully, that wasn't the case. I have a whole routine now when I want to sit down for a bit of daydreaming and ghazal-writing. I wake early, brew a cup of Arabian Mocha Sanai Starbucks coffee, arrange a plate of three biscotti and one muffin, and settle in. At night, I must have a glass of Argentinean red wine and imported cheese. OK, so it's really Folgers and frozen waffles and House Wine and Cheez-Its, but with the ghazal it's so easy to pretend.

There are four main things you need to consider when writing your ghazal. First, it is comprised of couplets, usually more than five but generally no more than fifteen. Second, there is a refrain—a repeated word or phrase—that is established in the first couplet that then appears at the end of the second line of each succeeding couplet. Third, there is a rhyme (a partial rhyme is OK, too) that appears right before the refrain in each couplet. And, as I mentioned before, each couplet should be autonomous; it should not depend on any other couplet to be understood or appreciated. The ghazal is often compared to a necklace. Each couplet is a gem or pearl that shines when plucked from the strand but is even more beautiful when viewed in its setting.

A couplet is, according to the *American Heritage Dictionary*, "A unit of verse consisting of two successive lines, usually rhyming and having the same meter and often forming a complete thought or syntactic unit." The ghazal is made up of couplets. There is no *set* meter or syllable count; it doesn't have to use, say, ten syllables (as the sonnet does), but you are encouraged to make each line *consistent*. It doesn't have to be exact—you can use your inner ear—but it should feel like it has rhythm. The lines should be of *approximately* the same length, meter, or syllables.

The refrain may be a word or phrase but is usually not more than three words. The refrain is introduced in the opening couplet. It appears at the end of both the first and second lines. It is also acceptable for it to occur at the end of the second line only, the end of the first line having offered a rhyme instead. In subsequent couplets, the refrain is always at the end of the second line.

The rhyme scheme is interesting because it doesn't occur at the end of the line as you might expect. Instead, it occurs right before the refrain. I can't tell you how much I love this rhyme scheme. It is completely unexpected, the rebel of the poetry world. The rhyme of the opening couplet is repeated at the end of second line *but right before the refrain* in each verse so that the rhyming pattern is AA, BA, CA, DA, EA, etc. The opening couplet sets up the scheme by having both the rhyme and refrain, and then the scheme occurs only in the second line of each succeeding couplet.

Each couplet should be complete in itself. The rhyme scheme and refrain provide a link among the couplets, but each couplet is a self-sufficient unit, detachable and quotable, generally containing a complete expression, a fullness of thought, a comprehensive idea—similar to a haiku. There is no "theme"; each couplet may contradict the previous one, represent another perspective on the idea, or address a new idea altogether. You could even rearrange all the couplets except the first into a new order and maintain the poem's integrity. The ghazal allows for the impulsive shifts in thought that are a natural part of daydreaming. No other form follows the classical rules of rhyme and meter yet simultaneously gives poets freedom to vary subject matter at will. It stands unique as a major, nonnarrative, lyrical form of poetry.

One more thing: Traditionally, the last couplet of a ghazal contains the poet's "signature"—her real name, pen name, nickname, or whatever. It might sound a little gimmicky at first, but this is a chance to offer some completion to a poem whose parts are unrelated. Try to incorporate this traditional element; it's pretty fun.

The age-old question: *Why this crazy ghazal thing? Can't I just sit around and count clouds?* I chose the ghazal for two main reasons: first, because it truly is a poetic form that lends itself naturally to daydreaming. When we set our thoughts truly free, they roam all over the place; this is not only expected in the ghazal, but demanded. And daydreaming is important and absolutely necessary to our happiness and mental health. When you take the time to write down your dreams, your random trains of thought, in such a way, not only have you created something tangible, beautiful, and meaningful—you also benefit from and remember any insights and *aha!* moments that may come your way.

Secondly, I enjoyed including an unfamiliar form, especially from a different part of the world. I know I can be ignorant of others—even of those just living across town from me—and it makes our own lives richer and fuller when we allow ourselves to benefit from the culture and history of others. It's just another little way of expanding your world without having to brave airport security.

Tips on Form

- When you've got your rhyme determined, make a list of potential rhymes in the margin, to the side, or somewhere where you can easily refer to it. This will make it easier and faster for you to write while sticking to the form. Remember: partial rhymes are okay.
- For the refrain, pick a word or phrase that is easy to work with, that can have different meanings, or that is common (and therefore easy to manipulate).
- Remember that both the rhyme and refrain should appear in both lines of the opening couplet, but then only the second line in the remaining couplets.
- Syllabic/metrical consistency is encouraged. This isn't difficult, because *you* get to determine what it is. It's not like the sonnet, which only allows iambic pentameter.
- The independence of each couplet can seem odd. Normally poets are expected to make "points," no matter how obscure or personal. But the ghazal is much more lenient and flexible than most poetry. Just go with it. Write where your mind takes you. You are likely to feel liberated, surprising yourself with unexpected discoveries.
- Ghazals often use the refrain as the title. It is difficult to title otherwise because the couplets are not expected to relate to any one larger thing.
- Remember Katie's suggestion (back in the sonnet chapter) of using an Excel spreadsheet. You might find it useful here, too.

For Further Reading

Examples of the ghazal are not as easy to find as most of the other forms in this book, but they do exist. One notable ghazal is Marilyn Hacker's. "Waiting," a gorgeous ghazal I was able to find on the Internet. Hacker is an internationally recognized poet who is known for using strict poetic forms in her work. Her collection, *Presentation Piece*, won the National Book Award, and her work is touching while at the same time technically sound; most of all, it's *readable*. She is one of my five favorite poets.

The book for incredible ghazals is *Ravishing DisUnities: Real Ghazals in English,* by Agha Shahid Ali. It contains many fine examples from such notable women poets as Diane Ackerman, Martha Collins, and Maxine Kumin. I read it for thirty minutes on the Stairmaster from Hell and it seemed like a mere twenty-nine minutes. My favorites are:

- "Regret" by Mary Pryor
- "For a Poetess" by Annie Finch
- "Destiny Haunts" and "Ghazal" by Kelly Le Fave
- "Consider" by Katherine Cottle
- Adrienne Rich has also written ghazals, but she has adopted a "free verse" form. She sets her poems in independent couplets but employs neither the refrain, nor rhymes, nor any sort of metrical consistency. Her work is fascinating and beautiful, but I think this is one of those times you should know the rules before breaking them. Rich certainly knew them first. She has a collection, *Ghazals: Homage to Ghalib,* that is worth the effort of finding.

Ghazal Soundtrack

Debbie has an amazing voice. When we were in college, she made money by winning karaoke contests. I can close my eyes and still hear her sing "Bobby McGee" and literally feel the hard wooden chairs of the bar at Striker's bowling alley.

Whether she is wishing things were different in the world and wondering what to do to change them, dreaming of her kids' future, or planning the upcoming evening with her husband, Debbie has always found music a special way to connect with her world while also calming and soothing her mind. In keeping with the spirit of the challenge to daydream, here are Debbie's top five songs for sitting back, relaxing, and letting her mind go:

1. Patty Griffin's "Fly" (also sung by the Dixie Chicks)
2. Tracy Chapman "Fast Car"
3. Cowboy Junkies "Blue Moon Revisited"
4. Joan Baez "Blowin' in the Wind"
5. Zero 7 "In the Waiting Line"

What Should I Write About?

One definition of the word *ghazal* is that it is the cry of the gazelle when it is cornered in a hunt and knows it will die. (This doesn't have to be taken literally; don't we all feel cornered by our bad habits and brought down by our own forces sometimes?) That is why traditional Urdu ghazals often have an atmosphere of sorrow and grief. To love and be loved is also a feeling commonly described in ghazals. There is quite often a mention of wine or some other intoxicant. Traditional ghazals often told of mystical experiences. Basically, with the stipulation that the couplets be independent, all human affairs from trivial to serious are fair game.

What should you write about? Whatever comes to mind. Don't close your mind to anything; that is the only way you can take full advantage of your open and free thoughts. You just might stumble upon a dream that is doable, an *aha!* that has been lurking in the back of your mind, or a solution to a problem that has been plaguing you.

A better question here might be *how should I write?* Daydreaming and letting your mind wander would be to write *about* literally anything. In one daydreaming session I could focus on anything from winning the lottery to Justin Timberlake to addressing the United Nations. I might remember my first kiss, my first regrettable mistake, or my first car.

How should you write? Freely. The form might seem restrictive at first, but I honestly believe that with just a little practice, it will be more revealing than restricting. Let your ghazal follow where your mind takes you instead of forcing your mind to follow your poem. When writing a ghazal, just like in a typical daydreaming session, impulse and intuition are more effective than rationality is.

I was not exaggerating when I said that I felt a full-fledged obsession coming on with the ghazal. It's seems to suit me perfectly: it offers me beloved form *and* glorious freedom. I took a trip with my son to visit my parents. While in flight, he was busy playing his video game, and I looked out the window. Here we were, floating lawlessly, illogically on clouds so thick they looked like snow. I took out my journal to write a ghazal. There were kids crying and flight attendants taking drink orders, yet I was still, inside and out. *How?* you may wonder. Because I wanted to be. As simplistic and impossible as it sounds, I was still and calm in the midst of a full flight simply because I wanted to be. I wanted this time—whether ten minutes or an hour—to be still and think, to let my thoughts float on the sky-snow with me. I wrote two ghazals right in a row.

NOW

I often wonder where I'll be ten years from now
wrinkles, fine. I just hope for different tears than now.

I like it when it thunders but rain never rains
God snickers, a cosmic joke—I'm in on it!—appears as now.

Dark green fat leafy limbs almost tap the window
call the tree guy—plumber, too—a thief nears my now.

She stood close for truth but left enough space for pride—
the distance from any mistake (that leers) to now.

What about a week a day even ten minutes?
Just give me red wine and different fears from now.

A black pre-dawn window shows her true reflection
not eyes, body, or mind—a Poet steers her now.

—Wendy

REALLY

After downing three Margaritas, did I just take that pill, really?
The one left from easy pain? did I want sleep—or numbness
*   really?*

It's always there when I need it, when I am too tired to be smart.
It fills the space. Until I replace it. Complete callousness, really.

Faith, love, loyalty, trust: a child's carefully plucked dandelion.
I mean, I have a MasterCard just in case; nothing's priceless,
    really.

I once thought a policeman was there for me; today's the day, I
    sighed.
There are lots of marbles in this pretty jar. You'll never guess.
    Really.

I was going to. I was going to shave, make steak, and be nice.
    But
tomorrow is yesterday. You say it (I'm weak): It's pointless. Really.

Because you always beat me at Scrabble and don't subject me to
    Risk.
Because you cheat, laugh, and play. I'd bolt if you were any less,
    really.

I want it all: reluctant fame, subtle fancy cars, to choose fake
    fur . . .
Fine. Ya got me. I'd get the longest mink she showed: I confess.
    (Really.)

It's the best worst thing to ever happen to you, my one Big
    Mistake:
proof, excuse, cause, and reason. It's a crown of thorns, Your
    Highness. Really.

I planted holly yesterday, dug into the earth with my own hands.
A shady spot with only speckled sun. Such sweet faithfulness!
    Really!

A strange resolve to Follow Through, do the right thing—she can
    say no?
Live true? I never thought Wendy could offer up such duress—
    really.

                                                            —Wendy

When you let your mind wander, it is open. When it is open, you have a fenceless view of what it really going on with you. I was up in the sky, the highest people that ever were, my son and I decided, and it was the perfect opportunity to daydream, to not restrict my thoughts. I often drift off in thought, but, with the ghazal, I have proof of where my mind goes. I know what is really bothering me, what I really wish would happen, and what really inspires me. Those are darn good things to know. I'm telling you: I'm hooked.

Current events heavily influenced Debbie's thoughts—and therefore her ghazal. She grew up in a loyal Republican family in Texas, and Debbie is a little more liberal . . . to put it nicely. Thoroughly frustrated with the political climate, she says, "When you mentioned that the ghazal can often have political connotations, I immediately thought of my dissatisfaction with the direction our country seems to be headed. I am so frustrated by the fact that our country is run by lobbyists who throw money for their big business cause to dictate policy."

Then at the grocery store, *People* magazine slathered Lance Bass's photo on its cover, screaming, "I'm gay!" That annoyed

Debbie, too. "Why can't we all just keep ourselves out of people's private business and not try to exploit their choices?" she asks.

She's also pregnant, expecting her second baby boy. Her first baby boy was diagnosed with Sensory Integration Disorder before he was two. "Obviously the impending arrival of a second son is weighing heavily on my mind these days," she says.

Another election year had rolled around, shortly before she was due—due for what? she couldn't help but wonder—grocery store checkout aisles were now celebrating the latest celebrity divorces, and Debbie's thirty-third birthday was right around the corner. There was so much on her mind that the ghazal was an appropriate poetic outlet. Debbie chose to let her mind wander—and rant and rave as it saw fit—through her mind's concerns, issues, and opinions.

BOYS

Hey little lady! Can I buy you a drink, what do you think?
Nothing like a good ol' boy.

New Kids on the Block, 'N Sync. 98 Degrees makes teenage girls
    drop to their knees
Never been a fan of those bands of boys.

You think differently than we do—let's go to war! That's what
    fighting is for.
Believing you are more powerful than you are gets you in
    trouble, my boy.

*One on my lap the other in my womb; I will have two and then
what will I do?*
Proud Mother of her boys.

Can you hear me? To you I am pouring out my heart.
Will you start to listen to me like a man rather than a boy?

*Birthdays become less enchanting it seems; another year has
passed, 33 here at last.*
Just a day where Debbie exclaims flatly, "oh boy."

—Debbie

"I actually spent weeks thinking of what that connecting line would be, and as always it seems, I was doing my thinking in the car on the few occasions where I was driving by myself," she says. She settled on "boy," because it seemed to represent everything that was weighing on her mind most heavily in one word.

Thinking of how to put her frustrations, worries, anxieties, and concerns into a poem helped direct her thoughts and give them a purpose, which in turn helped her ease her anxiety. She could let each thought come and go. "I found it particularly interesting," she says, "to read back a poem of all these couplets that didn't seem to have a single thing in common to find that in a weird way they sort of did."

The adaptability of the ghazal to address anything that is going on appealed to Debbie, as she is most often inspired to write by current events, whether they are happening in her home, community, family—or her health. Her next ghazal was inspired by her struggle with allergies. As she says, "The poem happened because I was up at 6:30 a.m.—a good two hours earlier than normal—because the damned fall elm and mold counts are so high, and I'm not taking any allergy meds due to the pregnancy, and I couldn't sleep!" Just the act of breathing was her entire focus. She decided to try to take her mind off trying to breathe . . . and just breathe.

BREATHE

Allergies and sinus troubles ail me
I wake, sleep at stake. I wish I could just breathe.

Great year; Enthusiast gives it a 90
Look at those legs! Full bouquet just begs, for me to breathe.

Tongue lolls out of her mouth
Drool falls as she drops the ball for another throw and tries to
*   breathe.*

You ask me what is wrong
Sometimes I just don't know, it isn't always so, my mind just
*   needs to breathe*

Love, yet impatience and frustration
A flower wilts, so much guilt; Debbie, before speaking sometimes
*   you must first breathe*

—Debbie

At first it was difficult to accept that each couplet didn't have to relate to or depend on any other. Yet, this also became the thing Debbie liked most about the ghazal as she worked on hers. It is a

[117]

type of poem that she can leave and return to. As she says, "Honestly, I don't think I have ever in my life spent more than twenty minutes writing a poem because I just get too distracted. I also tend to like my spontaneous ideas better than my carefully formulated ones." With the ghazal, twenty minutes here and there is all you need.

Posse Pointer

Debbie concentrated on the repeated element and the rhyme but decided to let the elements place themselves instead of forcing their placement. Her two ghazals have different rhyme schemes, but she was consistent within each poem. This helped her not get stuck in the form. It's okay to let your words determine the form as much as the form helps determine your words.

Tips on Daydreaming
(there is no real "subject" here)

- Writing about the excitement and business of a subway station while in a subway station is a good idea; however, to get the full benefit of daydreaming, you'll probably need a bit of peace and quiet.
- One great thing about a ghazal is that it can easily be put on hold and continued later. Since each couplet needs to stand on its own, you can lose your train of thought and come back; it's perfectly acceptable in the ghazal—practically *encouraged*.
- It might be beneficial to use some of your "dreaming" time to take notes on what crosses your mind, jotting images, impressions, wishes, concerns, ramblings, rants, and so on before writing your ghazal. That way, your mind is free to roam without having to fit into a form. (A repeated element that could serve as your refrain might even become evident in your "notes.") You might find this method particularly

helpful when first attempting ghazals, because it is hard to let your mind wander when you are concerned with "rules."

- When writing, challenge yourself to change your mood from one couplet to the next. If you find you are feeling particularly down in one, choose to be up in the next. If you are playful in one, be serious next. If you are brave in one, find how to be vulnerable in the next. Challenge your mind to wander and not just stick to one thing; travel all your internal hills and valleys.
- A ghazal accommodates any subject matter—politics, dreams, worries, health concerns, anxieties, musings, love, memories. Since each couplet can change direction with the breezes blowing through your mind, it is a good poem to sit down with when you want to write but are not sure what you want to write about. Just start. The poem will follow.

Give It a Try

Daydreaming is actually harder than it sounds. It means that you have to put yourself and your innermost thoughts in the number-one spot on your to-do list. It might even mean ripping your to-do list to shreds. And once you start daydreaming it is often difficult to sustain the mood. The laundry buzzer reminds you of household duties, the phone's ring of responsibilities, and the tick of the clock of family obligations. It might sound like an oxymoron, but it takes discipline and practice to be a proper daydreamer!

Dare to make yourself and your mind's music priorities. Set aside some time for nothing other than pure, unadulterated daydreaming—even if it's only twenty minutes a day. Then, take it a step further into indulgence and write a poem using the seemingly random notes that make up the symphony of your life.

You do have the time. How many hours a week do you waste watching TV? Surfing the web? Reading celebrity gossip? Okay, so those are vices of mine, but you probably have some spare time lost between the cushions of your life if you really look. What do you do with the average waiting time of twenty-three minutes at the doctor's office? What about your travel for business, those hours when you are in flight or alone in your hotel room?

If this just seems too whimsical and you have a tough time believing it is time best spent, use the time to deter yourself from a bad habit. Steer your mind away from that late night piece of chocolate cake, just one more cigarette, your final glass of wine, a full-fledged pity party, calling your no-good ex-boyfriend, or making even one more useless, wasteful purchase. If giving day-dreaming a purpose works for you, then give it a purpose. We *all* have a bad habit or two we could avoid by daydreaming.

Here are three questions that might help you get a serious day-dreaming session underway—the first step in writing your ghazal.

1. If you are taking time to daydream toward the end of the day, what would you change about the day so far? If you are taking this time in the morning, what would change about yesterday?
2. If you won the largest lottery payout in history, whom would you tell first and what is the first thing that you would buy?
3. Where would you go if you had unlimited funds and had to go *alone?*

Let's hope your daydreaming will become a habit and that you'll regularly take time out of your busy schedule to get in touch with your dreams, let your mind wander, and maybe even break some bad habits. Don't discount the value of allowing yourself to spend time doing absolutely nothing but noting the thoughts that float across the ocean of your mind. You realize what it is you really dream and what things you really want. As Janet Finch said, "Inside every human being, there is unlimited time and space. In our external life, we can be only one person. But in our imagination, we can be anyone, anywhere." Get in touch with some of your possibilities. And committing some of these to writing in some ghazals will not only help you catch thoughts, ideas, or passions as they dip and dive into your ocean, it will also make you responsible for the ones you do catch.

A Poetic Pause: How to Find Just a Little Extra Time

So how do you fit not only daydreaming but also writing poetry into an already full schedule?

Erin finds quiet time at work. She says, "For some reason, most days around 4 p.m. I hit a lull at work and find that I am able to think 'creatively' after thinking 'financially' all day."

Lori found a way at home to grab some extra time. She limits her TV time to only her favorite shows. She suggests, "Turn off the TV. I don't mean don't watch TV at all but limit yourself to your favorite shows. As soon as they're over, hit the 'off' button. Don't just channel surf or watch the next show because it happened to start immediately and you're still sitting there. You'll be amazed at how much time you can capture by doing this."

I do most of my writing at home. I wake before my family does and use the quiet morning hours to write. It was extremely difficult to make this a habit—I'm a nine-hours-a-night kind of gal—but now that I've done so, I feel anxious and forgetful all day when I don't, as if something is missing. The morning has a magic in it that sets the tone for the entire day.

I also find time by cooking: and I hate to cook. I sequester myself in the kitchen, announce "I'm cooking," grab a glass of wine and my journal, and I'm good to go. I don't make anything complicated. But while the chicken is baking or the pasta is boiling, I write. No one bothers me, because to come in the kitchen is to have to help out.

Heather and Michelle manage to find a moment of quiet here and there at home. Heather writes early in the morning if she is lucky enough to rise before her baby, and Michelle takes advantage of the times her daughter is taking a bath or engrossed in a cartoon.

On a side note, while I enjoy writing at McDonald's while my son is playing, Michelle's experience was different. She says, "Just for the record, I tried writing at McDonald's playland, but my list poem started to take on the tune of *Why I Hate McDonald's*. Then my husband showed up and started asking stupid questions and it started to sound like *Why I Hate My Husband*. McDonald's is not conducive to *my* creativity." Well, it's worth a try, anyway.

If you literally only have time for one lone couplet, consider composing a group poem with some email buddies. It's not only a great way to keep up with what's going on with them, but also a way to sneak in some poetry. You can write a group poem using just about any form. This is a group ghazal the Posse wrote:

OUR GHAZAL

No, not the Liberty Bell but Donne's bell tolled nearly three thousand times on the news today.

The price of a mink, the number of days in more than eight years,
*   the chime is too loud today.*

(Wendy)

She came to her senses only this morning
"I will not wear leggings with a dress," she vowed today.

(Erin)

What a day! I had no qualms about the temperature, tempera-
*   ment of my kids, or timbre of the ringing phone.*
Irritation ceased, nerves released, calmness and resolve, I am proud
*   today.*

(Heather)

"It's progress," they said, when the roadhouse gave way to the
*   road.*
But oh, the chicken fried or in your soup, green beans, potatoes &
*   cinnamon rolls—will they ever rebuild Stroud's today?*

(Lori)

2 a.m. . . . not stumbling home from the bar, rather stumbling
*   from bed to make a bottle,*
staring into the ever-trusting eyes of my newborn baby boy, imag-
*   ining all the ways I will be wowed today.*

(Jen)

I wish I had a new costume for the Halloween party today,
But thankfully I'm not a ghost and wearing a shroud today!

(Thelma)

*I don't always eat my green beans—regardless of starving kids—
    and still I want. Those who say don't do what it takes,
already do and surely have (too much). Well, get crackin, you
    know what to do. Time to make mama proud today.*

(Wendy)

*He's standing right next to me and I'm praying this moment will
    never pass away.
The train stops and my heart captures each movement, as he gets
    lost in the crowd today.*

(Kellie)

It is hard to find five minutes—much less an hour or more—
to write. But you will always find time for the things you value.
To write poetry is to dig deep for your soul; I hope you value your-
self enough to take the time.

Chapter Five

Live Now: The Haiku

The soul should always stand ajar. Ready to welcome the
ecstatic experience.

—Emily Dickinson

There was a time when I leaned on the haiku as a lifeline, a time where if I hadn't been writing—in haiku specifically —I don't know if I would have made it through as well as I eventually did. It was right after my son was born. I don't remember what exactly drew me to the haiku in particular— though surely the lack of time available to write and the lack of ability to concentrate on anything for more than twelve minutes at a time contributed—but I was almost inexplicably drawn to writing in this form. (Of course now I can look back and see that Whoever It Is You Believe In works in mysterious ways.)

The haiku helped me win back myself when my son was born. It was one of the most difficult times of my life to date. While I know *now* that most new mothers feel this way, *then* I really had no idea. Fellow Posse member Lori and I were talking over lunch the other day and I found out that she had an incredibly difficult time when her third child was born. I didn't know her then, but I was still surprised. I mean, here is this extremely competent woman who seems to function effortlessly in her roles as attorney, mother of three, wife, and friend. She always looks cute, is unfairly thin (and I'll just say it no matter how un-PC: especially for having had three children), never misses a school function, and I can't imagine her not being in complete control of any situation, whether it involves crying kids or legal briefs. I was surprised to learn that she found motherhood, and especially being a mother to her third infant, as challenging and overwhelming as I did.

We decided that this is one of the greatest myths of being a woman: that having a baby (or three) is anything but one of the most difficult things a woman will ever do, a life-altering event that takes an unimaginable, indescribable toll. It's not all cuddles and giggles.

So, while I had read my *Child* magazine faithfully and had several pages of *What to Expect When You're Expecting* earmarked and knew what I *should* expect, I was in no way prepared for what *actually* happened. I expected intense, overwhelming love, but I did not expect equally intense sadness and a frantic, debilitating sort of helplessness and anxiety. I had no idea what I was doing with a baby and wondered quite often what the Cosmos was thinking when I ended up with one. Had it just been the addition of a baby in my life, perhaps I would have been okay, but my marriage was slow in adjusting, my self-esteem was in the basement along with all my cute pre-pregnancy clothes, and I didn't have any family or friends I thought I could turn to. Many of my friends were expecting, and I didn't think it was right to burden them while they could still enjoy the ignorance that is the glow of pregnancy. My friends who had kids, I thought, never felt like this; and the fact that I did, I thought, made me the worst thing on the planet: *a bad mom*. I thought that if I told them, they would shun me from the Good Mom Club forever. My mom lived far away and my sister lived just as far the other way. I felt totally alone, except for a baby who cried all the time. And I do mean *all the time*, seemingly demanding more than I could give.

One day, out of desperation, I looked up how to write a haiku on the Internet (I kind of remembered, but I have always liked to know *exactly*) and started writing. I wrote them when he was crying; I wrote them those glorious twenty minutes when he napped; I wrote them in my head while we rocked for hours at a time; and I wrote them at 3 a.m. when he could get back to sleep but I couldn't. It was something that centered me and kept me in the moment. There were so many self-defeating thoughts; I concentrated on finding one peaceful, nice, or hopeful thing about the one moment I was in. I couldn't make it day-to-day or even hour-to-hour. I was surviving moment to moment. Sometimes I would sit and write ten or fifteen haiku in a row—almost obsessively. I forced myself to find something, anything, good or true and concentrate on that one thing. I truly believe the act of writing haikus helped get me to the other side of the depression I was battling. And make it to the other side I did.

I still write haiku, and I use this poetic form in particular to stop myself whenever I feel panicked, anxious, or teetering on the brink of something—something that I can't quite name, but just *know* will probably be bad—and notice that one thing that will stop the barrage of negative thoughts. It brings me back to where I am, which is always better than whatever I am imagining. Haiku force me to live the moment of *now,* which, in reality, is the only moment I can fully live.

Why a Haiku?

Haiku are everywhere. Debbie gets on this Austin, Texas, message board with other moms where there is a section called Mama-kus, which, as the name suggests, is full of haiku about motherhood. (It's austinmama.com if you live in the area.) I remember a haiku contest on one of my favorite radio stations that offered as the prize tickets to the some music festival. The winning haiku was a work of brilliance, describing how puke alters the feel of grass—a poem with *levels* for sure. Haiku have appeared in such TV shows as *Beavis and Butt-Head* and *South Park*. The late-nineties film *Fight Club* included a haiku on the subject of dissatisfaction with one's work in the modern world. Even the character Bowser in the game *Super Mario RPG: Legend of the Seven Stars* has his own haiku. You can walk into Urban Outfitters and probably find some kind of haiku book at any given time. *Salon* magazine once held a haiku contest on the topic of computer error messages. Haiku is a poetic form that has definitely permeated pop culture. There is a Haiku Society of America, a World Haiku Club, a World Haiku Association, and a *Modern Haiku* magazine, in addition to countless websites devoted to this form of poetry.

So what's the big deal? The big deal is such a little poem gives back something very big. Haiku are short poems with easy-to-follow rules, but one of these rules is that they must use the present tense or at least evoke a sense of something *happening* in the present. As a result, the writer must concentrate on something small and special that is happening *now*. Haiku bring your attention to the present moment, compelling you to experience joy, appreciation, and gratitude—and, if you can't muster that, humor—for the here and now. Writing haiku is a way to step back from stress and into appreciation, for we can only live one moment at a time.

We as people, but especially as women, have days that are more stressful than others. I swear my son will throw a fit because he can't wear red stripes *only* on mornings I have an early meeting. I won't spill my afternoon cup of coffee unless I'm wearing white pants. Of course, kids *never* get sick on Saturdays. It is often difficult to stop a morning or day from snowballing into thoughts that life just plain sucks. Writing haiku brings your attention to the here and now and encourages you to find some beauty, magic, joy—or at least some humor—in one livable moment. I think we can all agree that our lives would be more enjoyable if we could live moment by moment instead of entertaining all the regrets of yesterday and all the worries of tomorrow. Of course, that's much harder than it sounds. We do need help. Enter the haiku.

One morning, I was driving my son to school. It was very cold and dreary. Everything was that particular dreariness of a snow-laden sky, almost exactly the hue of a gray Crayola crayon. Because the sky was heavy, the morning felt heavy. Snow was coming and everyone knew it, and I could almost *feel* the anticipation in the way people drove and in the way they hurried across the street. Grocery store parking lots were full, and lines at the gas station were long, even that early in the morning. For once all the weather people had gotten it right, and the sky was waiting to get just a *little bit* fuller before letting go.

I was hurried along with everyone else, trying to fill up on gas, load up on the necessities of hot chocolate and popcorn, drop my son off at school, and get into my office before it actually started snowing. I was driving too fast, already annoyed with the problems it was going to cause—dangerous roads, heavy traffic—irritated because I had forgotten to weather-proof my new black boots, already overloaded with the work I would miss *if* the next day was a snow day, even though nothing was happening yet. I was just a bundle of anticipating-the-worse.

Then, the expected did happen—the sky literally opened up. But something totally unexpected happened too: It *thundered* as the snow fell in enormous bright white flakes. Honest-to-God *thunder,* at the exact same moment the first flake fell. I was suddenly and completely aware of my own small existence, and all my worries seemed small, too. To this day that is one of the most unusual and memorable mornings I have ever had, and it's an insight I won't forget. It's also one of the most special moments I've ever had with my son. We were both awed, and we felt so lucky to be together. As soon as I got to work, I jotted down this haiku and completely forgot all the annoyances that come with a Midwestern snow.

Is it God? he asks
No, I laugh, just thunder-snow.
Then: well, I . . . maybe

—Wendy

Lori was, of all the Posse, one of the most enthusiastic about the haiku. She welcomed the opportunity to live in the little moments of magic that so easily pass us by, and I think she might be hooked. After writing her first haiku she said, "The haiku definitely has therapeutic value. Writing the haiku made me reflect on a moment that otherwise would've gone unnoticed. And it gave me a lift to begin another workday. I need to write more!"

One morning, Lori was taking her three kids to school on her way to work. It was a thick summer morning, on its way to being an unbearably hot day. Lori was rushing a bit, trying to get her kids in the building before her work clothes got sweaty. "It was one of those 100-plus Kansas City heat waves," she says. "The kind weathermen call *very unusual*—year after year." As the kids were getting out of the car, they noticed a cicada sitting on the top of the license plate. All three leaned in to investigate. Even Lori was drawn in. She says, "Its wings were longer than its body; its head huge. We watched its eyes move as it watched us. Its legs fidgeted, but it didn't leave. What was the cicada doing there? Aren't they supposed to come out in the evening? Had it just alighted or did it ride with us from the house?"

She took the kids into school and continued on to work. She was all the way in her office, seated for the day, when she thought, "Aha! A subject." She took a few moments to jot down some impressions, thoughts, and phrases. She wanted to note what the bug looked like, that it was blazing hot outside, but mostly she wondered what he was doing balanced on the top edge of her license plate, and she wanted to come up with an answer. And as Lori says, "My haiku gave me the answer."

June bug on my car,
wings of spun-sugar melt, free
air conditioning.

—Lori

Lori continued to find inspiration everywhere she looked. She found a poem in the morning she was supposed to be able to sleep in, although her cat, Flint, woke her up anyway. She found inspiration in the sad state of her garden during a relentless summer drought. "I love the haiku," she says, "It's quirky and offbeat, which fits my own personality. And it's short. So many tasks in life seem endless. Or is it that we have so much to do, we can never finish anything? But you can write a haiku quickly, for an instant sense of accomplishment." My favorite haiku of those Lori wrote is this one:

I have the power
to make rain. Turn the spigot—
and thunderclap sky.

—Lori

This one was inspired by the special kind of summer heat that makes one feel powerless: powerless to keep plants alive, powerless to go outside, and powerless to feel anything but tired and nearly suffocated. But, Lori chose to feel a different way. She says, "Watering the yard in summer is my way of conquering nature. It is *empowering*." The sprinkler is an integral part of summer for Lori. She loves to watch her kids play in it; she loves to skip through herself when it is intensely hot, pretending it's rain; and she loves the way her plants perk up after a good soaking.

And what inevitably happens when she turns on the sprinkler? It rains, of course. As Lori says, "No matter how long it's gone without raining, as soon as I turn on the sprinkler, it'll rain. Mother Nature doesn't like to be upstaged, I guess. But I still like to think I had something to do with it." So, Lori has the power to make rain.

I love any poem that starts out with "I have the power," but especially a haiku that would have to explain that power with only twelve syllables left! Lori said that this particular haiku resonates with her far beyond turning on the sprinkler, and she keeps it where she can reread it. As she says, "Women have power. We don't always use it, and many of us don't even know we have it. We have the power to heal wounds and to make the sun rise—at least as far as our children are concerned. We have our intuition, our sixth sense. We can nurture and negotiate. In a figurative sense, this haiku is a mantra, a reminder to myself of this truth."

Even though Lori and I love to find our haiku moments, you might be wondering, *but why the haiku in particular?* If so, you're not alone. There are members of the Posse who were unconvinced at the beginning about writing in form. But writing in the haiku form has three main benefits. First, choosing your words and phrases specifically and carefully in order to fit in it all into just a limited number of syllables and lines forces you to experience what you are writing about in minute detail, perhaps noticing something you didn't before. Second, you have to slow down enough to notice one particular thing or moment clearly enough to actually write about it. Third, it is amazing mental exercise: it is hard, maybe even harder than most other types of poetry, because you must notice just one moment and not an entire day. After all, it's our moments that make up our days. And to make the most of our moments is to make the most of our lives.

You just might find a power of your own after a few haiku. Certainly you will find the power to see your *now*s as they happen, when you still have the chance to live them.

Haiku Soundtrack

Lori says, "I like music that lifts you up. It can make you simply smile, move you to dance, or, more seriously, take you to a higher place spiritually. I find that being out in nature has the same effect, so music and the haiku naturally go together." Here is her haiku soundtrack:

1. "Waters of March" by Suzannah McCorkle. This song, like the haiku itself, is an affirmation of life.
2. "Peace Train" by 10,000 Maniacs
3. "Orinoco Flow (Sail Away)" by Enya
4. "Zimbabwe" by Toni Childs
5. "Sunshine Day" by (yes!) the Brady Bunch Kids

So What Exactly Makes a Haiku?

Haiku appear simple because of their short length, but writing a good one takes practice, concentration, and time. Your World Famous Brownie Recipe probably wasn't perfected on the first try; but you most likely enjoyed the process of perfecting it. So while a haiku seems simple, I think you'll find it (delightfully) more challenging than you might initially think but entirely worth the effort. The more you write, the more your poems will improve and the better you'll get at noticing and appreciating the small, great things that surround you all the time. You'll get better at noticing *now*.

A haiku is a three-line poem. The first line has five syllables, the second has seven, and the third has five. Seventeen syllables, divided among three lines. 5-7-5: that's it. At least that's what Ms. Kelly, my fourth grade teacher said; and that's what I have always followed, because I like rules. If you are somewhat of a rebel, fear not: like most things, it's just a guideline; most of all, it's a way to help you keep things short and exact, true to the intent of a haiku.

Unlike other poetic forms, part of *how* to write a traditional haiku is *what* to write about. The classic haiku theme is nature. It is a unique way to appreciate and record the ordinary sights, sounds, and smells that Mother Nature gives us every day. The haiku also challenges you to focus: your haiku should describe one thing, not attempt to describe a season or an entire scene as a whole. It is a snapshot, as if you're calling someone over to see what you just captured in that small square of your digital camera. It is always in the present tense or at least evokes the feeling that what you are describing is happening *right now*. The haiku asks you to focus on nature and what it means to you, but only in one particular moment: now.

A haiku typically contains a "season word" (*kigo*). Instead of naming the season outright, you let the reader feel it or sense it. For example, instead of summer, you could use fireflies. Instead of winter, you could use icicles. For spring, maybe green; and for fall, perhaps gold. Or you could go with holiday imagery: Christmas for winter, Easter for spring, Independence Day for summer, and Halloween for fall.

Another interesting and challenging thing about haiku is that they are generally untitled. Because they are supposed to be complete and understandable in themselves, titles are unnecessary.

Haiku are emotional. The idea is that by showing feeling, you leave a definite mental image of what you are experiencing. Instead of saying something is lovely, you should describe what is lovely about it. The haiku should invoke feeling rather than dictate it. It should provide imagery you find beautiful rather than use the word beautiful.

Many of the haiku written by the Posse contain humor. Although some students of poetry distinguish between the senryu and the haiku by saying that the senryu is humor-based—whereas the haiku should maintain an intense emotional state without humor—we say life is too short, and will be making no such distinctions. What is important is how haiku help us appreciate what is happening around us, and how we use poetry to express gratitude for our lives *as* they are happening—something that sometimes necessitates a sense of humor.

To sum it up, a haiku is a three-line poem with the syllable count 5-7-5. It always takes place in the present tense, focusing on one thing happening right now. It is traditionally about something in nature, containing a "season word." The idea is to *show* how you feel about what is happening rather than *tell* how you feel about what is happening. That's what most textbooks say anyway—and Ms. Kelly.

Many haiku writers don't force themselves to stick with the 5-7-5 division of syllables among lines or even the total syllable count of 17. In fact, many think that a 12-syllable count is truer to the original Japanese form. Most do think that the first and third lines should be shorter than the second. What is essential for a haiku is not the syllable count but the poem's inclusion of a concise, perceptive, aware image about *now*.

Writing in this form will help you focus and re-center yourself. You can't go on and on about something or get lost in uncertainties or intangibles. You have to concentrate on what is right in front of you—what is happening now. You can't consider the "big" picture, but only one of a thousand small details that make the big picture as beautiful as it is.

Tips on Form

- A short, concise syllable count, three-line format, present tense, and nature-centered theme are essential to the traditional haiku. You probably want to shy away from any other poetic devices such as rhyme, meter, alliteration, repetition, and so on, but ultimately do feel free to experiment.
- Your "season word" can be any of thousands of words. Use your imagination to come up with all sorts of ideas about what season different words belong to. Entire works, called *saijiki*, have been written describing and classifying words and phrases by their season. Try brainstorming; come up with a list of possible words before you start. This part can be a lot of fun.
- "*Hai-ku*" means "beginning phrase," so while it is an accepted complete form now, it was originally intended to be the beginning of a longer poem. I find, especially at the beginning of putting something in haiku verse, that it is really difficult to stick to just three lines; I often use six lines, 5-7-5-5-7-5. I try not to go any longer.

Posse Pointer

Lori starts out writing in her head. She says, "I come up with words, phrases, verbs and arrange them in different ways, counting out the syllables on my fingers. This can be done anywhere: in the car, in the shower, while making supper or washing dishes." This not only helps you when you actually sit down to write a haiku, it also will help you notice possible haiku subjects no matter where you are or what you're doing.

For Further Reading

The haiku is one of the oldest forms you'll find in this book. Though "haiku" technically only dates back to the nineteenth century, its tradition goes back to sixteenth-century Japan. I like the feeling of writing in a form that has traveled the strands of time to act as a pearl on my particular strand, a form that will continue to capture the fancy of writers long after I'm gone, creating a necklace of sorts connecting us all.

If you want to read the work of a true haiku master, find work by Chiyo-ni. She lived from 1703 to 1775 and is one of the most respected Japanese haiku poets. One of the amazing things about Chiyo-ni is that she achieved fame during her lifetime in an age when women's freedom and creativity were restricted. *Chiyo-ni: Woman Haiku Master* is a great book on her life and her work. You will most likely be able to find many translated examples of her work on the Internet.

Some of my favorite modern poets have written haiku. Because haiku are most often untitled, I've listed poets that have written in haiku if no title was specified. You will note that often poets use the haiku as a stanza form in longer poems or write several connected haiku.

- Sonia Sanchez. She once said of the haiku, "When I have thought I had very little time to put some of my thoughts on paper, I've retreated to haiku . . . and felt a world of form that allowed me to live and breathe out my pain and joy."
- *Canicula* by Mary Kinzie. This is a collection of eight closed haiku that tell a story through metaphor.
- Look for haiku by Marlene Mountain, Anita Virgil, Alexis Rotella, Ruth Yarrow, Ruth Weiss, and Ruby Schackleford. Using your favorite search engine, you should be able to find

at least a few on the Internet, though, of course, the most reliable resource is your good old-fashioned library.

- There are haiku influences in Alice Walker's *African Images, Glimpses from the Tiger's Back*.
- One of my son's favorite books is *Least Things* by Jane Yolen. It is a collection of animal haiku accompanied by bright, stunning photographs. My favorites are the butterfly, lizard, and tree frog.
- *Haiku Mama* by Kari Anne Roy is a wonderful little book of haiku and makes a great gift for a new mother.

What Should I Write About?

Nature is the traditional theme of the haiku and a reason that it is one of the best forms for appreciating and living every single moment. As Lori says, "Its focus on nature forces you to stop and appreciate. Nature is, itself, an affirmation of life." Few things are more magical or inspiring than nature. When you really concentrate, and aim to truly *see*, you'll find a million things Mother Nature has to offer in each moment.

With that said, each person's seasons are as individual as the person herself, and the benefits of writing in haiku can go beyond conventional nature.

I do love the seasons but, personally, I am not one to spend a great deal of time pondering a blade of grass, the winter moon, or—gasp!—a sunrise. I do love living in a part of the country that offers four complete seasons, but I probably appreciate something different from what you might expect from someone who likes to write poetry. What do the seasons mean to me? Well, all those beautiful shades of gold falling from the trees in fall really mean that I've got to get out there with a not-so beautiful rake; winter is hardly a wonderland to me when it is slippery and bitterly cold; all the rain in spring gets annoying; and summer is simply too damned hot sometimes. So, what do I love most about the differences that each season offers? Shoes and cocktails.

THE SEASONS

knee-high brown suede boots
crunching, approach the red wine
man in his plaid scarf

numb toes in black heels
flannel suit warned gray and white
oh hell. brandy warms

wedges dress bare legs
enjoying chardonnay on
an honest pink day

metallic flip-flops
naked, alone on sand the
color of cold beer

—Wendy

Try as Debbie might, when she tackled writing haiku, nothing magical about nature jumped out at her. She couldn't muster the energy to care whether it rained or not, and she was too tired chasing a toddler and being five months pregnant to give a damn whether the hydrangeas were blooming. No matter how long she tried to be still and concentrate, it just wasn't happening. Yet she found a way to use her little moments in haiku that worked for

her. She used humor to approach the everyday happenings of having a toddler and being pregnant. Here are a few of her haiku:

Stinky diaper filled
Boy runs away shouting no!
Can he not smell it?

Sciatic pain shoots
Pregnant waddle has begun
Feel like I'm eighty

Scream, scream, yell and scream
No screaming! No yelling! No!
Scream, scream, yell and scream

—Debbie

While Debbie's haiku perhaps don't overtly appreciate something in nature, reveal deep insight, or provide perspective about what is happening around her, they do tend to make her laugh—the best, most natural de-stressor there is. As she says, "These poems take me a matter of seconds to write when I'm in that mode—and generally that 'mode' is a stressful day where I need to just step back for a second and laugh rather than let my blood pressure rise and my negative emotions get the best of me."

Jen's relocation to San Diego from the Arlington, Virginia, area was a tough adjustment. After living in Virginia for more than ten years, she truly considered it home. She enjoyed many long-term friendships—her high school best friend lived nearby— she had a career she was proud of, and they had just purchased a gorgeous new town-home. Then her husband got a fabulous job opportunity, and off to California they went. Jen found out she was pregnant—after they stopped "trying," of course—just a few weeks before the movers showed up. So Jen was leaving her job, her home, her friends, and her old version of family behind. She arrived in California with no job, no friends, and a belly too big to wear a bikini (in her opinion, anyway). I asked her for two weeks to try to write a haiku—or, at the very least, consider what she might write about—every time she started to feel depressed or negative.

The first one she wrote was because a California day was turning out cloudy and drizzly, ruining her plans to spend the entire day by the pool. But, on the lookout for haiku, she noticed something she might not have otherwise. As she says, "I looked out my balcony window at the gloom and saw a hummingbird at my plants." Any other time this sight would have gone by unnoticed and Jen would have continued feeling sorry for herself, ruining her day. But, because she had an "assignment," she wrote this haiku:

Flowers blooming in pots
hanging in the California breeze
a hummingbird's delight.

—Jen

Maybe she didn't like how the day was turning out, but the hummingbird seemed to like it just fine. Jen was dutiful for those two weeks. She tried to find joy in the little things, like when her husband took the long way home from Santa Barbara, detouring through LA, just so Jen could indulge in a Sonic cherry limeade slush:

Vast sea of tail lights
stop and go—mostly stopping
anticipation
Neon lights ahead
ahhhh, a cherry limeade slush
heaven in a cup.

—Jen

Rather than lamenting the fact that she wasn't working, she tried to appreciate the lazy, indulgent days by the pool, her only company an *In Touch* magazine: these were days she would never have had back in Virginia. She concentrated on the part of the day she likes the most (bedtime) and how the chirping crickets are so much louder in California, producing a unique, serene music set against the sea's crashing surf. She even used the haiku to write about a family trip to Legoland.

When her two-week haiku stint was up, she was surprised at the moments she recorded. They were all happy times, not one sad or down. There was something about poetry—and maybe haiku in particular—that encouraged her to find the good. It just didn't seem natural—or even occur—to her to write about her loneliness. Writing haiku didn't magically whisk away her homesickness or her lonesomeness for her friends, but, as she says, "I did feel better these past couple of weeks, so maybe it was there for a reason."

Shannon took a once-in-a-lifetime trip to Thailand. There were a thousand things she wanted to remember, but there was one thing she knew she couldn't forget. When visiting Bangkok, a passionate rally was held in support of the Thai Rak Thai political party. Thousands of people were bused in to support their prime minister.

The cab driver wanted to take Shannon and her friend to the rally. Sensing danger in the charged atmosphere they declined and decided to visit Khoa Sarn Road instead, where the streets are lined with shops, vendors, restaurants, and bars that all have guesthouses above for the use of backpackers. The two extremes struck Shannon, as well as the difference between the activities of those who lived there and those who were simply traveling there. As she says, "It was like walking into another world where there were no political issues, just travelers partying and buying cheap Thai things." Yet not more than a mile away, locals were rallying for a cause with fervor and passion. Shannon says, "As I sat out front at our favorite bar, in the center of the road, I was overwhelmed with a surreal feeling that I knew something most of these people did not and would not care to know the history behind (a harsh judgment on my part), although I was surrounded by people drinking and laughing and buying things. The contrast was overwhelming."

a rally for beliefs
not more than a mile away
a rally for play

—Shannon

Shannon wrote this haiku as a way to remember this one moment so that it wouldn't get lost in the hugeness of her experience.

Though the Posse wrote about a lot of different things in haiku, in each instance it was about appreciating one small, never-to-be-repeated moment. Kellie imagined herself vacationing on a beach, Nikki wrote about her son's first day at kindergarten, Debbie wrote mainly about motherhood in mostly funny ways (only Debbie can turn a poopy diaper into a poetic moment), and

Erin tackled one of the most annoying parts of her day: the time right around dawn that she has to let her little dog out to pee. Angie started to look for possibilities all around her, even finding herself drumming on the steering wheel for an entire two-hour drive. No, not to the radio, she was counting syllables, composing haiku in her head of the things she saw along the way. An ordinarily boring, dreaded drive went by in a flash of clouds, wildflowers, and budding trees.

Writing about nature is one of the ways the haiku is such an inspiring, calming, beneficial type of poetry to write. It forces you to appreciate one moment as it's happening, experiencing the magic in the ordinariness that surrounds you every day. It's hard to be upset with your kid when he's brought you the most perfect dandelion he could find in the yard. It's hard to feel stressed in rush-hour deadlock when you notice the shapes in the clouds. It's hard to feel inconvenienced by the rain when you notice how it makes summer streets shine.

Yet you can use the benefits of the haiku to write about many things other than trees and waterfalls. I think motherhood and all its extensions make wonderful haiku subjects, because, after all, what is more natural and awe-inspiring than motherhood? And, as Debbie shows us, it is motherhood that is often the reason we need to step back for a moment of decompression and laughter. I think sports are acceptable subjects for haiku, too. "Football" is a great season word for fall; "basketball" for March, or spring. And, of course, there are myriad things that you can relate to nature. Sonja Sanchez uses haiku to talk about love and relationships. I also think sex is a great haiku subject. It's one of our most natural, primal urges, and it is a perfect stress reliever, a great thing to concentrate on when you need to focus on something good.

Finding inspiration—appropriate "subjects"—for poems might be intimidating in the beginning. My philosophy is that you find what you're looking for. One afternoon, I was sitting in my office *annoyed*. A coworker had come in and said something totally innocent that I took the wrong way. The project I was working on was going nowhere. I skipped lunch because I wasn't hungry at the time but then I became *starving* after the cafeteria downstairs had stopped serving. I got the call that my husband was tied up with work, leaving me to pick up our son, causing me to miss my favorite aerobics class. And I just remembered I would have to stop for gas on my way home. I was *annoyed*. I knew none of this was that big a deal—just minor, everyday stuff—but I couldn't help but clench my jaw and tense my shoulders. Then, worst of all, I heard a clap of thunder. I whipped angrily around in my chair, prepared to see the downpour that would be the topper on *that* day—and was startled to see the most amazing sight.

diamonds on the roof.
how did they fall and sound like rain?
puddles spark a day.

—Wendy

I whipped around and saw that the puddles on the hotel rooftop that I can see from my office window were positively *sparkling*. Because it was a light afternoon summer rain, the sun was still forcing a few rays through the dark clouds. I took a moment longer than I ordinarily would have to consider the sight. I don't know if I would have internalized this in quite the same way if I hadn't been *looking* for haiku material. What I do know is that I wasn't quite so annoyed. I find that a lot of the time, when I honestly look for things to write about—when I actively look for the poetic in my life—these things come to me.

Tips on Subject

- The traditional haiku subject is nature, but how you relate to nature is as individual as you are. Have fun with it; experiment. Appreciate a sunset, laugh at an errant frog, or ponder a dead squirrel in the road.
- It's important to say what you want to say and not say what you think you should say. You don't have to like snow. You don't have to like the tulips in spring. Maybe you have terrible allergies. Write your own haiku. Like most things, it won't be convincing if you're not honest—and it will hardly relieve any stress if you are trying to write what you think you should instead of what you know.
- Remember that it should be written in the present tense, so, ideally, write your haiku as it is happening—but, seriously, who really has time for that? If a thought occurs to you, jot a note or two so you don't forget.
- Haiku are short and very quick to write. You can always revise later. Consider keeping a small notebook on hand so that if you need the time out and clarity that writing a haiku can offer, you'll be ready.

Here are a few more examples from the Posse. Take a moment to appreciate our moments:

Best friend, confidante
Sees into my soul and knows . . .
Which shoes I should buy.

—Erin

when was it we stopped
watching storms roll us over—
higher than thunder
flawed by lightening—and
now consult boxed weather to
decide what to wear?

—Wendy

Hair barometer
Says spring equals thunderstorms
Must use the Frizz-ease

—Debbie

Drinking sweet ice tea
While lying in the warm sun
My worries fly free.

—Kellie

"What is that?" I asked.
Sobs echoing down the hall:
Coats feeling useless.

—Thelma

No, you don't Old Man!
Puff your chest out, if you must—
powdered sugar on
dark chocolate bark—but
I won't, I won't get my black
turtleneck back out!

—Wendy

First day has come now
I really don't want to let go
You look a little nervous

—Nikki

convertible Porsche—
dangly diamonds, yellow silk—
I want such freedom

—Wendy

Give It a Try

The haiku is the perfect opportunity to step back from the big things of life and appreciate the little things going on right now. You can't get anything from the past unless you learn from it in the present, and you can't make the future what you want unless you are currently doing your best with the present. It's all about *now*. And to get the most out of *now*, you've got to appreciate it for what it is, not what it was and not what it might (or might not) be. Stress clouds our vision and doesn't let us see the sun right behind those dark clouds, the rays that could break through, dropping diamonds in puddles. Writing haiku gives you a sense of respect, gratitude, and appreciation for life and all that surrounds you *right now*.

Here are three exercises to get you started on your new haiku lifestyle—which, by the way, would never necessitate wearing sensible shoes:

1. Take a haiku journal on your next vacation. Try to write one every day. It will rival your scrapbook as your most treasured memory-keeper.
2. What is your favorite time of day? The mid-morning hour that your baby takes a nap? Your first sip of morning coffee? Dusk, when everyone is rushing home from work?

Write a haiku about that time of day. Try to write a different haiku every day for a week about that same time of day.

3. Write a haiku about the season you like the least. Do you hate the cold of winter? Do you totally dislike the bipolar nature of spring weather? Instead of concentrating on what you know brings you wonder, concentrate on that which you don't really appreciate. Maybe you will learn to, or at least laugh at the reason you don't.

I think you'll love writing haiku once you get started. You don't have to be a surfer living on the beach, one who spends summers kayaking, or a true camper with your own pop-up tent to appreciate Mother Nature. Beverly says her idea of "roughing it" is a hotel without room service. Yet she creates beautiful flower arrangements for her deck every spring and summer.

Here's another aspect of haiku writing that I have been finding beneficial lately: I think we all have a Thing—well, some of us (me) have many Things, but whatever—this is the Thing that you feel nervous or shy about committing to paper, something that you hesitate to write about because it's so big and important (possibly sad, scary, or regrettable) that it scares the you-know-what out of you to think of someone (maybe a specific someone) finding it and reading it. Or maybe you're afraid because you think that you can't do justice to it, that you wouldn't be good enough. Or maybe it's something you're not ready to face, maybe something you know deep down that you aren't ready to be completely honest about. Or possibly it's still too hot and you don't want to get burned by getting too close.

But, of course, your Thing is the thing you must write about—eventually. Poetry can help you deal with your Thing, whatever it is. It can help you decide how you really feel about it, giving you perspective and maybe once-and-for-all release. You may even see some humor or discover some hidden creativity while you're at it. But, like anything else, it—not only writing poetry but also facing your Thing—takes practice.

It's OK that there's something you aren't ready to write about; if it's that important, you want to be better before you tackle it. For me, haiku are the perfect way to practice writing until I'm ready. Haiku bring your attention back to all the beauty and magic that surround you every day, letting you be a part of something bigger than yourself for just a moment. Rest assured that you'll be ready to write about your Thing; but, in the meantime, take your mind off it until you're better. Know that, no matter what, the sun will rise, and the seasons will change—and that writing about those things is a perfectly legitimate and productive thing to do.

A Poetic Pause: Multitasking; Things to Do While Writing Poetry

Women are born multitaskers. We can juggle more things than the writers at *Vogue* during fashion week. In fact, it's no surprise that most of those writers are women. We could probably solve many of the world's crises—if only we had the time.

Poetry really can fit into your life—it doesn't require adding any additional bowling pins into the juggling act. I believe that if you really give it a try, it will make your life better by helping you be more creative, expressing yourself in your own individual style; more free, helping you deal with difficult things; and more content, teaching you to know yourself a little better. But, just to prove my point that you, your current responsibilities, and poetry can coexist peacefully and beneficially, I'll show you that there are things you can do *while* writing poetry. Here are just a few:

Whiten your teeth. It's no coincidence that Crest Whitestrips (or most other brands of over-the-counter teeth whiteners) take thirty minutes—so you can do something else while you sit there with that gross strip on your teeth. Why not use those thirty minutes to calmly and soothingly organize your thoughts into a poem? Even if you simply jot notes to use later, it's time much better spent. You'll have whiter, brighter teeth and a whiter, brighter mind.

Pretty up your feet. Sitting back with absolutely nothing to do while your toenail paint dries might just be the perfect haiku moment. Whoever gets to think of names for nail polishes—like OPI's Fireflies, Significant Other Color, Azure for Sure, Flashbulb Fuchsia, Pink Before You Leap, You Rock-Apulca Red, Never Lon-done Shopping, and Osaka-to-Me Orange—surely is an amazing haiku writer.

Get rid of some fine lines and wrinkles. What else are you doing while you enjoy the smooth skin benefits of a face mask? Surely not socializing with your family! That's the understood rule of funny-looking beauty treatments: you do them alone. It's a given; and if you ever write your own wedding vows, you should consider adding it in just so there's no confusion. You might as well curl up in bed, fluff up your pillows, and write something. I guess it's possible to whiten your teeth, give yourself a pedicure, put on a face mask, *and* write a poem, but don't make the rest of us look bad here.

Enjoy a cup of coffee. Or tea. Or hot chocolate—whatever your fancy. I like coffee. I've cut back to three cups a day—two in the morning, one in the afternoon—but it's all about willpower. I would keep my cup constantly full and warm if it were better for me. There's something about sitting with the perfect cup of coffee—creamy, not too sweet, not too bitter, just a little too hot—that is downright inspiring to me. If you ever have the incredible luxury of a weekend afternoon home alone, go ahead: put off cleaning the basement, sit down with a cup of coffee, and write. I am telling you: there is something about poetry and coffee that makes them just go together. It's the grown-up version of milk and cookies.

Poetry does fit in. You don't even have to make room.

Chapter Six

Hear Your Inner Voice:
The Villanelle

I don't create poetry; I create myself, for my poems are a way to me.

—Edith Södergran

Honestly, I had never attempted a villanelle before writing this book. I'd heard the term—from Creepy Professor Guy—but other than knowing it was a form of poetry, I had no clue. As I researched the mechanics and read examples, it was at first very intimidating. I was tempted to skip it or leave it out altogether.

I thought about the villanelle for weeks, trying to figure out how the form might speak through me and perhaps help interpret my life. It was the first chapter of this book in which I didn't have any direct experience with that type of poetry; I wasn't sure exactly how to do it, what to write—even where to start. I'll admit: it was daunting. I suddenly felt not only afraid of writing poetry, but also of writing a book. I mean, who was I to write this book? It's one thing to piddle around writing poetry in my spare time, but I don't have a degree from Harvard; I don't publish poetry; I can't even get all my laundry folded. But I remembered an Erica Jong quote: "Fear is a sign—usually a sign that I'm doing something right," so I kept thinking.

Part of the villanelle's structure is that it repeats lines or phrases. I focused on that aspect and wondered, *what is important about that?* The more I thought about it, especially during quiet times, like while on the treadmill or in the car by myself, I realized that there are lots of repeated lines and phrases in my life. Sometimes these messages sneak in when I'm not paying attention and let doubt leak in, and other times I call on them for strength.

I thought about the things, both positive and negative, that I repeat to myself and came to the conclusion that it is these recurring lines and phrases that make up the most important voice of all—my inner voice.

What do I mean by "inner voice"? Some call it intuition, inner guidance, the voice of reason, or self-confidence. It can also be guilt, doubt, or insecurity. I call all those things together my inner voice, that voice within, that only I can hear, that gets me out of bed or lures me back in to spend the day with the covers pulled over my head. It's the one that tells me whether it's a sassy-skirt-and-boot or oversize-sweater-and-baggy-pants kind of day. It's all the things I hear—all the repeated lines and phrases of my life—that blend into the one voice that guides me through each decision, big and small.

Where do these repeated lines and phrases come from? I'm not schizoid or crazy (exactly); I'm talking about messages—like advice, criticism, gossip, and encouragement—that stick with us for one reason or another. Affecting our life greatly, they can make us try harder and not get discouraged or make us give up and never start again. They remind us of successes or failures, lift us up or tear us down. These external messages that we internalize, sometimes without even realizing it, are incredibly powerful.

Some are from the past. There are phrases of childhood—perhaps taunts, teases, or downright cruel insults—that seem to have the ability to haunt and follow us forever. When we're strong, we use them to spur us to be better; in weak moments, they can keep us from trying. Sometimes these past voices are inspirational, like a particularly involved teacher, and help us ward off negative thoughts; while at other times these past voices are incredibly destructive. An abusive childhood can affect our own words to our children. A string of perceived failures can leave us telling ourselves it's not worth trying in the future.

Some messages are present voices. There are galvanizing headlines that hopefully get us off the sofa but often leave us feeling overwhelmed and hopeless. When we hear on the evening news about children dying and suffering all over the world, and indeed going hungry in our own cities, it's easier to tell ourselves that nothing can be done instead of trying to help just one other person. The constant barrage of the sad state of our world motivates some and depresses others, but it affects us all.

Then there are the messages of advertising that lure us somewhat unwillingly but convincingly to French fries and skinny jeans simultaneously. Skinny people are complimented, but others don't hear those nice words. Beautiful people are praised, but those who are less so do not benefit from the same kindnesses. We internalize messages of unrealistic perfection or miss out on words of kindness and praise. We ourselves contribute to the inner voices of others by what we say or don't say.

We can even internalize the messages we receive at work. The occasional professional critique can be taken too personally. Jokes can go too far, and we simmer for weeks over an off-handed comment made by a colleague. We may even adopt the prejudices of those we look up to in a professional setting. We strive to be better, make more, and move faster than our colleagues and tell ourselves any number of things—true and false—to help us make this happen. Sometimes we even let the size of our paychecks speak for us.

And so these messages—from our childhood, the evening news, magazines, work, even the chatter on the street—find their way through our ears into our minds. We latch on to some and repeat them over and over. Soon they, too, become components of our inner voices.

Another big contributor to the static of voices that we mold into our inner voices is the important people in our lives. One voice from the past that I take out to help me battle doubt is from Really Great Professor Guy. He encouraged me to write honestly and to pursue writing. I can't hear the phrase "nobody ever said life was fair" without thinking of my dad, either explaining why I couldn't have something I wanted or why I had to do something I didn't want to do; I often use this as a motivator to try harder or give it a go *one more time.*

As mothers, especially, we are bombarded with the words of the world, often quite unsolicited. Everyone has an opinion, whether it's when to send your son to kindergarten or what kind of socks your infant should wear—or whether to breast-feed or bottle-feed, but I can't even go there. We also have to be constantly on guard to protect our little ones from hearing things they shouldn't, whether from TV, older kids, or our own mouths. There are lots of words mothers could do without—like incessant whining—and lots of things we can't hear enough—like "I love you." If you're a mother, you've probably also experienced that moment of utter terror when it is not your words, but your mother's words distinctly coming out of your mouth, which you swore would *never* happen.

And what about women who are not mothers, whether by choice or by fate? How do they internalize the whispers, either of pity or accusation—not to mention the constant questions and invasion of privacy? How do they react when their lives are questioned? What do their inner voices tell them?

It is all these external messages and so many more that make up our inner voice, and your inner voice is not always telling you the right thing. Sometimes we turn up the volume on the wrong frequency. But the truly powerful thing about an inner voice is that it is *yours*. You—and only you—have your hand on the tuner.

I realized I could use the villanelle to note the repeated lines and phrases of my life that make up my inner voice. Perhaps, through the writing process, I could reveal what they do for me: are they building blocks, or are they the foot that kicks it all down? I thought of the villanelle as a way to hear the messages I use to constitute my inner voice, and tune in to what it is really saying.

One evening I found myself with a few hours of glorious solitude. I knew what I had to do—and it wasn't fold the laundry. I wrote a villanelle. And it wasn't nearly as difficult as I thought it would be. You know, like dreading your first day of school or meeting your boss's wife for the first time. It was enjoyable, and I was definitely high on personal accomplishment when I finished.

The best part was knowing that I could do it and knowing what to listen for as I went about my days. I became better at hearing my inner voice, recognizing the reasons for the things I was telling myself, and altering those messages when necessary. I now use that Erica Jong quote as one of the components of my inner voice to make myself keep moving.

But Why a Villanelle?

The villanelle is a form with some rules, a bit of structure. It's an older, traditional form that still has the power to be relevant in modern times—like a classic Chanel suit.

I love the challenge and mental calisthenics it takes to sit down and adhere to exact forms like the sonnet, ghazal, and villanelle. It is a feeling similar to doing a crossword puzzle or Sudoku. Writing a villanelle is, just like a puzzle, a way to arrange words; but you get something tangible, lasting, and personally enlightening when you've finished. I think it forces you to pick the *right* words and not settle for *just* words.

There is a repeated phrase or line that is used throughout the poem and that, to me, is perfect for noticing the things—uplifting and defeating—that we say to ourselves on a daily basis. It is perfect for acknowledging those voices—either inspirational or deflating—that influence our lives so.

Writing a villanelle can help you hear your inner voice, and you need to listen—because sometimes your inner voice needs a little fine-tuning. A villanelle will help you hear whether the messages of your life that constitute your inner voice are helping you or hurting you. It will also help you shape your inner voice so that it serves its function: making you the best *you* that you can be, never letting you settle for less.

This was my very first attempt at a villanelle. I thought about some of the messages I've heard all my life, and the phrase "right before the at" was the first phrase that jumped into my mind.

My mom was very strict—a strict grammarian, that is. Breaking curfew was easier than leaving a dangling participle in that house. And an incorrectly used gerund? I'd hear about it for an hour. She was *particular* about our speech. She used to say that people who cursed in regular conversation were either not smart enough or too lazy to think of something else to say. Now, she did leave room for her own "damn!" said in times of to-the-brink frustration—but if, and *only* if, it were not combined with any other word but left to hang in the air like drooping bleeding hearts. This was the only exception; and, of course, it was only for her. The first time my brother said the F-word, it was like he was tearing down everything my mother stood for in one delib- erate swoop of the tongue—which, of course, was absolutely his intention. And the thing that I remember most about her grammar- correcting ways was "right before the at." Anytime we'd ask, "Where is [insert lost item here] at?" she would respond, with- out fail, "right before the at." It used to drive my sister, brother, and I absolutely f-ing crazy.

I decided to use this phrase as my repeated element. But I didn't know exactly where to take the poem from there. So, I thought about my mom and the things she tried to teach me (try- ing not to dwell on the ridiculous role grammar still plays in my life). I saw how she truly was gifted in the art of helping us find the things she could, but not the things she knew we could—and should—find on our own. After all, most things can be found right before the at.

WHAT CAN ALWAYS BE FOUND

Looking, looking, one purple crayon in hand
"Where's the red one at?" I ask, tapping her on the shoulder
"Right before the at," she replies, not bothering to stand

"But where is God at?" I ask, sifting through dirty sand
"Wherever you look," she says, as the dusk gets California colder
Looking, looking one sunset on the horizon in hand

"Where the hell is my other white boot at?" I loudly demand
hands on hips, blue-up-to-eyebrows cocked, ridiculous, before her
"Right before the at," she replies, not bothering to stand

"Where's the meaning at?" I implore, "I can't possibly understand."
"Hear it, don't just read," she says, putting the receiver in the holder
Looking, looking, one tattered Emily Dickinson volume in hand

"But, I love him. Where can he be at?" I ask desperately, and
she sighs. and lays her hand on my shoulder.
"Right before the at," she replies, not bothering to stand

"Where's the other one at?" he asks, in a defiant stand,
then stomping down stairs, each foot a boulder
Looking, looking, one red spider-man sock in hand
"Right before the at," I reply, not bothering to stand

—Wendy

I'm okay with this phrase being one my inner voice calls on. It reminds me that I'll always find what I'm looking for—when I honestly look. Sometimes I spend so much time being mad at what's missing that I forget to actually look for what I want—or, most importantly, what is already there. Other times, expecting it to be easy, I give up too soon. So I try to remember: Where is [insert desire here] at? Right before the at. I'm extremely lucky that my mom's voice doesn't eclipse my own but instead adds to my strength.

Kellie was inspired to write her villanelle by the voices of her father and grandfather. Both are deceased, and it is their strength, optimism, and ability to cheer everyone around them that Kellie remembers most.

Both endured long, painful illnesses but never let their pain or troubles bring them—or the rest of the family—down. Kellie remembers, "My grandfather had both legs amputated, on dialysis, borderline diabetic . . . and when you called him on the phone, he would joke around and say, 'I'm okay, I can't complain.' My father shared the same positive attitude about life as did his father. A preacher stated, at my father's funeral, that he did not realize my father was the one on the sick list because he laughed and joked with him throughout his visit. My father had a captivating smile and a contagious laugh that will be cherished forever."

The part of Kellie's inner voice that reminds her to slow down, look around, and be thankful is drawing on her father and grandfather's message: "It's not as bad as it seems," something they used to tell her often as they defied illness to break their spirits. She has internalized this mantra. As she remembers these important men of her life and their inspiring outlooks, she is reminded, as she says, "to just go step by step and take one day at a time."

IT IS NOT AS BAD AS IT SEEMS

"It is not as bad as it seems," he'd say,
As he peered through the blinds;
Take it step by step and day by day.

Life happens in moments, be steadfast and pray?
Each sunset leaves cares behind.
"It is not as bad as it seems," he'd say.

I slow and look, but still go astray,
As I search the corners of my mind.
Take it step by step and day by day.

Yes, anchor yourself without delay;
And pick your battles yet be kind.
"It is not as bad as it seems," he'd say.

Like butter on hotcakes: time melts away -
Smells of home are hard to find.
Take it step by step and day by day.

Balance is key, so work hard and play;
Prepare for the daily grind.
"It is not as bad as it seems," he'd say.
Take it step by step and day by day.

—Kellie

Kellie says, "I still hear them say this today, even though my father has been gone for eight years. I often think of home, where he'd sit in his chair and watch television, as the aroma from my mom's cooking filled the house. Little things tend to remind me of home and yes—they are definitely hard to find." That's when she tunes in and hears that part of her inner voice: when she needs the strength to go just a little longer—when she needs to be reminded that things are not as bad as they seem and are so often just about to get better.

Although both Kellie and I recalled voices from influential family members that helped us be better—voices that contribute to a strong, motivating inner voice—the villanelle can also be beneficial to writing about negative voices. Writing about the negative messages directed at you—from family members or from any other large presence in your life—can help you single them out.

When you see them in writing, it can encourage you to accept how harmful they are, drawing your attention to how often and how strongly you recall the words—no matter how long ago they were spoken—and how you use them to berate yourself or, worse, others. When you are more aware of them, you can tune them out more easily or call upon better, more positive voices to overpower them.

To write her villanelle, Lori drew upon the voice of a wise woman she heard a while back. The actual words are years old, but the message is one that spoke to her then, and it influences the way she balances work and family to this day. It happened at a women's leadership conference. As Lori recalls, "The topic of the symposium was the work–life balance. I was recently married and just starting out in my career, so this was a pressing issue for me. Can you have a career and successfully raise kids? Can you give back to the community and still have time for yourself?" Those were questions that Lori asked then—and still asks now as she navigates her way through the ever-changing landscape of work and family.

There was one speaker who offered her the wisdom she needed to come up with the answer and still offers the answer now, when she asks herself if she's still making the right decisions concerning work and family. This woman, Lori remembered, seemed to have achieved it all. "She was an African-American woman, a retired executive, a civic leader: wife, mother, and grandmother," Lori remembers, "She was also very funny." The advice Lori heard that day has remained part of her inner voice. This villanelle is what Lori's inner voice tells her when she needs a little direction along the way.

WOMEN OFTEN WONDER

Women often wonder if they can do it all.
I feel like when I juggle, there is rubber and there is glass.
"The answer is you can," she said; her voice filled the hall.

Your children are the glass; never let them fall.
But bounce a few of the rubber ones into the weekly trash.
Women often wonder if they can do it all.

Does she need a feeding? Have I missed a call?
My body was so heavy, then came the crash.
"The answer is you can," she said; her voice filled the hall.

Life comes in phases, some big and others small.
This, too, shall pass.
Women often wonder if they can do it all.

Even now I'm struggling just to crawl
and everything's moving so fast.
"The answer is you can," she said; her voice filled the hall.

Ladies, take it from someone who has seen and done it all.
Very little matters; few things last.
Women often wonder if they can do it all.
"The answer is you can," she said. "Just not all at once," her voice
*   filled the hall.*

—Lori

"With her wisdom in mind," Lori says, "I dropped my volunteer work and went part-time when I started having children. I still work on pacing myself. And I still think of her often."

Maybe you are thinking, *why a villanelle? It seems too hard. I can't write a good one and it'll take too much time anyway.* Sounds to me like someone who needs to work on her inner voice. Why the villanelle? Because you *can* do it, and because you should strive to challenge yourself as long as you live. And because writing a villanelle can help you single out some of the messages that play like a CD on permanent loop in your mind. You will get something out of it if you open yourself up to hearing the components of your inner voice. Your inner voice guides you through your days, your decisions, your challenges—through your life—and you owe it to yourself to make sure it's showing you the right way.

So What Exactly Makes a Villanelle?

A villanelle is like red shoes. They don't go with *everything* but once you *do* find an outfit, red shoes always make it smashing. The villanelle takes some thought. You'll find that not every phrase that pops into your mind will work, but once you do find that magic combination, you'll be able to write a truly amazing poem.

A villanelle is a poem with six stanzas; the first five stanzas consist of three lines and the final of four. A villanelle is nineteen lines total: five triplets and a final quatrain, if you want to use fancy words. Here's where the repetition comes in: the first and last line of the first stanza take turns repeating as the final line of the next four stanzas and finally end the poem as the last two lines of the final quatrain.

The villanelle also has a rhyme scheme. It is aba, except the last stanza, which twists it up a little. The poem is centered on the two rhymes used and the two refrains, the repeated phrases or lines. Relax, it isn't as complicated as it seems. Once I got into it, the first one was definitely the hardest, but it was much easier after that.

Good news: you can follow a meter if you really want to, but you don't have to; what is important about this form are the repeated lines, not the meter. If you do choose to employ a consistent meter throughout, it is up to you what that meter is. Of course, many do not put a count or meter at all and simply follow the rhyme scheme and repetition, the villanelle's two most important elements.

Here is the layout of the villanelle:

A1
b
A2

a
b
A1

a

b

A2

a

b

A1

a

b

A2

a

b

A1

A2

a,b represents the rhyme pattern—all the a's rhyme and all the b's rhyme. A1 and A2 are specific, repeated lines. This layout shows you the position of each of the elements of the entire poem.

Tips on Form

- Good news: once you've got your refrains (your repeated elements), you're halfway there! Choose with care. Make sure they have resonance and are memorable in some way. As Margaret Ryan says, "It's great if their meaning seems to spread out from them like ripples from a stone thrown into a pool."
- You can choose to repeat the entire line, or you can alter that line slightly. It is up to you, but the repetition should be obvious. Feel free to experiment; it might help your repeated lines hold different meaning as the poem progresses.

- You can also try to play with the punctuation in your repeated elements. The lines can be exactly the same, but, with different punctuation, the meaning can be altered easily and dramatically.
- Choose easy rhymes. You only get to work with two rhymes, so give yourself a break and try to use words that will be easy to work with, especially for your first attempts.
- Consider making a list of rhymes when you know which words you'll be using (this could happen after the first stanza or before you even begin) so that you can have ready word choices. This might also help you get a feel for your poem and know if your first words might just be too difficult to work with before you begin.

Posse Pointer

Kellie advises first thinking about the repeated elements, A1 and A2. She says, "These two significant lines provide the fundamental meaning of the poem; therefore, they should be given substantial consideration before you begin writing. What message do you want to convey? After you have determined and arranged A1 and A2—the core—you are now ready to build."

For Further Reading

"One Art" by Elizabeth Bishop is one of the most well known villanelles. It's not yet in the public domain, but you can try to find it at your local library. It is featured in *The Complete Poems 1927–1979* by Elizabeth Bishop.

Bishop claimed that writing her villanelle was a gift, that writing it was as easy as writing a letter. In reality, she wrote at least seventeen drafts of "One Art." I almost didn't include that part because I hate to be the kind of woman who doesn't allow another her half-truths, so I hope you'll use it as encouragement to keep writing, revising, and living—just as Bishop did. In fact, Bishop often spent many years writing a single poem. "I'm not interested in big-scale work as such," she reportedly once told fellow poet and friend Robert Lowell. "Something needn't be large to be good."

Reading villanelles by recognized, skilled poets will help you get a feel for its vibe and internal rhythm. After reading a few examples, I bet you'll reach for the pen and paper.

- "Rockin' a Man Stone Blind" by Carolyn Whitlow. This poem has a skillful rhythm that just begs you to read it over and over.
- "Daughters, 1900" by Marilyn Nelson Waniek
- "Villanelle" by Marilyn Hacker
- "Mad Girl's Love Song" by Sylvia Plath. If you make the effort to find just one and read it, I suggest this one.

What Should I Write About?

As Margaret Ryan says in her book *How to Write a Poem*, "We are complex creatures, and we are often so busy *being* ourselves [that] we can't really *see* ourselves." The villanelle asks that you take time out from so constantly *being* yourself to *hear* yourself, which will help you *see* yourself more clearly.

The villanelle encourages exploration of powerful recurrences in our lives. These recurrences are often verbal—messages from family, media, those we admire, teachers, preachers, society, or bumper stickers on cars as they race past us on the interstate. We soak them up, and they trickle out of us and influence what we see in the mirror, what we believe ourselves capable of, and how we see the world around us. These verbal recurrences make up our inner voice—that voice that tells us how to get up in the morning and whether or not to wear red shoes.

Take advantage of this opportunity and listen not only to what the world is saying around you but also to how you mold the messages into what you tell yourself.

During the course of our poetic adventure, Angie encountered another big adventure: moving her family of five away from her family home, where all three children were born, to another city four hours away. She was also leaving her parents, who lived just a few houses down the street. The move was challenging, because Angie (by her own admission) is a planner and controller. "I am a planner," Angie admits, "which is great when I am in the role of PTA President, but not so good in other aspects of my life. I can get unbearable when my plans fall through or, worse yet, when someone changes or gets in the way of my plans."

Not only were Angie and her family moving, but they decided to build a new house. Anyone who has ever built a house from the ground up knows that the process is anything but under your control. As she says, "I planned and planned, but things did *not* always go my way. The builders were on their schedule, not mine. My husband was on his own schedule, living away from us for work while the house was on the builder's schedule. And I was living back in my parents' house with my three kids, definitely not on my own schedule!"

"Letting go of things that were not so important was a lesson I struggled with over those six months," she says. "It was hard for me to completely trust a future that I was not directly planning." Finally, she realized she had to tune out the part of her voice that demanded control and tune in to the part that was telling her to trust and let go.

TRUST ME, LET GO

Trust Me, the time will come
He tells me that all the time, but time is rare
Letting go of the control that controls me

Planning to plan the plans for my life
He tells me not to worry and He will take care
Trust Me, the time will come

Dealing with the struggles and strife
He tells me it won't always be fair
Letting go of the control that controls me

Try to be the best mother and wife
Taking on more than my share
Trust Me, the time will come

Worries that seem larger-than-life
Changing plans I've planned to dare
Letting go of the control that controls me

Moving out, moving on, moving up
Giving Him the final despair
Trust Me, the time will come
Letting go of the control that controls me

—Angie

Writing this poem, especially with its repetitive elements, helped Angie focus on the one part of her inner voice that helped her make this recent transition. Having a tangible record, she can refer to it if she ever feels the pressure of control sneaking back in.

"In my teens and twenties, my inner voice used to be that little devil on my shoulder that told me it would be okay to do whatever and see if consequences came later," Angie says, "like the 'what if' scenario when you had little to lose. Now I feel like it is more of a spiritual connection, not just my conscience." As we get older, our inner voice changes as much as our outer bodies do. It behooves us to keep track of what it's saying, just as we aim to keep our bodies in good health. "My inner voice these days," Angie explains, "doesn't just tell me right from wrong but helps me focus on who I am and what I want to do with my life, from mothering to being a wife to owning and now operating my own business. It reassures me when I need it and tells me when to back off when I need that too." Using poetry to reinforce this spiritual connection helps you not only hear what you need to hear but also determine where it's coming from. "Is it divine guidance?" she wonders. "Most of the time I think it is, although who doesn't try to take the credit herself?"

Listen to what you are asking or telling yourself right now. Is it really you? Is it the *you* that you want to be?

Villanelle Soundtrack

There is one time I am glad to hear my own voice loud and clear: riding in a convertible, alone on a hot summer day, with the top down. Here are my top five songs for singing when I don't care who's listening:

1. "I'm the Only One" Melissa Etheridge
2. "I Will Survive" Gloria Gaynor
3. "Fighter" Christina Aguilera
4. "Redneck Woman" Gretchen Wilson
5. "Survivor" Destiny's Child

Beverly used a combination of voices from her past and present when writing her villanelle. Raised in the South by her grandmother, Beverly's upbringing was old-time South: full of white gloves, table manners, women who didn't work (and, more importantly, didn't want to), and big, perfectly pruned elephant ears in the front lawn. And that is the life she was *supposed* to perpetuate. Yet life had other plans for Beverly. She didn't stay in the South—and, horror above all horrors, she found herself a *career.*

Even still, the South never really left Beverly. She still appreciates an impeccably set table (don't even *try* to bring a can—any can—to her table), fashionable shoes, and three-season landscaping. There is a certain attitude that has stayed with her. She has a friend who good-naturedly calls her an "uppity Southern woman." It was this attitude that Beverly started to write about.

"Then," she says, "I realized that I know an awful lot more about uppity southern *ladies* because that's what my grandmother thought she was teaching me to be. For those who were not raised in the South, you may not know that there is a vast difference between a lady (what we should all want to be) and a woman (something somehow lesser)." It was difficult to hear her friend calling her an "uppity Southern woman" without also hearing her grandmother's voice—a voice long gone—that would have preferred *lady*.

ONCE-UPON-A-TIME SOUTHERN ~~WOMEN~~ LADIES

Southern Ladies Never
Stomp angrily across the marble floor
But glide effortlessly through arched doors

On the way to important places
To keep equally important dates
Southern Ladies Never

Raise their voices stridently and
Pound their fists demanding more
But glide effortlessly through arched doors

As they depart gracefully to
Attend well appointed events
Southern Ladies Never

Haggle prices in common markets
Or search the sale racks for Dior
But glide effortlessly through arched doors

And into cherry-red cars off
To the new boutique on Second Street
Southern women rarely ever
Glide effortlessly through arched doors.

—Beverly

Beverly, on her "selfish days," laments the life of leisure, free from concern, that she was *supposed* to have—a life she purposefully denied. Yet she knows deep down that the life she *chose* is the life that is worth more, even if some of the comforts are missing. By reflecting on the lady she chose not to be, Beverly found her villanelle—and a bit of her inner voice spoke a little louder.

Beverly acknowledges her "uppity Southern woman" voice because that is the voice that has steered her toward a life that she is proud of, realizing that a lady wouldn't have nearly as much fun, and a lady simply wouldn't have nearly as *much*. As Beverly says, "Writing this poem freed me, as I realized that the life I was taught to live had little substance and the life I *do* live is much richer!" Beverly was able to fine-tune the lady out of her inner voice and hear the woman loud and clear.

After I wrote my first villanelle, I immediately wanted to start another; it was so refreshing and powerful. However, I hit a block in thinking of something to write about. I couldn't think of a single thing, so I went through my journal, as I often do when I can't think of anything to say. I found an incomplete list poem entitled "Things That Go Together." One of those things was champagne and regret. It got me thinking about some of the mistakes I've made—especially the ones that were a lot of fun.

I love champagne. The very first time I tasted champagne was with my husband, on our very first New Year's Eve together. It was Dom Perignon. How could a girl not get hooked? There has been but one opportunity in my entire life that I have turned down champagne and that was when I was pregnant, attending a friend's baby shower where mimosas were served. (We have always espoused the philosophy that just because we couldn't drink doesn't mean everyone else shouldn't for us.) But, without fail, every other time in my life that champagne was offered, I have indulged—and, honestly, indulged too much, every time. But that's just me. It hasn't always been the best decision, like the one New Year's Eve when I decided that I would only drink champagne the entire night, convinced that the New Year would then be full of champagne (both literal and figurative). I was hungover until . . . oh, *July.*

Some of the best times of my life have involved champagne: my wedding brunch; the one and only time I've been in the MTV studios; New Year's Eve, 1998, when I looked the best I've ever looked; and the afternoon a friend and I sat in a hole-in-the-wall bar drinking the most terrible champagne I have ever had by the glass for no good reason at all.

Of course, after the consumption, or, rather, the *over-*consumption of champagne comes the morning-after regret—and I'm not just talking about the splitting headache that feels like you've stabbed a stiletto heel into your temple. I'm talking about realizing that you sang "If I Could Turn Back Time" karaoke-style, with no karaoke machine in sight; I'm talking about not remembering the names of the New Best Friends you met in the bathroom as you bonded over lipstick. Even still, I feel awkward and embarrassed for a day or two and then move on—and do the same thing the exact moment someone pops a cork or I see even a bad bottle on the by-the-glass list. It's just me. So the internal voice I heard here probably said, "Yes, I'll take another."

CHAMPAGNE AND REGRET

It seems, I thought, some things just go together
rubbing my head, looking out the window—
champagne and regret, complaining and the weather.

Prayer and the last minute: life happens like a falling feather
breeze or gust, always as slow is fast, as fast is slow.
It seems, I thought, some things just go together.

I always learn, but I never know better.
Easy lessons are forgotten, yet some things I thankfully know—
Beastie Boys and convertibles, complaining and the weather.

Denim and cashmere: the lies of him the secrets of her,
to keep or free to love or hate to stay or go.
It seems, I thought, some things just go together.

It's probably all illusion, as we see our tether,
empty or full smart or dumb, we reap what we sow—
black lace and sex, complaining and the weather.

Champagne and regret: serve it up! I'll hopefully never say no,
*   whether*
Saturday or Wednesday, much to the Thursday's woe.
It seems, I thought, some things just go together
me and my best mistakes, complaining and the weather.

—Wendy

There are some things about me I wish I could change and am actually working on changing, but I'll never be perfect—how boring if I were. This is something I don't care to change: I will never turn down champagne and I will most likely always have something to regret the next morning. Some parts of me are stupid, embarrassing, and overindulgent, and those are the parts that sometimes I like the best. Even if the results are questionable, I'm okay with that so long as I accept complete responsibility. Some of my best mistakes have made me who I am—and, of course, will make the best stories for my grandchildren—and the best of those mistakes have helped me hear my own voice more clearly. So, yes: I'll take another. I'm not willing to tune that voice out. I'll take the champagne, even if I have to take the regret, too.

Tips on Subject

- A narrative is difficult in the villanelle. If there is a story you want to tell in this form, using repeated elements, try to focus on snapshots or moments and not a traditional storyline with a beginning and end.
- You might consider introducing your thought in the first stanza, giving it different interpretations or meanings or building upon its significance in the second through fourth stanzas, and then finally offering some sort of conclusion in the final stanza. Because the final stanza is the only one with four lines, it accommodates this purpose and might help you make sense of your subject.
- There is a certain air of obsession with the villanelle; all the repetition almost sounds unhealthy or unbalanced. This is the way I read Plath's "Mad Girl's Love Song." Whether you are preoccupied with death, God, or purple shoes, it is your poem and you should write about whatever is important to you.

Give It a Try

It's amazing what you hear when you listen. Your inner voice is always speaking—you just have to quiet down enough to listen. You can find out a lot. When I started to listen to myself, I found that I spoke at obvious times, like when I couldn't sleep or when I was alone in the car with the radio off, but also at the oddest times. For instance, in my weekly kickboxing class, I found that a certain person's backstabbing gossip kept coming to mind, along with all the things I *wish* I had said. That incident was more than two years ago, and I didn't know that it still bothered me so much. During church one Sunday morning, something about the way the sun was shining through the floor-to-ceiling windows reminded me of a small church my dad used to pastor in Fairfax, Oklahoma. I often wondered as a child why I couldn't physically hear God if he was talking as much as everyone said He did. Then I realized, sitting there, that of course, He does—but sometimes it sounds a lot like me.

As I listened more, I became aware of the ways I am critical with myself. I started hearing my own berating negativity every time I reached for a chocolate chip cookie. Of course, guilt was loud and clear every time I snapped at my son or raised my voice to him. When I looked through magazines (a serious guilty pleasure of mine), I didn't only see pictures but also heard whispers of jealousy and inadequacy.

Yet as I listened to and actually heard my inner voice, I heard other things as well if I listened hard enough. I heard myself patting myself on the back when I got to work on time or when I made a good parenting decision. I heard myself being complimentary when I put together a truly unique, stylish outfit without buying anything new. I even heard myself ever so quietly sometimes actually *like* myself. So I decided to try to concentrate on these voices. I still hear all the other stuff, but the more I listen the easier it gets to let my inner voice be nice.

Here are three ideas to get you started writing your villanelle. And even if you never actually finish a by-the-book villanelle, as long as you start listening and your inner voice comes through a bit clearer, it's all worth it anyway.

- Think of an influential person of your childhood. Was there a certain phrase he or she used to say to you to calm you or ease your fears? See if you can relate this phrase or these words to anxieties or fears that you have as an adult.
- Do you have a personal mantra? Something you tell yourself when you are up against a challenge?
- What's your favorite curse word? I have a friend who can use the f-word in any context you can imagine: noun, verb, adjective, adverb, anything: it's a true gift. What's your favorite? Notice when you most often use it. Writing poetry can be fun, and it doesn't have to be respectable. I rather prefer it when it's not.

I won't lie: writing a villanelle is difficult work. But so is hearing yourself; and, in both instances, the more you practice the easier it gets.

A Poetic Pause: Ways to Share What You Write

If you feel like sharing your poetry, there are ways to use what you write without coming across as cheesy, overly sentimental, or gushy. Let me be straight with you here: a poem to your daughter on her fourteenth birthday will probably not suffice for the insanely expensive jeans she really wants. Likewise, there are no more than eight—no, probably more like six—men on the *planet* who would honestly appreciate a poem. But there are some lovely ways you can use a poem you've written if you're so inclined.

Scrapbooking. I am amazed when I look at Erin's scrapbooks. She could document a trip to the grocery store and make it seem like an exotic vacation. I wish I had a baby book like she has put together for her son; it's almost as beautiful as he is. A poem you've written adds a personal, unique touch to a layout. List poems work well, because they take everyday things and make them special. Erin used her list poem "Why I Adore Cale" on a page with pictures of her son. Haiku are also a good form to try. Their brevity makes them nice accents to a page, and their playful nature works well with photographs.

Christmas cards or ornaments. A cute little Christmas rhyme makes a wonderful, personal Christmas card, especially if you are one who likes making cards. A cute cutout and colorful bow on the front, a poem inside—and you're done. The sonnet or ode work well, because they rhyme and sound poetic to any ear. You can also get clear ornaments from any hobby store and write a holiday poem in gold or silver paint-pen directly on the ornament. I gave my mom an ornament with a poem about our Christmas traditions when I was just out of college and totally broke. She still hangs it on the tree.

For the big ones. Funny or serious poems are a great way to mark big birthdays—sixteen, twenty-one, thirty, forty, fifty, and so on. But, again, make sure to put it with a desired gift. Something like a list poem to your daughter entitled "What I Wish for You on Your 21st Birthday" would be fun as part of a twenty-one present birthday. (My mom did this for me when I was eighteen and it is still hands-down the best birthday I've ever had. I had just gone to college and was incredibly lonely. She started eighteen days before my birthday and sent me one gift the first day, two the second and so on. On my actual birthday, I was greeted with a box of eighteen individually wrapped gifts.) A funny poem to your husband on his fiftieth is a good idea—especially if accompanied by you in something skimpy. The list poem or sestina are great forms to work with.

An accessory to an unexpected girlfriend gift. This can be funny or serious. For a good friend, perhaps an anti-love sonnet on Valentine's Day with a box of sugar-free chocolates or an ode to wedges on the first day of spring with a certificate for a pedicure. You can have short poems engraved on jewelry boxes or around the sides of a frame. It's okay to be a little cheesy with your girlfriends. Life's too short. I once gave Angie a journal with a poem on the inside front cover. She's had it for about ten years now and is finally using it when she writes her own poems.

As I mentioned in the chapter on haiku, a haiku memory book written while on vacation makes a wonderful keepsake of a favorite holiday, honeymoon (first, second, third . . . we don't judge in the Posse), or family vacation. You can write spontaneously while on location or take notes and transcribe them once you're home. Barnes & Noble or amazon.com usually carry gorgeous, handmade, hand-bound journals. You could also use a picture book and put your poems in the spaces instead of photos—or combine both.

You can also add short poems in photo collections that you hang on the wall. Pottery Barn, Restoration Hardware, and Target usually carry collage frames. Intersperse poems handwritten on nice cardstock among your photos. This is especially great if your children are exposed to poetry and begin to write their own. I don't know a grandmother alive who would not fawn over a collage frame filled with treasured photos accompanied by a "Why I Love Grandma" list poem.

Chapter Seven

Lift Yourself Up:
The Letter Poem

Any time is a good time to write a poem.
—Gertrude Stein

I have always had a love for letters. In fact, my middle finger on my right hand has a "writing bump" that I am convinced is the result of gripping my pencil too tightly while writing letter after letter as I grew up. (I could also attribute it to my mean third-grade teacher, Ms. Hurty, who made me copy math equations during recess, but the letter-writing thing is a much more romantic explanation.) Having moved around quite a bit growing up, I've written my fair share of letters. I consider myself quite lucky that I've received almost as many back. Letters were an integral part of my youth. In fact, I can remember significant events by how much stamps were at the time. Some curse the penny stamp. I find comfort in the fact that a penny can still accomplish so much.

We moved around more than most, the result of having a father who was first a pastor with always a bigger congregation to save, then a chaplain in the Navy with always-another order to fill, and then a pastor again. Add to the mix parents who are simply restless souls (something I imagine they would deny as each move promises something infinitely *better*) always looking for *something* (I've never been quite sure what), and the end result is a childhood spent literally on the move. The result of that is a lot of letters.

Most of the time I found the prospect of moving exciting. When, in the third grade, we moved from Fairfax, Oklahoma (population less than 2,000) to Tustin, California (population innumerable), inexplicably, I was neither scared nor nervous. I couldn't believe I was going to see an ocean with actual waves and feel real sand between my toes. Yet, as I grew older, the moves got harder. The first time I was miserable as The New Girl was in the fifth grade. It was the first time that making friends was challenging, because it mattered that I had an accent (left over from Oklahoma and Texas), it mattered that I didn't have the Members Only jacket *everyone* was wearing, and it mattered that I wasn't allowed to stay up late enough to watch *The A-Team*. Stamps cost twenty-two cents apiece.

Because this was before I started writing poetry, I wrote letters instead. I would pour my whole lonely, ten-year-old heart out to my friends and send it away for less than a quarter. And no matter how difficult a day I had, coming home from school to be greeted by a letter from a faraway friend was enough to lift my spirits. I mattered again. Someone *remembered* me.

The move to Germany my junior year of high school was the toughest—stamps were a quarter. I bet I wrote a thousand letters that first year. I am grateful my parents made that move, because it gave me a much larger view of the world—of what one could do and where one could go—but then, not so much. I *really* didn't fit in. I talked funny, used too much hair spray, and needed to seriously rethink the whole granny boot thing. Although I did write poetry often, I also wrote a lot of letters. It was almost as if I was trying to write enough to pave a way back to the States, desperately wanting some kind of physical connection with those who liked Def Leppard as much as I did and recognized the fashion brilliance of white lace hose and a denim skirt. I remember my first day in the American high school, sitting in algebra class, writing a letter to my BFF Angie, when a girl in dreadlocks and a Cure t-shirt (I did not know who The Cure was and had never seen a white person with dreads) came up to me and said, "You're new? Writing letters so soon? You'll *never* make it."

I will never forget how much 25¢ could buy. I was so stubborn, clinging to my pink acid-washed jeans, that every plain, white envelope I saw with my name on it made me feel like I at least belonged *somewhere.* Eventually, as I let go of Poison for The Cure and embraced the United Colors of Benetton, my letter writing slowed down. However, there are two things I will always be grateful for: the fact that my dad never forgot to mail a letter on his way to work, and that Angie replied to every single letter I wrote her.

When I left my high school boyfriend for college in the States, I wrote many a love letter to him, and he wrote even better ones back. Stamps still cost me a quarter. I kept my love letters in an old shoebox until a jealous college boyfriend found them and threw them out. I mourned that loss for a long time. Not the loss of the letters themselves and certainly not the loss of a high school boyfriend, but the loss of a *personal effect,* and the loss of a time when love was simple enough to put into words, when there was actually another person on the planet who deemed me worthy of love letters.

I still write the occasional letter, even though I've lived in the same city for more than ten years. (I also complain loudly about the price of stamps—forty-one cents!) I write my husband when I have something to *say* that I can't actually *say*. It works well because I get to say what I really want to without interruption and obnoxious, barely disguised eye rolls. I can reread and revise. I can be smart and organized. I can even throw in a pithy anecdote if I've got the time. I can never think of snappy comebacks in the heat of the moment, but, oh—give me a piece of stationery and thirty minutes and I can scorch the page. Sometimes he gets the letters and sometimes he doesn't. Well, even when he gets them, whether he *gets* gets them is probably up for debate. But, either way, what *I* get is the release of anger, guilt, resentment, or whatever it was that was weighing on me enough to warrant a letter. Whether there was any actual resolution or not is less important; just getting it out *always* makes me feel better.

In all my letter-writing history, there was one thing in common: I had a need to say *something* to *someone*, to let words out so they didn't stay inside and weigh me down. To my faraway friends, I said, *don't forget me*; to my boyfriend, *I'm lonely*; and to my husband, *try to understand me and love me anyway.* When I let those words out, I was free: free to make other friends, free to go about the life I had without being crippled by what I had left behind, and free to be myself and expect love in return. In each instance, I was a little lighter after writing the letter.

Liz Carpenter, once press secretary to Lady Bird Johnson, said, "What a lot we lost when we stopped writing letters. You can't reread a phone call." I think it's so true, even though I admit that I haven't postmarked nearly as many letters since I got my first e-mail account. You technically *can* re-read an email, but there's something about a handwritten letter that is delightfully personal, curiously sweet, and simply brave: it's a grand, though small, gesture to fold up a small part of yourself and send it away for less than a dollar, when you never know if you'll get anything in return.

With a letter-poem, you aren't required to send anything away, but you always get something back: an unrivaled opportunity to lift yourself up.

Why a Letter Poem?

Writing a letter poem is an incredibly brave thing to do—even if it is never delivered. You are singling out something that you need to ask, say, or tell—and a recipient. It's not only a poem, it's an *action*. Go ahead and pat yourself on the back before you even get started.

There are two main ways in which you can use the letter poem to lift yourself up. The first way is by letting something go that is weighing you down. We all have experiences that can weigh us down. Some of these take place in childhood—like being relentlessly teased by a bully, or a drastic change in family finances, or growing up without a parental figure—and leave us feeling insecure and unsafe far into adulthood. Some of these happen as adults—an unhealthy marriage, or the time we pushed a dream aside to pay the mortgage, or the loss of a loved one—and leave us in a tailspin, feeling trapped by circumstances.

There are also things that, while neither large nor affecting in the grand scheme of things, that can still ruin a day: guilt at raising your voice to your children, anger at the man who cut you off on the interstate, resentment toward a coworker who got your well-deserved promotion—even frustration at the damned computer that keeps freezing up in the middle of anything important.

Certainly many of these things could be described as "not our fault." Although, any self-help book, any woman over the age of sixty, or any talk show host will say that it is *you* who is allowing *you* to be affected by [insert situation/person/feeling here], it is a sentiment so overused that we have become numb to its truth. We become numb to the power we really do have over ourselves. You do have the power to let go what is weighing you down, and a letter poem can be a step in that process.

Recently, I had a heavy feeling in my stomach. It was something that, logically, as an adult, I knew wasn't supposed to bother me as much as it did, but I just couldn't shake the funk I was in. In my thirties, I was feeling abandoned because my parents were leaving me.

I mentioned that my parents moved around a lot. Well, they did—and they still do. They moved close to me, only an hour away. Prior to that, I hadn't lived near my parents (we're talking sometimes an ocean away) in almost fifteen years. When they moved to my area, it was one of the best things that had ever happened to me. I felt like my life was fuller with them around. I *loved* it.

Mom and I got our hair done together and spent Saturdays shopping and getting pedicures, and I loved having dinner out—just the two of us. I also got to spend the occasional Saturday with my dad, drinking beer and watching college football. My son would spend weekends with them exploring the "jungle" behind their house. I had never been close to my grandparents because we were always moving, so I liked being able to give him something I had never had. Then, pretty much out of the blue (for me, anyway, because I didn't *want* to see it coming), they told me they were moving.

Even though I was supposedly an *adult* and had only had them near me for a short four years, I was devastated. I felt like I was five years old and lost in the grocery store.

But I didn't feel justified in telling them how I felt, because the move was good for them. I felt stupid for feeling so abandoned. I was a grown woman, for gosh sakes! I didn't want to make them feel guilty. They have been, and still are, great parents. My mom once braved a German dermatologist who didn't speak a lick of English because I thought I had too many pimples. My dad once assured me that if I really wanted to, I could be the first Miss America to wear glasses—and I believed him.

But *I* still felt weighed down by the situation. It was the type of thing that became more debilitating the longer I ignored it. I cried at the grocery store for no discernable reason other than that I was walking down the pasta aisle and remembered that Mom wouldn't be there to make meatballs for us anymore. I had an embarrassing spell in my office elevator because an instrumental rendition of "Wind Beneath My Wings" was playing.

So I sat down one night and wrote my mom a letter. In this letter, I told her exactly how I felt about her leaving. I put the letter away for a few days before using it to write a letter poem. When I got it back out, I realized the sestina would work well. There were words I kept using over and over. I divided the letter up into the six general things I wanted to say and wrote my sestina from there.

Dear Mom,
I haven't said much about your leaving, moving away
because I knew it wouldn't matter, it's just more time

of the way it's always been. But it does matter; it matters to me
because I feel left, and even though I'm no longer a child,
I am desperately afraid of the mistakes
I'll make when you take your everyday love.

I screw up the most when you're gone, in love
and in life. That one summer when you were kilometers away
it was day after mistake after day after mistake.
I wasn't proud of my "wild time."
I was lost; I was a child,
who needed a mother to be ashamed. sad. and disappointed in
   me.

you know you couldn't really know, being so far from me
don't you? I wanted someone to love
me because those who were supposed to love their child
best were too far away
and couldn't be reached with the difference in time
zones. I hate those made-me-who-I-am mistakes.

Letting her go, was my heaviest mistake,
but I didn't know how to do it, I didn't know the me
you knew. I collapsed and died and almost fell too far that time.
You would have said yes, I could do it, I had enough love,
because I could keep what I had and you'd give some away,
but you couldn't—all lines were busy, mother to child.

You weren't there, even though I was your child.
So I got married, too young for sure (for you, not a mistake).
I needed a family, one that wasn't an ocean away,

one that could physically hug, scold, and give what I lost back
*   to me.*
The first boy who asked, the first one who meant love,
I owed him: he caught me just in time.

Then! that time, that lovely, seasonless, fleeting time!
You were near me. I was your everyday child,
and I believed that I was capable (capable!) of life and love.
The fact that he left wasn't my mistake
but his. In a small black dufflebag, I could pack me
up, and you were just fifty-six minutes of hills, hay, and hawks
*   away.*

You think of me in a Good Place so it's easier to go away—
again—(remember that time when I magnified your mistakes,
because I was afraid to leave?) Well, call soon. Love, your child.
                                                —Wendy

Only after writing the poem did I realize it has little to do with meatballs, hair appointments, or pedicures. I realized I was just plain *scared*. I had come to depend on her quite a bit in those four years and, as unreasonable as it may sound, was frightened at what things would be like without her.

Reading what I had written was like standing on a busy street corner and suddenly realizing I'm wearing a see-through skirt. It was uncomfortably revealing. It became clear that lots of moving, in addition to the most current situation, contributed to my sense of desertion, rejection, and helplessness. *I love my mom* and would be proud to be half the mother she is. But that didn't make my feelings any less legitimate. Acknowledging my real feelings about being left (this time and other times) cleared away some old junk I never even knew was in the basement. I understood that I'm in charge of letting things go because I am the one who ends up weighed down.

Since my mom has moved, I've talked to her nearly daily on the phone and visited a few times. Rereading the poem is uncomfortable. It's so raw and full of emotion. I was tempted to edit and rewrite it so it wouldn't be so painful (for her or for me). It felt like a child-size cut that needs a superhero band-aid.

I resisted the urge because it is 100 percent how I felt at the time. Keeping it as is reminds me that I grow, learn, and get better all the time—and that I'm quite often stronger than I think. *Never* edit down a poem you've written as part of a personal journey to the point where you change its meaning. It's the worst kind of censorship. In fact, I believe that you should never significantly change such a poem after the one-month mark. You said what you said for a reason—and if it's difficult to read, it's probably simply because it's true. Such a situation doesn't call for editing; it calls for a new poem.

The second way to lift yourself up by writing a letter poem is by writing to someone important in your life. This is great because not only are you lifted up, but your intended recipient (*if* you decide to send your letter poem) is lifted up as well. You can write a letter poem aiming for forgiveness, gratitude, or love. Your next thank-you note could easily be a thank-you letter poem. Expressing gratitude for a special person in your life can be as uplifting as letting something negative go.

This is exactly what Kris decided to do. She wrote a letter poem, in sonnet form, for her best friend Katie. Kris says, "I wrote about Katie, because I have such strong feelings for her. I mean, what do you say about someone who you can call at 3 a.m.

when your water breaks six weeks early and your husband is halfway across the country? Someone who—though she never had children—goes through labor with you *and* goes to the ends of the earth to get your husband back in time so that he can make the birth of your first child?"

Kris met Katie nearly fifteen years ago when they worked together. It was Kris's first "real" job out of college. Katie had been around the block a few times. Some might find it interesting that Katie is only three years younger than Kris's mother, but their relationship has always been sisterly. "Perhaps it's because we met as adults," Kris says. "I don't know what I'd do without her. Even though I've been married for six years, she's *still* my In Case of Emergency Contact person."

Katie
Where do I begin?
Labels attempt to describe you
Mother, aunt, sister, friend
But these don't capture all that you are or all we've been through

New jobs, old loves, mammograms, and kidney stones,
Shopping trips, lingering dinners, me a new bride
The passing of your father, the birth of my daughter, and a debil-
itating broken bone
Odd coworkers, difficult in laws—it's been a wild ride

Funny, capable, genuine, and kind,
Loving, dependable, loyal, efficient—I'm still not done
Someone who always helps you out of a bind
And most of all, fun.

There just aren't words for what I want to say
Except that I am so thankful for your friendship, each and every day
—Kris

"Poetry can be a wonderful tribute to someone," Kris says. So Kris took the unique opportunity the letter poem presented to let Katie know just how much she means to her. She shared the poem with Katie, and both felt blessed, lucky, and a little more uplifted as a result.

But why a poem? Can't I just stop at the letter? you may be wondering. Of course—writing the letter will be therapeutic and cleansing by itself. But taking it further into poetry makes it more uniquely *you* and gives you an extra step in a process designed to lift you up. A letter poem takes the process that much closer to your core.

What Exactly Makes a Letter Poem?

The one and only instruction for writing a letter poem is that it be to someone or something. There is no mandated *form*. The letter poem is not so much a *form* of poetry as a *type* of poetry, a place to focus your thoughts. Those are probably the shortest instructions in this book! Ah, but it's always the things that *seem* easy that rarely are.

I, of course, recommend writing a letter poem in form. The process of acknowledging and rejecting words, phrases, images, and perceptions to fit a form forces you to go through all the words, phrases, images, and perceptions of what you are writing about. You will not only have a better grasp of your subject but of you yourself. The great thing about a letter poem is that you get to pick the form.

You can even come up with a form of your own. Decide every line will have ten syllables, that every fourth end word rhyme, or that the lines alternate between twelve and fifteen syllables with every other word a rhyme. It is another way of making the letter poem specifically from you and will also give you the intense exposure that writing in form offers.

With that said, there is a place for free verse in writing a letter poem. I think writing in free verse is one of the most difficult things on the planet. It's like Halloween. I'm afraid of walking into a costume party and having to explain all night long that, "See, I'm a One Night Stand. The wooden square around my waist, the lampshade on my head. Get it?" A sonnet, sestina, or ode is a poem because *it is;* free verse I feel like I'd have to explain—and there's a reason I haven't dressed up for Halloween in twenty years.

Free verse can be very effective in a letter poem. However, you must be extremely vigilant when writing in free verse that you are disciplined in going through all that is necessary to arrive at your truth. Everything technically "fits" in a free verse poem, so you may not experience (or reexperience) as much in the process. If you do decide to write in free verse for your letter poem, analyze each and every line just as you would any poem you wrote in form.

Whether writing in free verse or in a form, write an actual letter first. Put *everything* you want to say in there. Decide that you will never send it so that you will say everything, leaving nothing out. This is your letter, and you need to say whatever it is that you need to say without fear of judgment, retaliation, or self-consciousness. Whatever it is, believe that you have the right to say it, and then *say it all.* Let the letter sit for at least a day.

When you return, read back over your letter and try to be more specific and descriptive. Instead of "I felt hurt when you left," try "I felt depleted when you took your things." Instead of "I love you because you are kind," try "I loved you most when you gave the man on the corner a dollar and a cigarette." Make it emotional and vivid. Then, leave it again.

When you return, look over what you've written. Does a form jump out at you? Do you have a favorite form you retreat to time and time again? Will it work here? Read your words until something inside you tells you what kind of poem you should write. I absolutely guarantee that if you listen hard enough, your soul will speak.

If it is free verse your soul decides, concentrate on each word as much as you would a poem in form. Get rid of everything that isn't really necessary. Try to eliminate every adverb that you can. Most of the time adverbs are like excuses—obnoxious and unnecessary. Instead of "very depressed" try "bottomed-out." Instead of "really happy" try "ecstatic." In fact, try to cross out every single "very" and "really." Replace clichés and overused words with something original. Get out a thesaurus if you hit a dead end with something. When in doubt, take it out.

Aim for phrases that conjure up images and sensory experiences rather than straightforward declarations. Experiment with odd punctuation or fragmented sentences. Consider changing the order or shifting parts to make it more dramatic. Carefully determine your line breaks. In free verse, you can end them anywhere you choose. Reading it aloud may help you decide where a line break works best.

After these steps, your initial letter should now be a letter poem—delivery optional.

Tips on Form

- When considering which form would work best, look carefully at the words you use in your letter. If you notice a pattern, maybe the villanelle would work; if you keep using the same words over and over, you could work well with a sestina. If you are having trouble figuring out how to make it look, feel, or sound like a poem, consider using the arbitrary syllable division of the haiku.
- You can name your recipient in the title or make a formal "to" and "from" a part of the poem to help the "letter" feel come across.
- The letter poem is another form that benefits a great deal from editing, revision, and rewriting. Everything you might write in a letter may not have a place in a poem.

Posse Pointer

I feel strongly that your initial letter, the inspiration and basis for your poem, should be written in longhand. There is something personal, intimate, and unique about handwriting. Like fingerprints, no two hands are the same. By physically writing your letter, you own what you are writing. Modern conveniences aside, a pen is sometimes more honest and soul-baring than a computer. If you absolutely must resort to the computer to compose your actual poem, that's fine; but still try to handwrite your letter.

For Further Reading

Perhaps most poetry can technically be considered letter poems, as there is often tangible inspiration in the form of the person writing them. One of my favorite poets, Emily Dickinson (I am both pathetically impressed and abnormally obsessed with her use of the em dash), often addressed her poems to people or things. She was also a prolific letter-writer. Some scholars maintain that some of her letters were actually poems, and she often did include poems in her letters. Much of Dickinson's work can be found on the Internet, because it is in the public domain. *The Complete Poems of Emily Dickinson* and the *Letters of Emily Dickinson* are both available in paperback in many libraries.

Here are some additional examples of letter poems:

- Dorothy Parker also often addressed her poems to others; she usually named the intended in title: "For a Favorite Granddaughter," "For a Lady Who Must Write Verse," and "From a Letter from Lesbia" are some of my favorites. If you ever have an empty moment, Google Dorothy Parker. Her life was incredibly interesting.
- "A Brave and Startling Truth" by Maya Angelou. The poem was written for, and delivered in honor of, the fiftieth anniversary of the United Nations.
- "Daddy" by Sylvia Plath
- "A Letter to Dafnis: April 2nd, 1685" by Anne Finch, who often wrote poems to her husband.
- "A Letter to Theo" by Annie Dillard. From her book *Mornings Like This*, this poem is an actual letter from Van Gogh, translated by Johanna van Gogh and turned into a poem by Annie Dillard.

The Letter Poem Soundtrack

Here are five songs I happen to like quite a bit that also might help you see how you can uniquely and creatively express your thoughts to (or about) someone as you might in a letter poem.

1. "Mother, Mother" the Veronicas (okay, so it's really a phone conversation, but it works here)
2. "Anchorage" Michelle Shocked
3. "You're So Vain" Carly Simon
4. "You Oughta Know" Alanis Morrissette
5. "To Bobby" Joan Baez

What Should I Write About?

The letter poem is similar to the list poem in that it can help you see the possibilities for poetry all around you, but it's also one that you may have difficulty beginning because the possibilities are *so* open.

Maybe you've got something you need to say to your boss. Perhaps you feel resentment toward your parents for a childhood incident. If you are estranged from someone in your family, this is a great moment to spell it out. There could even be an episode long past in which you didn't say what you really wanted to—well, here's your chance. Maybe it's time to finally say good-bye to that negative influence you keep letting hang around. A letter poem also provides an unparalleled opportunity to apologize to someone you may have wronged or extend forgiveness to someone who hurt you. Take the opportunity for introspection and the chance to let something heavy go.

Of course, this person you need to address might be you, which is what I decided to do in one of my letter poems. I intended it for my twenty-three-year-old self. It was a pivotal time as I look back. I made a lot of important, defining decisions that have affected my life to this day. I still haven't made peace with some of those decisions. I think *what could have been if only . . . what might have been if I would have . . . how things would be different if not for . . .*

As I wrote my letter, and then my letter poem, I considered how the advice might also be useful to one of my nieces. She is seventeen, a senior in high school, so close to being a woman that a passerby couldn't tell the difference. I considered what I would not only say to my twenty-three-year-old self, but also what I would say to her, someone who can still avoid some of the mistakes I made.

AN OPEN LETTER

Pay attention to doubt, as it is sometimes disguised as intuition;
follow through, because everything eventually comes to fruition.
Screw Plan B—it wasn't A for a reason;
never settle while youth is in season.
Live in the downtown of a city you can barely afford;
breathe its energy, dance its symphony in minor chord.
Travel enough to know where the leaves turn best;
live and love and laugh enough to compare sunsets.
Love will lead to sex—this is true of most of what we do—
but, as you probably know by now, the opposite is rarely true.
Get a signature drink that doesn't require a mixer;
but never mistake it for truth or love's elixir.
Fall in love with someone who reminds you of e.e. cummings,
experience enough of love and poetry to recognize his qualities.
Never give your heart to someone who laughs at your dreams,

curses at the dinner table, or even one time isn't what he seems.
Live by yourself for at least one year;
dare to know yourself and every fear.
Remember money will buy you some thing,
but will never make you worth anything.
Sing out loud every time you hear your favorite song;
have as many as a summer day in a convertible is long.
Smile when you are called beautiful but only believe it when you
*   think it;*
you'll only know if the movie is as good as the book if you've
*   read it.*
Learn when you stumble so you'll have padding for the big fall;
dream big, tall diamond fantasies but never say yes to get them all.
Know that you will hurt, worse than you imagine you will,
but you'll get on with it—there are two sides to every hill.
Use your library card at least twice as much as your credit card;
when you're cold and lonely, you'll have the comfort of The Bard.
When your heart makes a friend, your hands must follow through
*   with letters.*
To send away one more birthday card than the last, makes each
*   year better.*
Determine your own style and the mirror will never lie;
cashmere and silk, yes, but class is one thing you can't buy.
Grow, change, and evolve—but keep one interesting vice,
and never look at the past long enough to give rhyming advice.
*   —Wendy*

Though it reminded me of one of those chain emails—we all know by now to wear sunscreen—it was fun to write, even if a little uncomfortable to rewind ten-plus years. By the time I got to the end, I realized that there was no point in looking back—the movie is the same, after all, no matter how many times you push the rewind button. Besides that, all the things I wish I were different, or ways I wish *I* had been different, were all things I could still change. I didn't feel weighed down by the past; I felt uplifted. I've still got plenty of time. My twenty-three-year-old self is gone, but my thirty-something-year-old self has all the power.

Nikki chose to deal with something very painful in her letter poem: the death of her aunt, a family member she was extremely close to and who was an enormously positive influence in her life. In Nikki's words: "Aunt Arla was my mother's sister. She was perfect. She was a hairdresser; she was funny; she was grounded; she was down-to-earth. And I will never feel loved like she loved me."

Arla died suddenly from cervical cancer. She waited so long to see a doctor that she died mere months after being diagnosed. She died two months before Nikki had her first son. Though it happened more than five years ago, her death is still difficult for Nikki.

Nikki is regretful. "I was nineteen when she died," she says. "I wish I could have spent more time with her. I was so naïve when she died that I did not realize she was actually going to die. I wish I could be with her for a little longer; I wish I would have laid in the bed with her for three days straight just to love her."

She is also angry. "I have been very angry that, of all the people in my life who do bad things and live horrible lives, she, a living angel, had to be the one who died," she says.

But most of all, Nikki simply misses Arla. She says, "She did so many little things in my life to help mold me to be the way that I am today, and *I do not want* to live without her."

So, Nikki decided to write her letter poem to Arla and finally tell her.

Dear Aunt Arla:
Remembering your smile and laugh and face—I am so sad
Remembering you touching my pregnant belly—I am so sad
And then finding out that day you were gone—I am so sad

My kids never got to know and love you—I am so angry
There's bad people that could have gone not you—I am so angry
Why did you wait to go to the doctor—I am so angry

I was too busy for the barbeque—I am so sorry
Odessa was too far to drive some days—I am so sorry
I didn't see you for months at a time—I am so sorry

I didn't take advantage of your beauty while you were still here.
I would give up anything in my life right now just to have you
*   there.*
You were the most perfect person I will ever know.
I should have done more to let it show.
I know you loved me because I could feel it and sometimes still do.
I wish I could let you know how much I love you.
I wonder how I am going to make it through the rest of my life,
without the life in your eyes and the love in your heart.

I am so sad.
I am so angry.
I am so sorry.
I miss you so much.
Love,
Nikki

Nikki had to let go of not only her aunt but also her feelings of sadness, anger, and guilt. The letter poem helped her begin that process. "It was rough," she acknowledges, "because every time I thought about the things that I didn't do and didn't say, I realized all over again that I will never be able to do or say those things."

Writing to Aunt Arla helped lift Nikki above her heavy feelings by letting her say all the things she wanted, but never got a chance, to say—and in a personal, intimate, real way. "I think that a letter poem is a great thing," Nikki says, "because I really want to talk to her again, and I feel like that is what I was doing. It is so hard to miss her that it was a relief to speak with her again."

Your feelings are valid because they're yours, but the heavy ones only weigh you down. Whether it's anger, guilt, remorse, resentment, regret, or the scariest of them all, hatred, composing a letter poem can help you let it go.

Heather chose to write a letter to her two girls, a subject that always lifts her heart. Oh, who are we kidding? Every mother knows that life with children is hardly ever poetic. It's messy, loud, and busy. But it is possible to slow down enough to be grateful for your kids, especially when you take the split second it takes to realize they're only kids for that split second.

As Heather said in the letter to her girls that she based her poem on, "The things I love about you are endless. Some of the things written here are interchangeable, and some describe each of you and your wonderfully differing personalities. The most important thing is to know how deep my love is for both of you, and this letter is a reminder of those things on the days when I want to pull my hair out and run for the hills!"

Dear Girls,

I love it when you dance around the room to a song from your book.

The times when you make up songs about fairies, butterflies, and flowers.

The times when you whistle as loud, as long as you can.

I love it when you smile and say, "Mommy, you're beautiful."

The times when we play dress up and beauty shop

The times when you paint my nails every color of the rainbow so "I can go to work and tell my friends, 'my daughter did this for me.'"

I love it when you tell me stories that go on as long as the car ride will take it—sometimes it's an hour.

The times when you explain with such authority that an expert would take pause and consider the idea—at least for a minute.

The times when things are described with such imagination an artist could create art from the list.

I love it when you draw me beautiful pictures to put on the fridge or keep in my purse.

The times when you "write" me letters and then "read" them to me so passionately.

The times when you send letters in the "mailbox," deliver them, and then open them with surprise.

I love it when you snuggle into my shoulder—even when it includes a little nip.

*The times when you blow me kisses, when it is time to say bye
bye.*
*The times when you run up to me and hold up your arms so I
may pick you up.*

I love it when you are helpful, even when I don't need it.
*The times when you smile and do something so blatantly
naughty, I want to laugh out loud instead of send you to
time out.*
*The times when I want to wring your neck and you flash those
beautiful sapphire blue eyes.*

*I love it when you stand at the window and scream to go
outside.*
*The times when you repeat a word over and over and over and
over . . .*
The times when your words and inflections sound curiously familiar.

The list is endless and will continue to grow
as you two grow into the beautiful girls I know you will be.
I am truly blessed to have witnessed you
and am proud to be the mother of my girls.
I love you,
Mommy

—Heather

At first, Heather intended to write a poem addressed to her mother. "I wrote the letter to the girls," she says, "because one to my mom would have been really negative. I thought I would write one to the girls that was positive to change the pattern of the mother/daughter relationships in the family." Though a letter to her mother surely would have been therapeutic, so was making a conscious choice to focus on something positive instead of something negative. Every time you sit down to write a poem, you have that power. Dealing with the negative has its place, but so does celebrating the positive. Poetry offers you the unique opportunity. "I feel like I have given a gift to myself and to the girls," Heather said, after writing her letter poem.

Tips on Subject

- You can address some pretty hefty stuff with the letter poem: an abusive parent (alive or deceased), an indifferent spouse, a rebellious child, or someone you may have wronged. This is a great way to use poetry to help *you* specifically. You could even consider addressing a harmful addiction *directly*.
- If you have an extremely painful subject in mind and aren't quite ready to face it, practice writing to simple things first. Write to an inanimate object, a person from your past, a famous person you admire, your dog, a cloud—or whatever. Ease into it if you have to.
- You can also express gratitude, love, and appreciation in a letter poem, just like in an actual letter. You are uplifted by recognizing the positive influence in your life, and if you decide to share it, the recipient is lifted even higher.

Give It a Try

We've all got some unfinished business in our lives that can weigh us down a bit. If you can't think of anything, you aren't really trying. As women, we tend to carry the weight of our world on our shoulders—and not just our world, but also the worlds of our families, friends: even the weight of worlds long gone. Sometimes it gets too heavy. Let it go. You have the ability to do it—and in fact you are the only one who can do it. All it takes to get started is a pen and paper.

There is likely also someone in your life to whom you could express thanks. It is easy to get too busy to let people know how we really feel. There is no better time than now. Name a positive influence in your life you could write a letter poem to—and uplift yourself and another at the same time.

If you need just a little more guidance or simply some practice, here are three ideas for getting started on your letter poem:

1. Write a letter to your younger self—say, you at age sixteen, twenty-one, or thirty. Are there mistakes you wish you had not made? Advice to avoid such pitfalls? Are there mistakes that you are glad you made?
2. Think of the single most influential person in your life (this person doesn't have to be living). Write a letter poem saying thanks.
3. Is there someone from your past whom you have wronged? Write a poem of apology and ask for forgiveness. There aren't many things heavier than guilt.

Your first attempts might feel more like letters than poetry, but keep at it. No matter the finished product, it is the process and what you have gained from it that is important.

If you decide to write and let something negative go, consider putting your poem away in an actual envelope and seal it shut, symbolic of something that you've dealt with and moved on.

Gather your courage, take one small step forward, and let go of what's weighing you down.

If you decide to focus on celebrating someone's positive influence, consider sharing your poem. It doesn't have to be perfect or poetically brilliant; but that you took your time and energy in such a way will make that person's day, week, year—it will, in fact, probably always be remembered.

A Poetic Pause: Making a Poetry Book for Kids

This is one of my favorite ways to use poetry: making a poetry book for kids. You can have it professionally bound, approach it as an "altered book" idea, or go to Paper Source for a kit, but if you are less like Martha Stewart and more like me, there is an easier way to do it. I am talking about a laminated, spiral-bound book that, depending on your page count, should cost you less than $20 to make, start to finish—and, seriously: that anyone can do. Here's how:

Call Kinko's, Office Depot, or other place you know that offers lamination and ask their size requirements. Then cut down the paper you will be using—you can use construction paper, card stock, or scrapbooking paper; because it will be laminated, it doesn't have to be terribly thick—to the correct size.

Place poems on the pages. You can handwrite them or type them on cardstock (or other paper) and glue them on. Use borders, photos, drawings, stickers, stamps, cutouts, and so on as accents. You can make it as colorful and busy or as sophisticated and simple as you choose.

Then take it to a place that offers lamination and spiral binding (I use Office Depot). It usually only takes a few days. Kids from eighteen months to seven years old will love it. They love the singsong nature of rhyming and the way poetry flows in a more musical way than straightforward prose does. Older kids can even make a book themselves.

Here are some specific ideas/themes:

- Take pictures of your child's favorite toys and make up silly rhymes.
- Write haiku about the seasons and use pictures your child has drawn.
- Make it one long list poem: "I Love You Because . . ." and use actual pictures of your child.
- If your child has a current obsession—like trains, dinosaurs, or superheroes—use this as your theme. You can write sonnets, villanelles, or ghazals (they love the rhyming and repetition) and use stickers, coloring book pictures, or magazine/newspaper clippings.
- If you are expecting a new addition to the family, make a poem book about your family, writing a sonnet for each family member. (Or consider making this book if a close friend or family member is expecting.) If you have older children, enlist their help with writing and pictures, and in laying out the book. It will help them welcome the newest family member while also creating a priceless keepsake.

Such a book makes a memorable, sweet, personal gift for holidays, birthdays, or just because. It's one book that will never find its way to the 5¢ box at your next garage sale and will instead likely be handed down from one generation to the next.

Chapter Eight

Get on Your Spiritual Path: The Prayer Poem

That's why I pray and poetize: to be able to see my brothers and sisters despite my own (often petty) agonies, to partake of the majesty that's every Judas's birthright.

—Mary Karr

When I was a teenager, I was sure. I was sure of typical adolescent stuff, like knowing *way* more than my parents; I was even relatively sure of myself, like knowing that I absolutely *could* be a Supreme Court justice *and* Miss America. Sure, I had typical adolescent insecurities on the outside (facial blemishes, an "athletic" build, and the fact that we could never afford designer jeans) and on the inside (being the "smart" girl who sometimes got tired of studying so hard, the "new" girl who just wanted to belong, and the "good kid" who just wanted to be herself every now and then). But, for the most part, I was sure. Perhaps the most startling and the most impressive, as I look back on those years, is how sure I was of God.

Growing up, the biggest person in our household was my dad, which is funny because on a tall day he stands at 5'6". He wasn't loud, intimidating, or mean. He wasn't rich, famous, or important—except to us. He wasn't flamboyant, odd, or flashy. Yet, as we grew up, he affected the direction we all took. My brother rebelled against him, my sister is still a Daddy's girl, and I, in my own way, wanted to be just like him. I wanted to be as sure of the world as he was.

He was a Southern Baptist preacher, leader of the First Baptist Church of Poteau, Oklahoma. So, yep, I was a PK—Preacher's Kid. We went to Sunday school and church Sunday morning, class and church Sunday night, church Wednesday night, and I had a youth Bible study on Tuesday nights. I easily spent ten hours a week doing church-related activities. In addition, I went to church camp in the summer, youth ski trips on spring break, and more revivals than Tammy Faye Baker. There are three main pastimes in small Oklahoma towns: football, gossip, and church.

Being a PK in a small town is an unusual experience. Because my dad was the pastor of the *First* Baptist Church, we were kind of like the First Family of Poteau. I may not have had paparazzi following my every move, but there were plenty of prying, peering eyes from little old ladies who would report all happenings of the town, big and small. (My brother took the car without permission and got caught because the closing cashier at the grocery store—there was only one main one—saw him and told her friend, who just happened to be the church pianist.) What we wore, how we talked, where we went, and with whom we went was always under scrutiny.

We were literally voted in. It sounds cruel and archaic, but we "interviewed" as an entire family. We came to Poteau for a "visit," stayed with a family in the congregation, my dad performed a sermon one summer Sunday night, and then we sat sequestered in the small church office as an official oral vote was taken. I guess since they voted us in, they felt some amount of personal responsibility to make sure we stayed who they thought we should be. We were held to a higher standard; a standard decided by some Small Town Law of Old. There's a reason most PKs are either goody-two-shoes or flat-out, no-holds-barred wild: expectations are hard to live up to and downright impossible to live down.

We lived in Poteau for five years, the longest we lived anywhere as a family. Though I remember instances of racism, classism, and lookism (Poteau always seemed on the verge of some type of eruption, and I don't think it can be entirely attributed to the lack of choices at the local movie theater), I also remember Friday night football games, cruising down Main Street, and Holton's Department Store. This is where I experienced my first kiss (right outside the church!), my first best friend, and my first Mary Kay makeover. Though certainly confining—it was like the world didn't exist past Ft. Smith, Arkansas—such a small space was also reassuring; I could touch its sides.

Here, the world made sense. My dad stood tall on the pulpit and made sense of it. And not just the easy stuff like why you should pray, go to church, and tithe, but the hard stuff like why God allows destructive technology, loss, and personal suffering—all things that, while I knew they were happening, didn't happen to us. I believed that everything that was was a part of God's master plan—a plan I didn't have to understand. I believed in miracles I didn't see. I believed that prayer could change a world I didn't really know. Because he was so sure, I was sure.

Then we moved to Germany and something happened.

To this day I don't know what it was. Maybe it was because we weren't together as a family anymore. (My brother stayed behind for college.) Maybe it was because we were removed from under the microscope. Or maybe it was because we were in a world whose sides we couldn't touch anymore. I don't know. But, by the time I left for college two years later, my dad had left the church and the United States had entered the Gulf War. My dad stopped believing; I was on my own; and people I knew were leaving for *war.*

I've never been as sure since. I've never really asked my dad why he left the church. Selfishly, I'm resentful that, because he started questioning, I had to question. It's actually very easy to follow what the Bible says—especially if you've let someone else interpret it for you. It's much more difficult to determine your own spiritual path. For the past almost twenty years, I've been searching for the same type of spiritual certainty I had in my youth. I've sought it in different churches—some so large I was convinced even God could get lost and some so small I don't know if He fit—and I've sought it in other people; I've sought it through good deeds and I've even tried to swallow enough to pretend I wasn't searching for anything.

But I am searching. I need spirituality, and I believe that it is a necessary part of a successful life. I could be author of the next *Oprah Book Club* selection, win the lottery, and spend my time building schools in Darfur, but if I didn't find my spiritual path and follow it, my life would be meaningless. By "spiritual path," I mean figuring out how my life follows ideals that make not only the world but also my home a better place—how I fit into humanity as a whole on the positive side, as well as how to be a good mom. I happen to believe in God. But I don't believe that any *specific* faith is necessary to find and follow a spiritual path. Each person's path is unique. Mine is curvy and hilly; others may follow a straighter path.

I don't even know if my dad prays anymore. But, through it all, that's the one thing I have consistently done. At times I have been sure of my direction, like when I look into my son's laughing eyes, find myself absorbed by the first snowfall of the year, or give my last dollar to the man on the corner. But, for the most part, I'm still wandering around asking for directions. Sometimes I find it in a prayer poem.

Why a Prayer Poem?

First of all, don't think you have to chant "ohm," channel Mother Teresa, or hole up in a monastery to write a prayer poem. In fact, the quest for a spiritual path in the midst of your life as it is happening is perhaps the most admirable quest of all. As Ding Ling once said, "Happiness is to take up the struggle in the midst of the raging storm and not to pluck the lute in the moonlight or recite poetry among the blossoms."

I believe that to function at one's highest level, one must determine how to make spirituality a moving part of everyday life. There must be morals, ethics, and values that you believe in so you know when you're proud of your life. There must be a spiritual path that helps you keep these values in sight. It is a unique kind of path that you pave as you go. The prayer poem can help you lay down the stones, keep you looking straight ahead, or give you a light when it gets dark.

It has nothing to do with church or the entity that you pray to but everything to do with *you*. Only you can determine the direction and destination of your spiritual path. To stay on it means that you are living the life you want to live, a life you are proud of, a life that adds something positive to the lives around you. A prayer poem doesn't have to be an actual *prayer*. It is anything that gets you in touch with your spirit, that deep secret place where you determine your spiritual path.

Instead of a traditional prayer, Lori used the prayer poem to delve into what it is she believes in—her values, what makes her proud of her life, what keeps her on her spiritual path. As she says, "I asked myself, *what am I about? What do I believe in? If I died tomorrow, what would I want my children to know about me?*"

Spirituality to Lori isn't a prayer you say in church or even one you say on your knees at the side of your bed at night, it's what you tell yourself each and every day to keep yourself moving forward; spirituality is what you do in life that makes you and your family proud—spirituality is what you believe in. This is what Lori believes:

ONE WOMAN'S CREED

I believe in love and laughter,
life, death, and the ever-after.
I believe in the healing power of touch—
hugs, kisses, tickles, and such.
I believe in education, books,
dinners at home, and food that I cook.
I believe in the power of written words,
finding your voice, and feeding the birds.
I believe in good design—
graceful curves and a clean line.
I believe in the restorative power of dirt,

basalt, granite, and my black satin skirt.
I believe in history, dance,
music, art, and even France.
I believe in affirmative action, evolution,
freedom of choice, and my own revolution.
I am a lawyer, wife, mother of three,
and this is my wisdom, my mantra, me.

—Lori

"This poem took a lot of rewriting and editing over several days," she says, "I tried to distill it down to my most essential beliefs." Lori thinks it is a practice necessary to one's spirituality to devote serious thought every once in a while to essential beliefs. It is an affirmation of one's whole self. "We tend to identify people by what they do—career, motherhood—and it's easy to lose yourself in such all-consuming pursuits," Lori says. "But women are complex creatures. We should give ourselves credit for *all* we are. My poem keeps me close to what is important to me—which is essential to leading a purposeful, directed life."

The prayer poem is an excellent tool for determining your daily beliefs, and it can keep you on your spiritual path. The prayer poem is also an excellent tool for determining what it is you really need.

One week before my birthday, an early Sunday evening found me making my annual birthday list. First were the red patent pumps I had been lusting over in Nordstrom. A close second was a new pair of Seven jeans. Coming in third, a facial and massage. An ivory cashmere cableknit turtleneck, Mac lip gloss in Angelwing, Chanel nail color in Sensuelle, and a brown tweed newsboy cap rounded out the list.

I looked over my list and thought, *is this what I really want? Is this what would really make me happy? No.* The answer came quickly and clearly—and in a voice that seemed to come from a very deep place. None of these things would give me a happy family or a loving, respectful, nurturing marriage. None of these things would make me a better mother. None of these things would help me accomplish any of my professional pursuits. None of these things would enhance my life in any way.

I turned my focus inward and thought about what I really wanted for the next year. I opened up my heart and soul beyond what I wanted and into what I *needed*.

MY BIRTHDAY LIST

freedom from cashmere want. to spend a Wednesday
fall afternoon in a blue convertible,
laughing at orange leaves, writing poems in the clouds.

strength to do what's hard so the rest will be right.
to hold my shaking arms out wide as long as
it takes to catch my dreams in a hot summer rain.

love for the man on the corner with the sign.
to list and list as snow silently blankets
the twinkling trees of winter's early twilight.

faith to blow out the candles and turn on the
light. to plant brilliant possible bulbs in spring's
cold, hard, giving earth with my own two dirty hands.

—Wendy

Writing this prayer poem was difficult because it was to admit something was missing. It was to admit I needed something I couldn't run out and buy. There was no store that sold what I needed. But it was also reassuring, in that I found the peace and comfort prayer has always offered me by opening up to needs bigger than my wants. *God knows what you need best when you tell Him,* I kept remembering my dad say. This prayer poem was like a big neon arrow pointing me in the right direction.

(I also hid the age I was turning in the form. I didn't need to date it, because it tells my age with every word; it was a personal way to detail where I was when writing the poem.)

Can't I just pray? Why a prayer poem? you might be asking. Of course you should pray if that action works for you, but a prayer poem doesn't have to be a traditional prayer; it is a way to get on and stay on your spiritual path, especially if you don't normally pray and especially if you feel like you've lost your way a bit. As Lori demonstrates, it doesn't have to take the traditional "Dear Lord," tone or style. Through a prayer poem, you seek to reconnect with your spiritual self. It takes effort and reflection. It simply does not happen unless you make the commitment to do so. The prayer poem gives you a way to foster the connection, another source to water your creative and spiritual garden. It's something that has personally helped me, and because I am certainly no guru, and definitely no more enlightened than you, I think will help you, too.

Thinking of spirituality and how it betters your life can be overwhelming. It's like trying to decide what to wear in the morning. When you open your closet and see a mass of hangers, clothes, and shoes, it can be frustrating and tempting to fall back on those black pants and red shirt you always wear. But if you take the time to consider what you have going on that day, or the weather, or how long you'll be on your feet, or your mood (and so on), it's easier to choose something that will be comfortable and attractive the entire day. It's particularly easy if you've thought about it the night before. Likewise, it's a lot easier to make spirituality an influential, beneficial part of your life if you think about it consistently and realistically. If you look outside when you've decided to wear your new suede shoes and it's pouring down rain, it's tempting to throw your hands up and call in sick. The prayer poem reminds you that sometimes all you need is an umbrella.

What Exactly Makes a Prayer Poem?

A prayer poem is like the letter poem in that it is a *type* of poetry where you can employ any form—or none at all. It is simply a spiritual experience you've turned in to a poem. I would never tell you how to pray, what to believe in, or where to find peace. In the same vein, I could never really tell you *how* to write a prayer poem. What I can tell you are some things a prayer poem is not—or rather some misconceptions you might have.

First, you do not have to be in a state of nirvana or be experiencing total inner peace to write a prayer poem. You don't even have to be a good person. Often during turmoil, confusion, and rebellion are the best times to write a prayer poem. It's when you sit in the eye of the storm that sometimes things become clear.

Secondly, you don't have to talk to God. Address whatever/whomever it is that makes you feel a part of life as a whole, makes you aware of your soul, and offers you inspiration to be a better person. This could be God, Mother Nature, Allah, Zeus, or the Full Moon—whatever.

Thirdly, this doesn't have to be a nice, peaceful, or even respectful poem. I get mad at God and rant at the inequality, suffering, and insanity of the world. Just like in my relationships with every other important presence in my life, I feel better *getting it all out*. A prayer is as individual as eye color. No two blues, browns, or greens are exactly the same, and if yours were any different, you wouldn't really be you—and you wouldn't see the world in the same way. I talk about honesty a lot—but realize that you really won't reap the benefits of a prayer poem without being honest. Colored contacts look great, but they don't really change your inner eye color.

It is okay to wonder and ask about the inequities and injustices of the world—even those in your own life. The great thing is that if you keep at it, if you keep re-approaching the prayer poem, you will eventually feel a moment of peace—it truly is inevitable, but it is *not* instantaneous.

A prayer poem is a spiritual experience, not a religious experience. There are no prerequisites or mandatory beliefs. All that is required is a commitment to opening yourself up to a world you can't see, faith that you were put here to find a path and follow it, and a desire to get in touch with your spiritual nature to live your most authentic life.

Unlike the sonnet or villanelle, you can't get on the Internet and find out how to write a prayer poem. But you can use form. If your focus is nature, consider the haiku. If there is a repeated thought or question, the villanelle might be just the one. If it is a particularly emotional situation you are dealing with, the sonnet might help you say what you need to say. If it is simply a session of musing, of random philosophical thoughts, perhaps the ghazal is the perfect medium. Because I think using poetic form enhances writing, thought, and the emotional process, I encourage you to seek one out. However, prayer must come from the soul, and maybe your soul is a free verse kind of gal.

If you do decide to employ free verse, be extra vigilant about your word choice, just as if you had to fit a form. Analyze each line to be sure it is just right, even though there are no formal rules to follow. Challenge yourself to be as succinct and true as possible. Reread and revise. Resist the urge to accept the first thing that you write.

Tips on Form

- Use your own words. Just because I call this a prayer poem doesn't mean that you need to use lofty, "spiritual" words.
- Think of it as a conversation. Addressing someone/something that you perceive as too far to reach can sound stiff and unnatural, so talk as you would to someone/thing you are comfortable with. A prayer poem is intensely personal and should sound like it.
- Try to get it all out in one sitting. I know it's difficult to find that block of time, but this exercise is most beneficial when you can follow it through. Even one day can make you think and feel differently. You can always revise and edit later.
- Consider dating your prayer poems. How you pray, what you pray about, and the tone you use are unique to this one instant. By next week, and certainly by next year, your poem will be as different as you are. You can learn a lot from old prayer poems, and their lessons will be more obvious if you know exactly when they were written.

For Further Reading

I hardly ever read the newspaper. But on New Year's Day 2006, I was delivered the paper by mistake. In it, there was a poem—*Prayer*—by Maya Angelou. I read it and was immediately affected. I found myself rereading it aloud as if it were my own prayer. A spiritual moment descended upon me right there in the middle of my den. It certainly had a lot to do with her beautiful, touching words and true sentiments, but also that I was reading it on a day of such hope and promise. I knew suddenly that it was not a mistake at all that I would receive the paper that day. I tore it out and have kept it with me ever since.

Maya Angelou is an amazing woman, poet, and person—did you know she was the first black cable car conductor in San Francisco, or that "Maya Angelou" is a name she gave herself as a stage name, or that she has been nominated for a Tony Award as well as the Pulitzer Prize? You must read *I Know Why the Caged Bird Sings* or, for an unrivaled poetry experience, listen to the *Maya Angelou Poetry Collection (Unabridged)* audio book (she reads her poetry herself) while driving alone for miles.

There are many excellent examples of prayer poems that can also be easily located. If you are searching on the Internet, you will probably have better luck finding examples with searches like "spiritual poetry" or "spiritual poems" than "prayer poem(s)." Here are a few examples I was able to locate:

- "Prayer for a New Mother" by Dorothy Parker
- "A Dreamer Prayer" by Mary Harper
- "The Word of God" by Catherine Faber
- "I'm Alive, I Believe in Everything" by Lesley Choyce
- "Prayer" by Sara Teasdale
- "Welcome Morning" by Anne Sexton

Soundtrack

I can hardly separate my days in the church from the music. Especially as a youth, I found music transcending. (Yeah, I'll admit it: I've been to a Stryper concert, owned a Petra cassette tape, and know the pre–"Baby, Baby," pre–Vince Gil Amy Grant.) I remember when my voice blended effortlessly with others, when a song had the power to send sinners down the aisle to be saved (when sinners actually could be saved). I can close my eyes and feel the hard, rough, faded, blue cover of the hymnal and see its gold, once-shiny letters. I'm also at a place where I can separate the religiosity from the spirituality and appreciate the raw power of music. Music is to spirituality what 400-thread count sheets are to bed: not *necessary*, but, with it, the whole experience is better.

Here are five of the most meaningful songs from my time in the First Baptist Church in Poteau, Oklahoma:

- "Just As I Am" (lyrics by Charlotte Elliott) is my favorite hymn. It's the only one I could probably still sing—all six verses, too.
- "El Shaddai" as performed by Amy Grant (also very popular on the Miss Cinderella pageant circuit). There wasn't a dark, starlit summer night at church camp without this song.
- "Close to Thee," (lyrics by Fanny Crosby)
- "Answers Don't Come Easy" by Leslie (Sam) Phillips. I would sit for hours alone in my room listening to this song.
- "Dear Refuge of My Weary Soul" by Anne Steel

What Should I Write About?

When I started writing this chapter, I thought, *what have I gotten myself into?* Telling people how to pray or what to pray about is like telling someone whether to spank their kids or not. I know what I believe, but whatever I say is bound to piss someone off.

It's a touchy subject, but the truth still remains: I believe in prayer and I believe in poetry. I also believe that an individual sense of spirituality is necessary to living one's best life. There must be something—a faith, belief, conviction, or set of principles—that makes one strive to be a positive influence and add something good to the world. But it's unique; no two people can possibly follow the same path. The prayer poem can help you find your path and follow it, as well as find your way back when necessary.

The prayer poem was one of the most difficult for the Posse to write. It is difficult to pour your heart out in prayer and in verse, knowing that someone will be reading and maybe even judging your words. The prayer poem is a poem that is most beneficial when written for your eyes and heart only. It cannot be censored and remain a true prayer.

Erin found the beginning stages of writing a prayer poem difficult. "Honestly, it was a little uncomfortable to put those types of feelings down on paper," she says. Yet, she bravely considered the prayer poem and how it could not only relate to but also *affect* her life and spiritual path. "When I think of spirituality, I think of my relationship with God," she says—so it was God she turned to for help. She was at a point in her life where she wasn't sure of her direction as a wife, mother, and human being.

"This poem is about the pressures of being a 'good' wife and mother and juggling that with a career," she says. "It's also about the frustration I feel over the lack of support where I need it most. It's also about forgiving myself for the *major* mistakes I have made in the past and trying to make the right decisions moving forward." She needed God's help, so she turned to both the villanelle and God and asked for help in a prayer poem.

HELP ME FIND A WAY

Help me find a way
To push my frustrations aside
And enjoy this life.

Torn between what I should and what I want
It's a bumpy ride.
Help me find a way.

My mistakes linger and taunt
Grant me the shore at high tide
To enjoy this life.

Pressures like semi-precious stones flaunt
Their gaudiness—I cannot hide
Please help me find a way.

I aim for courage, fall short, and haunt
The places easier to reach inside
I want to enjoy this life.

Can't I have all this I want?
Release the want to which I'm tied;
Help me find a way
To enjoy this life.

—Erin

"Writing the prayer poem," Erin says, "allowed me to put down on paper the things I need to remember, think about, and ask for help with on a regular basis." It was not only the act of writing that was helpful to Erin in remembering that she must lean on God for guidance on her spiritual path, but rereading her poem was also helpful when she needs the reminder. As she says, "It has been helpful to me to go back and read this poem, because I can stay mindful. To me, a prayer poem can be a great way to remind yourself of those things for which you need grace."

My prayers and prayer poems usually take one of four routes: I am either saying please, thank you, why, or help. Truth be told, my priorities are often out of whack, and I say please and why more than thank you or help. One night, I was feeling out of sorts—like nothing was going right. I was feeling overwhelmed by my home, feeling like I was falling short of what I needed to do to be a good wife; my son was getting into trouble at school, soccer, *and* home, so I felt like I was the Worst Mom Ever, always doing the wrong thing and messing up something terribly important; I was worried about finances; I was stressed at work, involved in a no-win project that I couldn't help but take personally; and I was lonely and feeling very sorry for myself because I couldn't think of a single girlfriend who could drop everything and come right over. I wanted to just sit down and cry. I felt like no matter what I did, it was going to be wrong. It was like road-tripping while following an upside-down map.

It is at these times that I pray; and I prayed that night. I know I should pray during all the good times too, and I try—I'm still trying—but a realization of what it was that I needed came to me. All I needed was a little courage to make just one good decision. So this was a *please give me* type of prayer.

PLEASE GRANT ME COURAGE

to say no and I,
to speak truth, not hide and peek
behind pretty verse.
to save my very
last dollar and give away
the one before that.
to untangle the
knots I tie, to set free what
I hold, clutch, strangle.
to see my flower-
box dreams, especially when
my eyes are open.
to never let his
spirit be broken, for he
would always be cracked.
to look out from the
cliff I've been standing on for
these three years—and fly.
to travel alone,
barefoot, and shape clouds on the
steep and rocky climb.
to affect one life
each day—this day grant me the
guts to make it mine.

—Wendy

Did you recognize the form? I used the haiku. I chose the haiku because what I needed was basic—courage—and I didn't want the simplicity of my plea to get lost in a bunch of unnecessary words—

or in the mess that is my life. I needed a form that would force me to say only what was necessary, honestly and simply.

I didn't immediately develop huge courage muscles, but writing my poem did give me the courage to keep going, to resist the urge to give up. I wrote and prayed instead of crying. It helped me remember I can only make it one day at a time, one step at a time, one decision at a time.

Kellie chose to say thank-you in her prayer poem. Kellie's spiritual path is something she considers every day. She has a strong daily faith in God and without it couldn't live her life the way she was meant to live it. She says, "I have grown to realize religion is not limited to or defined as Sunday rituals, but it is in fact a lifestyle."

When considering her prayer poem, the things she wanted— even needed—first came to mind and she started out asking. But once she really thought her prayer poem through, she changed her tune. She says, "I started out asking, but quickly changed and decided to thank Him for all He has done, is doing, and will do. It forced me sit back and reflect on how blessed I am."

Lord, Thank You
Thank you for being Alpha and Omega.
Thank you for opening my eyes and revealing the truth.
Thank you for catching each tear and reminding me this too
*   shall pass.*
Thank you for hearing my prayers both spoken and unspoken.
Thank you for loving me despite my disobedience.
Thank you for being my refuge, during the raging storms of life.
Thank you for being my compass, when I lose my way.
Thank you for being my strength, as I tire from the daily struggle.

Thank you for restoring my joy, after the world tries to take it away.
Thank you for forgiveness and for my being forgiven.
Thank you for your grace and mercy afresh with the rising of
the sun.
Thank you for being the ultimate source of love and peace.
Thank you for life and life everlasting.
Thank you for your protective suit of armor.
Thank you for your infallible and unchanging Word.
Thank you for being the great physician who's always available
and right on time.
Thank you for showing me; even though I am lonely, I am
never alone.
Thank you for being the living water flowing through desolate land.
Thank you for being the great I AM.
Thank you for the mansion not built by the hands of man.
Thank you for being Alpha and Omega.
Amen

—Kellie

"The prayer poem provides the writer a chance to reflect on those things which are most important in life. I personally get caught up in asking for things, instead of thanking Him for what He has already provided," Kellie says. Writing this poem allowed Kellie to redirect her thoughts and express gratitude. It also serves as a reminder in case she ever momentarily forgets all that she has to be thankful for.

"I believe," Thelma says, "there is a purpose for every life, and we have been gifted to follow that purpose, but sometimes the gifts are not discovered." One's spiritual path, as Thelma follows hers, is to discover those gifts that enable us to affect good, even if in one small corner. "I think the prayer poem is one of the most beautiful there is," she says, because it can remind you of your gift or keep your eyes straight ahead to keep looking.

"Most of my prayers are a bit spontaneous and inspired by something I see or think about," says Thelma. So she wrote this prayer poem in the same spirit over the course of a day, keeping the paper on the table, jotting down ideas and thoughts as she went about her daily chores. ("I like writing that way, as it gives me something to think about instead of my own problems," she remarked.) As a result, her poem was, as she says, about "the real things I see as I drive on my way, usually to the school [where she works]. Not all in one day but a matter of a few days." It turned into a why, please, thank-you, and help prayer—all rolled into one.

A DAY

I see the pictures of my loved ones lined on the wall
I pray, "God you know I love them, will you bless them one and
     all?
They all live so very far, thank you for being omnipresent; I know
     you are there.
Will you stay close beside them and keep them in your care?"

I think I am dressed and ready for the day,
But no, I can't go out to face the world dressed this way,
Because I'm dressed in clothes of doubt and that will never do,
I need to walk in faith, so I'll have to change my shoes.

As I drive along, I see an old bearded man standing on the street,
I know at one time he must have been so very clean and neat.
They say there's good in every man, and he must be honest and
     sincere;

He holds a sign that simply says, "Why lie? I need another beer."
Lord, I pray
Bless this man and help him find a better way.

There's the girl on the corner so scantily clad,
Is she looking for love that she never had?
Or maybe a true love she had and then lost,
Trying to find it again regardless of the cost.
Help her to see that your love is true,
And turning to you is the best thing she can do.

Then at the school the kids are out to play,
Some already tired and crying tho' it's early in the day.
They miss their Mom and Dad and are ready to go home.
Lord, help me as I play with them make the day not seem so long.

Thank you, God, for your blessings today,
And bringing me safely home. I sit down to relax
And turn the TV on, then I hear the cold, hard facts:
Wars, chaos, grief, and pain, brought on mostly by the greed of
   man.
Help us as we try to help others find peace in the world, and in
   our hearts again.

—Thelma

"Sometimes I see people and wonder, how did they come to be where they are; what is a matter of God's plan and what is a matter of choice?" Thelma says, "I try to withhold judgment and wonder what circumstances have brought the person there. And say a little prayer." This poem was her prayer not only for herself but also for her family, for the strangers she sees on the street every day on the way to the school, and for our world at one of its most desperate times. It reminds her to keep looking for her gifts, something sometimes as simple as saying a prayer for a stranger.

I keep my prayer poems and refer to them often. They are like road signs on my spiritual path. I inevitably backtrack along the path or wander off completely, but when I re-read them, I'm reminded and reassured enough to keep going. I remember to stop and be thankful, to use caution with my words, and to yield to others whenever possible. And someday I'm sure I'll look back and be thankful I asked for courage when I needed it most.

Those four sentiments—please, help, thank you, and why—are good places to start if you can't immediately think of something to write about.

Tips on Subject
- A prayer poem can be intensely, perhaps even uncomfortably, personal. Know that if it is difficult to write, you are probably on the right track.
- What you are writing about is more important than who or what you are writing to.
- Choose a subject that is bigger than you—something that you feel is beyond your capability to handle yourself. (Though I bet you feel differently after writing it.) This one works well with the really big, really hard stuff.
- Remember that prayers—and therefore prayer poems—are not right or wrong. Write about what you know you need to and in whatever tone is right for you.
- Your subject might indeed be quite difficult—but open yourself up to receiving answers, assurance, or acceptance. You can only receive it if your heart, mind, or soul is open.

Posse Pointer

Even if you lean toward writing a traditional prayer poem like Kellie, also consider writing an "I Believe" type of poem like Lori. As she says, "It would be interesting to repeat this exercise every ten years or so to see what changes and what stays constant over time. But even if it's done just once, this kind of 'what I believe' poem should be a required assignment for every woman in her lifetime."

Give it a try

I hope you don't miss out on the prayer poem experience, thinking that you are not spiritual enough or religious enough or good enough. Everyone believes in something, and everyone deserves a belief. Everyone also has the potential to live a spiritual life, to abide by principles that put her on the plus side instead of the minus side. You must stay in touch with your spiritual side and keep track of your spiritual path to live the most effective, authentic life you can. To help get you started writing a prayer poem, I am going to challenge you to experiment with writing in different places, in addition to giving you ideas of what to write about.

• Drive by a church and find somewhere that you can legally park or sit for fifteen or twenty minutes. It can be any church: the fancy church downtown or the small one ten miles out, a church you regularly attend or a church you've never seen the inside of. Give yourself at least fifteen minutes to take in the entire scene. Write down the first six words (or phrases) that come to your mind. Don't censor yourself! Let it sit for at least a day. Use these six elements in a sestina.

- Stand in your kitchen and list twenty things you have to be thankful for. Use this list to write a list poem.
- Watch the evening news, from start to finish, wherever you watch TV most often. Ask *why?* If you keep asking the same questions or wondering about the same injustices, try the villanelle. If not the villanelle, try the sonnet.

Even if it feels unnatural to pray, make the effort to get in touch with your spiritual side and get on your spiritual path. It's not about commandments, prayer books, or sermons but instead about what you need to do to feel good about the direction you are going in life and about what you do on a daily basis to add good to the world. Say a prayer, write a poem, and see where your path leads.

Poetic Pause: How to Read Poetry and Why You Should

Telling you how to read poetry, and why you should, in such a short segment might seem far-reaching. After all, entire books are devoted to the subject. Yet here I go—because not only can writing poetry help you live your most creative, expressive, and authentic life, but reading it also offers immense pleasure and can add something you might be missing.

No one should read poetry because she *has* to. That's like pretending you like classical music. How often do you go to the movies, select a book, watch TV, or listen to the radio because you *have* to? It is okay to expect poetry to entertain—to expect the experience to be pleasurable. Like the rest of the arts, poetry should be accessible, instructive, *and* enjoyable.

Reading poetry is actually very easy, because you don't read poetry, you experience it. You don't have to understand it to enjoy it. It's about emotion and the giant strand that connects us all—

not so much about individual threads. These days, poetry is read out of necessity (usually involving a grade), under order. Well, just like you can now eat cereal for dinner if you like, you owe it to your adult self to seek out poetry and find out what you like. I absolutely, unequivocally promise that if you look long and hard enough, you will find poetry that you enjoy reading.

First you have to find poetry to read. Where to even start? There are so many different kinds and styles. I adore certain poetry by men, but I decided at the beginning of this book to only include women's voices not only because we are overlooked and looked over too often but also because I find the voice of a woman particularly inspiring and easy to identify with. If you are looking for somewhere to start, consider these female poets: Christina Rossetti, Emily Dickinson, Sylvia Plath, Edna St. Vincent Millay, Adrienne Rich, Elizabeth Bishop, Marilyn Hacker, Lucille Clifton, and Kay Ryan. (I've mentioned other poets throughout this book, all worthy of Google searches.) You can search for them on the Internet or use your local library database.

If there is a certain subject that appeals to you—motherhood, spirituality, love, or nature—you can search amazon.com with that keyword and find anthologies, which are great ways to encounter many different poets and styles.

Now that you have some idea of *where* to start, here are some ideas on *how* to read poetry.

First read the poem in its entirety. Sometimes readers give up or struggle with misunderstanding—or not understanding at all—lines and meaning. Read it through. Try to *feel* it instead of *understand* it.

Next, read it out loud. Poetry's tradition is oral, and even though modern poets write with the intent of being read and not recited, poetry's flow and rhythm sometimes only make sense when heard. Read each and every word slowly; pronounce and enunciate each one.

Now read it again and look up words you don't know. Then read it one final time as an *active* reader. Conjure up images in your head. Decide for yourself the story, point, or lesson. Let the poem take you somewhere.

Now, after reading it four times with an honest effort in each step, decide whether you like it. If not, move on. Don't waste any more time with it. That one just isn't for you. If you decide that you do, record it somewhere—either handwritten in your journal, or on an electronic log on your computer. Read it again and again. Just as *you* aren't the same year to year, your favorite poems will grow with you.

If you encounter a poet you like, consider researching her life and reading her works in chronological order. And by all means, buy your favorite work in hardbound books. You can buy them new or used (for much less than you might expect), but buy what you like expecting to read it again and again. The best poetry changes each time you read it, because *you* change.

Now that you have the beginnings of how, why? Amy Lowell wrote a timeless essay, "Why We Should Read Poetry," which at press-time could be found at about.com. As she says, "Why should one read poetry? That seems to me a good deal like asking: Why should one eat?" Poetry expresses that part of human nature that is common and necessary to us all; it is the simplest, most profound essence and expression of our being.

Whether you can afford Manolos or Payless, woman cannot live on material things, on material concerns, alone. If so, as Lowell says, "every bookshop would shut, every theatre would close its doors, every florist and picture dealer would go out of business, even the baseball grounds would close." There is something within each of us that strives for more, that yearns for pure and true beauty—like poetry. And poetry is that beauty that tells the story of the human soul, not the story of human happenings.

Poetry tells the story of what matters most: of love, of loss, of sorrow, of fear, of terror, of joy, and of every other human emotion that is shared by any other human being. It's the one thing that has the capability to connect us all.

Reading poetry connects you to a larger world, reminding you that no matter what you are going through you're not alone. Poetry shows us that even the bleakest, most war-torn world has the potential for peace. Poetry gets past all the difference and lands in that spot where we're all the same.

You should also read poetry because it will help you write better poetry. And why, really, should you write poetry? Because the world needs more of it—and not just your world (of remembering what you're thankful for, of love, of heartbreak, and of searching for direction), but the entire world (of wars, famine, and poverty). The next great poet may not come from the halls of Harvard but may come up from the laundry room or that beige office building downtown. In all probability, you will never write a true work of genius—but indeed, genius cannot be written unless we write.

So seek and read. You'll discover a beautiful, hopeful, intense, and expressive world you scarcely knew existed—yours.

Chapter Nine

Learn Something New Every Day: The Epiphany Poem

If I feel physically as if the top of my head were taken off, I know that is poetry.

—Emily Dickinson

Beverly's was during a conversation with her husband, Jen's during her first staff meeting, Lori and Katie when they were approaching birthdays, and Debbie's over a cup of coffee with her dad. It hit me in the car and then, again, while writing. Kellie was struck after the death of her father. By what? An epiphany.

But what exactly is an epiphany? It's a term that is tossed around quite a bit, but what is it? And can it really happen any old time?

The idea of "epiphanies" is a concept that has captured many an imagination in literature from Proust and Joyce to Thoreau and Emerson—in *Les Miserables,* for example, Jean Valjean's epiphany, when the priest he had robbed forgave him and gave him the candelabra he had tried to steal, was the beginning of a new and rewarding life.

The epiphany has a religious background. Those familiar with Christian beliefs have probably heard of the Epiphany Feast that celebrates the manifestation of the divine nature of Jesus to the Gentiles.

The concept of epiphany is also common in popular culture. An amazon.com search returns more than 25,000 books with "epiphany" in the title, covering everything from romance to self-help. Epiphany is also the name of Bible study software, accounting software, and a web browser. It was even the name of a restaurant co-owned by Kevin Costner as well as of a California wine.

What is this curious, grand notion that finds a home in literature and religion, on our computers, and even in our wine goblets? *Webster's Collegiate Dictionary, Fourth Edition* defines epiphany as: (a) A moment of sudden intuitive understanding; flash of insight (b) A scene, experience, etc. that occasions such a moment.

One night I was sitting up late, paying bills on the computer (never fun). The house was a wreck—dishes in the sink, unfolded laundry on the couch, makeup and hair products on the bathroom counter—and my son was up an hour past his bedtime. I was in the midst of some serious internal complaining and asking *oh, why me?* Suddenly I looked around and inexplicably thought, "I have a lot to be thankful for." This overwhelming truth came on strongly and unexpectedly. Suddenly I knew that, even when I thought it wasn't enough, I had a lot. Everything I was complaining about was really a blessing. An epiphany? Maybe. It definitely changed my attitude that night.

When my son was about three, we were sitting in church, and he turned to me and said, "Mommy, I don't like coming to church because I think the lights will crash down." Our church is a gorgeous building with high arched ceilings and probably fifty chandeliers that hang down with shining lights. I suppose what I found beautiful and serene, he found uncertain and scary. As I looked into his eyes, I realized suddenly what it is to be a mother. He needed me to reassure him—yes—but I could also see, beyond a shadow of a doubt, that he thought me capable of preventing not only this potential catastrophe of crashing lights but any other catastrophe that might arise in his life: monsters at night, disappointment, Max not wanting to be his friend, loss, and so many others. I suddenly grasped the scope of what it is to be a mother. Another epiphany? I think so. I felt heavier and graced all at the same time.

What made them epiphanies and not just random insights was the fact that I learned something important, something that truly did change my way of thinking. They were indeed moments of sudden intuitive understanding: flashes of insight. But they always took place while I was doing normal, everyday things, always in the midst of my routine. The key was that I was open to the insight, and I *needed* the lesson.

My perception of an epiphany was that it must be fantastic— an angels-singing, light-shining kind of moment. But the more I read my favorite poetry and the longer I thought about it, I realized that epiphanies are simply lessons or "insights" that change us (even if for only a moment), which we learn and acknowledge as we go about our lives. It is, most of the time, not grand at all; epiphanies come to us as we go about our daily duties—that is the essence of epiphany. It is not the incident itself that is fantastic but rather our reaction and willingness to absorb it and learn from it.

What better way to not only open yourself up to receiving epiphanies but also to record their awesome effects than through poetry? What epiphanies will you have once you're open to receiving them? What do you think you need to learn?

But Why an Epiphany Poem?

Women are naturally intuitive creatures. We instinctively know when our child's cry is one for attention or the real thing. We sense danger; we pay attention to unease. We often know when something's up in our relationship far before the actual admission. There is female intuition; have you ever heard of male intuition? We are more in tune with our surroundings and often more open to receiving insights and knowledge from not only within but also from unidentifiable forces without. We accept "a sudden flash of insight" and are open to learning something from the experience. All women are capable of such self-knowledge—for epiphanies are *always* personal—some just need a little practice realizing an epiphany when it rears its beautiful, welcome head.

Enter the epiphany poem. When I was discussing this chapter with Lori over lunch, she asked, "Are you talking about epiphanies that occur while writing or writing about epiphanies that occur?" "Both," I replied. And that is what is so amazing and valuable about the epiphany poem.

Writing poetry is about opening your soul to yourself. Whether writing a list poem about something seemingly ordinary that you are now looking at with a magical eye, a sonnet to help you delve deep into feelings and figure out how you really feel, or a ghazal, indulging in a bout of daydreaming, poetry can offer you a sudden insight into a part of yourself that you had kept hidden, didn't even know was there, or that just needed a little help seeing the light of day. Epiphanies can certainly occur in the midst of writing.

Epiphanies also occur in the midst of living. Madeleine L'Engle once said, "Inspiration usually comes during work, rather than before it." I think the epiphany is inspiration's sister: Epiphanies usually come in the midst of living; and the more you live, the more you experience. Poetry is the perfect medium for recording epiphanies, because you don't have to explain exactly; you can rely on feelings, perceptions, circumstances, and images. You can honestly *describe* and not worry about constructing perfect sentences or making worldly sense.

You are experiencing epiphanies all the time whether you are aware of them or not. Putting your mind in the way of writing an epiphany poem will open your eyes, heart, and mind to these lessons as they occur. Writing about it gives you an honest, accommodating, and lasting outlet for describing the experience, including what exactly it meant to you. Such a poem is proof that life works and that you are receiving the lessons you need all the time.

Beverly describes an epiphany as, "the majestic *aha!* when the dawning of a new thought shifts my perspective so much that I just can't return to my old thinking"—which is exactly what happened to her during one ordinary day through one ordinary conversation.

Beverly is a grandmother, mother, wife, and teacher. She teaches at the university level, specializing in teaching teachers. In her various life roles, she encounters a lot of problems she feels the need to fix. Whether it's daughters wondering about potty-training methods, a husband pondering his career choices, or students under the gun to make decisions that affect the direction of their lives, Beverly wants to solve them all.

During a conversation with her husband, her *aha!* moment occurred. "My epiphany," Beverly says, "was that I don't have to have all the answers and I am not responsible for solving everyone's problems. The best gift I can give, instead, is to listen so that they can work through their problems to find their own solutions." As with most epiphanies, it may sound simple and much like plain old common sense, but it was a shift in perspective that convinced Beverly that she needed to slow down and stop carrying the weight of the world on her shoulders.

Ping—sprong—whoosh
Oh god, the pressure . . .
I have to find the answer
I have to figure this out
I have to know what to do
My Roger-rabbit brain
Ping-ping-sprongs
One thought leads . . .
To another thought . . .
And another—faster—faster
Oh god, the pressure
There are so many problems
I have to find answers
I have to figure them out
Someone may need me
I need to know what to do
Sitting in bed, exhausted
Roger-rabbit stops
Ping ping-sprong—whoosh!
Oh god, the release . . .

I don't need the answers
Someone may need me—
Just to listen

—Beverly

"The poem," Beverly says, "was a wonderful avenue for grounding the epiphany so that it will become a daily reality in my life." Writing down these insights (no matter how seemingly insignificant at the time) can help you remember what you learn along the way. As Beverly says, "By connecting and integrating the various scattered experiences of life, you can create an ever-evolving self. I think that if I hadn't had the occasion to write the *aha!* in poem form, I would not have experienced the extra measure of joy in examining the epiphany closely to formulate exactly what I learned." Remembering all the little lessons is one way to experience big growth in your life.

I recently had an epiphany sitting alone in my car. It's a lesson I seem to have to keep relearning in different ways. I quite often forget how much control I have over my own life. It's easy for me to feel so overwhelmed by work, family, and already-made choices that I pass up opportunities or resist change because it seems too hard, and I am terribly fearful of what is unknown. The result is a life that I'm merely having—not *living*.

I was sitting in my car waiting for the library to open on a Sunday afternoon. A mother and her daughter were walking through the parking lot. The daughter was complaining about some situation at school with her friends and said, "Oh, well. It is what it is." Her mother replied, "What it is, is a beautiful day."

I hear the phrase "it is what it is" a lot. My husband uses it often, as what I perceive as a sort of self-imposed, convenient Zen attitude that says that some things can't be changed—so why expend unnecessary effort trying? I recently read it in *People* magazine in a story of how a young celeb ran into her ex-boyfriend at the MTV studios. The situation was awkward for her, and the article quoted her as saying, as she sighed, "It is what it is."

I hate the phrase. It's like nails on a chalkboard when I hear it. It sounds like the speaker is giving up or accepting some unwanted, terrible fate. It sounds meaningless, hopeless, and complacent. That story in *People* annoyed me most because I was thinking, *what about the fact that you are young, beautiful, rich, and famous and were in the MTV studios? That's what* is, *not some run-in with an ex.*

Yet, all of a sudden, in my car, I understood the phrase exactly. (And I do not think it was coincidence that the insight came from a mother.) That was my *aha!,* my epiphany. The phrase isn't annoying at all; I just never understood it. It is what it is, because it is whatever I see. My epiphany, as I sat alone in my car, was that there are good, simple things, that surround me every day, that I am choosing not to see because I spend much of the time seeing the small, annoying things. I see what's being lost instead of what's being gained. I see the effort instead of the reward. I see the pain instead of the growth. It doesn't mean giving up; it means accepting the choice to see that it is what it is. And that is when you gain control of your life.

IT IS WHAT IT IS

discovery
the perfect pine cone
under a green soggy leaf
found because we looked

mystery
how does a tulip
find its home in the brown brush
along the highway

promise
blue eyes flint and spark
worlds open as his small voice
wonders: but what if

beautiful
a breeze wisped my hair
bothered, I looked up and saw
the sun in the sky

hopeful
a bad knock-knock joke,
a line at the library,
the windows rolled down

Mine.
minutes, hours, days, years
still in my hand for magic
and I've got my pen

—Wendy

I first tried the villanelle to record the experience, because I kept hearing a phrase over and over, but I couldn't get it to work. I finally settled on a string of haiku, because I was experiencing the small moments of magic available in every single day if I choose to see them.

Like most epiphanies, it seems simple and basic, but I truly had forgotten that the life I was experiencing was *mine*. I had forgotten that I have complete control over that life. I had forgotten that I can make it anything I want—and I want it to be *poetic*.

I didn't record this particular epiphany in verse right when it happened; actually it was about a week later. Yet putting it into a poem takes me right back to that moment in my car like no other method could—I feel that resolve to look around and choose to see that it is what it is, which is pretty damned great. I do wonder how the poem would have been different had I written it right away, but now that I've got the epiphany poem in my arsenal, another such insight won't pass me by.

Katie recently had an epiphany just when she needed it most. For whatever reason, eyeing sixty hit Katie harder than she expected. "For some reason, the late fifties is a kind of passage that I cannot ignore," she says. "I had trouble turning thirty, as it seemed to be the true end of what I considered 'my youth.' I breezed through forty without even batting an eye. I think sixty holds the same life change for me as thirty—a step from 'middle age' into *something* that is not defined as elderly but is certainly not middle age."

Katie's emotions—apprehension, restlessness, discontent, perhaps even a little fear of what this *sixty* thing is all about—are very unusual feelings for her. In the past, whenever she has felt like this, she has simply packed up, moved, and given herself a new start. A new place, a new job, and new surroundings have never scared Katie; on the contrary, newness has always made her feel energized. Since birth, she has never lived anywhere longer than five years. She says, "I love to move! I love packing and sorting and looking at my life as it appears in boxes and pictures. I love new surroundings; I love new jobs—I believe it keeps me young at heart."

Yet, for the first time, moving didn't seem like the answer. Though nervous about this strange *sixty* thing, all of a sudden Katie looked around and realized she liked her home, her job, her friends—basically, her *life*. She didn't want to move. But she still felt like she needed to do *something*. "I need new dreams for this next phase—whatever it is," she says. As a self-professed "change junkie," what is a girl to do? Well, Katie started by writing a sonnet called "Addicted to Change."

ADDICTED TO CHANGE

Change is an amazing joy—such a joy
Newness and wonder delight with each first start
Electric as a child's first wind up toy
Boredom and emptiness and I shall part

Change the challenge the fresh black brown warm earth
Brings me to a virgin place to plant anew
New can bring fear and nervousness to birth
Risk has no meaning when caught in the flow

Change by choice is no more fun than by chance
Time to dream can sometimes cause me to pause
Being forced like following in dance
Often the easiest you see because

Time to start anew is glorious indeed
Choose change and jump and skip forward be freed

—Katie

It was the writing process that offered Katie her epiphany. Katie says, "Through the poetry process I was able to understand just how important *change* itself is—it is like washing a blackboard and being ready to write on it fresh." Katie realized it was *change* that she craved—but change that *she* controlled: not that her body or the passing of time controlled. Instead of packing it all up, Katie saw opportunities for change all around her. "I realized I was 'down' in a way that a move would normally refresh," she says, "but [I realized] that I could create the feeling with a few smaller changes: repainting a room, organizing some paperwork, or taking things to Goodwill."

Discovering she could satisfy her need for change and excitement without actually moving was a "revelation" to Katie. And, between repainting rooms and her newfound hobby of writing sonnets, she's figuring out her dreams for this next phase—right where she is. Katie used the sonnet to work through her emotions and learned something necessary—indeed was the grateful recipient of an epiphany. "I will remember that entire afternoon for many years—the writing of it," Katie says. "When writing, I had the feeling of elation and joy, a kind of jumping out of my skin."

But why an epiphany poem? you may still wonder. *Why not simply record the experience in prose?* Perhaps, especially at the beginning, not all your epiphanies, all your life lessons, will make their way to poetry; but you might find that some of them cannot be honestly expressed any other way. An epiphany poem can record your experience as the emotional, rather than rational, experience that it was. Through poetry, which does not have to make sense to anyone but you, you can recall the moment—and the lesson—more vividly and more honestly.

In addition, as your hand gets used to recording such fantastic instances in verse, your mind will get used to recognizing a lesson when it comes your way. As you write more epiphany poems, you will live more in tune with their occurrences.

Finally, when you write the experience down in a poem, which is arguably the most personal form of writing, you make yourself responsible for acknowledging that an epiphany occurred and for applying the gift of a necessary lesson to your life.

Whether you are describing an epiphany that has occurred, like Beverly, or whether you experience the insight while writing, like Katie, poetry can help you seize the lessons, the epiphanies, that are sent your way.

So What Exactly Makes an Epiphany Poem?

Don't worry: you didn't skip an important class in Intro to Lit or snooze away an entire lesson in high school English and missed the epiphany poem. Chances are you've never heard of an epiphany poem. There are no how-to books in the library. The epiphany poem, like the letter poem and the prayer poem, is a way to direct poetry, a way to look into your life as you are living it and find the inspiration that is already there. An epiphany poem is simply a recollection, recording, or realization of an insight that has occurred.

Form has its place in the epiphany poem. Such instances frequently take place in the awe of, or when surrounded by, nature. So the haiku is a possible form to adopt when writing an epiphany poem. As Katie illustrates, sudden insights can also occur when dissecting an emotional problem into parts (think stanzas), so the sonnet can work beautifully and effectively. We often learn something new when looking at something we see every day. Often the end of a list poem—the surprise, the magic—is an epiphany.

Not surprisingly, when recording a special memory through the sestina, we may remember something we had forgotten—or even that we never consciously accepted or acknowledged. This type of epiphany could have affected not only the memory but also the way we have lived since. When we open our minds to whatever path it follows—light or dark—by allowing ourselves to daydream, epiphanies can occur. Indeed, epiphanies most often catch us off guard, when we're not anticipating anything. Hence, in composing a ghazal, we may become aware of a deeply hidden or carefully guarded desire, dream, or direction. Certainly that qualifies as an epiphany.

So form easily and comfortably finds its place in the epiphany poem. A form can lead to an epiphany just as an epiphany can best fit a form. Yet there is room for free verse, too. Poetic form has its place in aiding you in expression and process, but free verse must be considered too—especially in something as personal and unique as an epiphany.

No two people will perceive the same situation, circumstance, picture, sculpture, scripture, or person in the same way. Likewise, the same set of circumstances can offer two people an epiphany, yet the insight or lesson will be different for each. Writing an epiphany poem is an incredibly personal process, and you should adopt the best method for you. I feel comfortable in form. It helps me find my way to my words; it helps me cut out what's unnecessary; and it challenges me beyond what I sometimes think I am capable of. That's *me*. I appreciate and welcome order and structure in my crazy, messed-up life. *You* might find that sometimes something can only be expressed *as* it comes to you. The epiphany poem just might be one of those times.

Tips on Form

- Consider jotting impressions, phrases, words, perceptions, and so on describing your epiphany before you begin writing a poem. Perhaps a form will present itself.
- Consider your epiphany as an entity in and of itself: was it an emotional, intellectual, mental, physical, or religious experience? Perhaps that consideration will suggest an appropriate form.
- If you decide to employ free verse, review and edit your poem more than you normally would. It's easy to overlook unnecessary words or miss a better visual in free verse when we accept the first try.
- Make sure your words are true to your epiphany and to you. Lofty, spiritual, ethereal words are not necessary and, quite honestly, are sometimes untrue and misleading. The words you choose are yours and must convey *your* experience.

Posse Pointer

Debbie suggests getting started right away, if you encounter a subject for an epiphany poem. She says, "I think it's important to sit down and put pen to paper (or fingers to keyboard, as it is with me!) as soon as possible after the moment has occurred.

That way your impressions on the event will be as raw and fresh as when you experienced it, and, hopefully, that will translate through to your writing."

For Further Reading

Gwendolyn Brooks is a favorite poet of mine. A poem I have always liked reading is "The Lovers of the Poor," which seems to me to be an epiphany of sorts for Brooks. It is as if she is suddenly aware of the racism that surrounds her and has surrounded her. Written during the Civil Rights Movement, this poem is symbolic to me of an entire country coming to terms with a series of troubling insights about itself.

"The Mother" and "A Sunset of the City" are two other poems I like, which seem to me to offer a single insight. Winner of the Pulitzer Prize for *Annie Allen,* Brooks put into her poetry a beat and rhythm that I enjoy reading. Many of her poems can be found on the Internet.

Just as epiphanies are subjective, considering another's poem an "epiphany poem" is subjective. Here are a few of my favorite poems that read to me like the writer has discovered something influential about herself. They also make me think a little harder about myself, perhaps leaving me more vulnerable to epiphany's bolt.

- "I Felt a Funeral in My Brain" by Emily Dickinson
- "Black Rook in Rainy Weather" by Sylvia Plath
- "Instant Glimpsable Only for an Instant" by Jane Hirshfield
- "A Winter Bluejay" by Sara Teasdale
- "The Double Image" by Anne Sexton (If you read only one of these poems, I strongly suggest this one.)

What Should I Write About?

Like the list poem, all you need to write an epiphany poem is your life as you are living it—believe me, you will never be the recipient of an epiphany concerning someone else's life. Like love and the perfect parking spot, epiphanies usually don't happen when you are looking for them. They generally occur while you are going about what you need to go about—and just when you need them most. Perhaps gifts from above or simply momentary, enlightened heightenings of awareness, epiphanies relate specifically to us—to our lives as they are being lived. They teach us something. They're aimed like an arrow, and we are the bull's-eye.

An epiphany can offer a lesson about any part of your life— intimate relationships, family, professional direction, dreams, aspirations, motivations, how actions affect others—so you can write about anything. Whatever spark hits you hard enough to start a fire in your life is an appropriate subject for an epiphany poem.

Unfortunately you can't wish an epiphany upon yourself. But I do think that what you are open to receiving will eventually come your way—though it might not take the exact form or offer the exact lesson that you anticipated (or even wanted). Listen hard, look intently, and feel deeply—and a subject for an epiphany poem will present itself. It is another way that poetry can help you live a more in tune, receptive life before an actual poem is even written. Since the lessons epiphanies offer can only apply to you and your life, all you have to do is live with the receptiveness and openness to accept them and learn from insights as they come your way.

One ordinary morning, as Debbie was talking to her dad over breakfast, she was the recipient of an insight, an epiphany, into their often-complicated relationship. "My dad stayed with me one night while my husband was on a long trip to New Zealand," Debbie recounts. "The next morning he sat down with me and started talking for an hour straight! We're always rushing around in the mornings, so it was so hard for me to listen—especially since I'd heard so many of these stories over and over again." She found herself zoning in and out, not really listening, and already anticipating the frenzy when her son woke for the day. Then, in one split, ordinary instance, the conversation turned, and Debbie realized something she had never realized before. Here is her poem:

I sit before him listening though not
My mind wanders to the clock the minutes ticking by
My son should be awake soon
He'll need to be fed and dressed for school
I need to take a shower
Get myself ready for the day
I hear the stories of his life
He starts from the beginning and brings me forward year by year
I have heard many of these stories before
I try not to catch his eyes
As I quickly avert mine to glance at the clock again
We come to a new story
One where he felt obvious pride for an award he received
A speech he gave
The roaring of an audience as they stood in ovation for him
He stops He begins to cry
I do not know what to say to this man I call my Dad
So I ask if he is having a good memory
He brings the story of his life to a close with a story about me
I was on a stage singing in front of a crowd that cheered
Much as the one he remembered cheering for him
And he says that at that moment
He was more proud than he's ever been
Because he knew I had something special
Something he always saw in himself
But in me the opportunities seemed greater

Given the stories that preceded my own debut in comparison to his
I stopped looking at the clock
And felt ashamed for not realizing
Through all of our differences
Through all of our arguments and hurt feelings
All my Dad wanted was for me to be proud of him too

—Debbie

"When I am in writing mode," Debbie says, "I am more intro-spective about things, and perhaps that leads to being more sen-sitive to the world around me." Thus, looking for an appropriate subject for an epiphany poem, she was open to what might be offered. Debbie says, "It was interesting to me that such a situa-tion arose right when I was looking for a subject matter for this type of poem. Maybe going through this process enabled me to see the situation with my dad in a different light."

Writing about the experience not only helped cement its importance in Debbie's life and perhaps positively influence future interactions with her father, but also helped her let go of some of the guilt she felt from the instance. Had she not written about it, she says, "I would have thought about it and kind of stewed over it continually in my head and made myself feel even more rotten about my reaction and boredom." Choosing to write about it, she says, "was so cathartic. I wrote the words and had a good cry. It helped me move on from feeling guilty about the whole situation."

Writing an epiphany poem helped Debbie understand her father a little better and helped her move forward with the lesson intact.

Kellie's epiphany, too, had to do with her relationship with her father. The occasion of the insight was many years ago, when her father passed away. "It was an *aha!* moment," Kellie says.

Her father's death was devastating to Kellie. "My father died eight years ago," Kellie says. "I know time heals pain and heartache, but until then—one must learn how to live with it." When her father died, Kellie didn't know if she had what was necessary to keep going. So many areas of her life seemed to end when his ended, and the grief was overwhelming and debilitating. She says, "I give God all the credit, because I did not have the strength or courage within to carry me through."

Then there was a sudden, clear moment when she realized she *had* to keep going. It was her *aha!*—a gift from her father's passing. Kellie remembers, "I knew I was an adult, but in a sense my head and my heart were not in agreement. My life changed instantly. It was as if someone told me for the first time I was all grown up. The lesson I learned," Kellie says, "was that I was no longer someone's responsibility, but now a responsible adult, responsible for myself and responsible for my family. I was no longer just Kellie, but Auntie Kellie, big sister Kellie, and Ms. Kellie."

FROM EARTH TO HEAVEN

He took his last breath on earth and his first in Heaven.
In that moment I realized . . .
I was no longer someone's responsibility; I'm responsible.
I can no longer blame others for my actions; I'm accountable.
I can no longer play hide-n-seek; I have to stand and endure.
I can no longer depend on other's to chart my way; I have to plan
and navigate myself.
I'm no longer only a student of life; I'm also a teacher.
I could no longer live solely on the prayers of others; I have to
know God for myself.

I cannot wait until summer to go outside and play; I know tomor-
    row is not promised.
I can no longer live in a fairy tale; my life is what I make of it.
All these things were known—
Just in that moment they were realized—
From that moment forward they have been confirmed.

—Kellie

Kellie has long used poetry to record her life lessons. "Poetry allows me to knock down walls, peep around corners, excavate, and shine a light on those things I have hidden from the world and tried to hide from myself," she says. When her life lessons come in the form of an epiphany, she depends on poetry to help her define the experience fully. "Poetry," she believes, "allows you the opportunity to go beyond the superficial. Initially, you think you understand an idea/thought in its entirety, but as you dissect the moment, you learn so much more."

That sudden, clear moment after her father's death helped shape the person she has become as well as the person she still hopes to be. By writing about an epiphany that has shaped her life to this day, Kellie not only remembered what she lost but also everything she still has. "Today I am inspired to go on," she says, "because I am not only living for myself."

Jen too had an "Oh, my gosh! I'm a grown-up!" moment, an epiphany that made her realize that she was now an adult responsible for her own life as well as those of others. Though she is a wife, this epiphany did not occur while with her husband; though she is a mother, it didn't occur when she was tucking her kids into bed at night; she is a working woman (and now a *boss*), and her epiphany occurred during her first staff meeting.

"I held my first staff meeting after becoming the new boss," she says. "I was standing in front of the meeting, in front of about forty people, and everyone was looking at me waiting for me to say something . . . to *lead* them." It was then that she knew that she was an adult and not just responsible for her family but, now, for those who expected to follow her. The biggest, best epiphany, though, was the realization that she could do it.

HEAR ME ROAR

Sitting side by side
Not having to say a word.
My soulmate, my true love.
I am his wife,
No longer just a girl.

Watching my sons play,
Not a care in the world.
My angels, ever-trusting.
I am their mother,
No longer just someone else's child.

Standing in front of the room,
All eyes on me.
My staff, looking for guidance, direction.
I am their Leader,
No longer just a follower.

Such pressure!
Such responsibility!
HA! I CAN DO IT!!

I AM a wife, mother, leader!
Hear me roar (meow).

—Jen

Jen actually wasn't thrilled with the way the poem turned out. "I honestly just ran out of time and creative juices," she admits. However, though it's not, as she says, "a masterpiece or Internet poetry-contest material," it still served its purpose of providing her with a means to record an experience and, most important, the insight that came with it. She also recognized the role poetry can play in the acknowledgment and internalization of such lessons. An epiphany, she says, "doesn't have to be about a life-changing event or decision—it can be about anything that just hits you. I think they happen every day, but looking for things to write a poem about made me recognize them more."

Birthdays come once a year, and their dates are never surprises, yet there's something about them that prompt us to question where our lives are going, and the "big ones" often offer the best opportunities for epiphanies—for the chance to receive the gift of direction. Katie was hit when she turned sixty, and Lori was hit when she turned forty. As she says, "I was facing forty and questioning everything I was doing—or not doing. Something was missing. I was restless. I wondered, worried, lost sleep. It was a true mid-life crisis."

And then it came, when she wasn't even looking. "When I wasn't thinking about it at all, the answer came," Lori says. "I was missing a creative outlet. I had kept a journal after college but, much like exercise, I had abandoned it somewhere along the way. I've even got a journal that a friend gave me, sitting mostly empty." Perhaps it was this process of writing poetry, the reality of turning forty, or a combination of both, but Lori had her epiphany. She knew what she needed to do—and it came to her in her sleep.

EPIPHANY

I almost quit, then
it came to me in a dream
one still, quiet night

A whispered secret,
it came to me in a dream:
"you need to write."

—Lori

"I chose the haiku," she explains, "because, like that form, there is something magical about an epiphany. Your soul knows what it needs. The magic is in being able to hear it." Lori plans to get out that mostly empty journal and, as she says, "open it, like a fine champagne, on my fortieth birthday and begin again."

I had not written a ghazal before this book, but it has quickly become one of my preferred forms in which to write poetry. It seems that when opening up my mind without the constraints of maintaining a true subject, *something* almost always occurs to me. I was sitting in my favorite spot one morning, looking out my back window. An old, dying rosebud (they only live about twenty years) takes up the entire thirty-six-pane window. Especially if I have a cup of just brewed coffee, I can unwittingly spend an hour doing nothing but sipping and contemplating that tree. That morning, I decided to do *something* rather than *nothing* and write a poem about it. The ghazal fit, because there were so many different things to say about it.

Even as I was writing, I was surprised at what was occurring to me. Memories I had forgotten, fears I had buried, and wants I had ignored came to the surface. Each line seemed like an epiphany to me. Madeleine Costigan once said, "I have a lot of excitement in my life. I used to call it tension, but I feel much better now that I call it excitement." That's how I think of epiphanies: I've had these insights all along, but now that I can label them as something as large and important as an *epiphany*, it makes me not only much more aware of them and their lessons— but also makes me feel pretty damn smart.

ROSEBUD TREE, 2006

Outside my back window is an old rosebud tree
I spend much time dwelling, staring, wondering, looking at that
*   old rosebud tree.*

Dark, tired, and alone, I wonder where God is—
In the buds that purple every spring or the dead branches of my
*   rosebud tree?*

Our first spring here, the whole window was a bright bloom
I never knew such sweet surprise, given to me by a rooted rose-
bud tree.

His first tree to climb, I saw him from the window:
I knew someday he'd climb highest as I looked upon another
*   rosebud tree.*

I am most uneasy when green and color mix
It's the arbitrariness of a season's end for a blooming rosebud tree.

In the mornings, before the sun dictates the day
Her limbs draw shadowy pictures of elusive words, my muse this
rosebud tree.

When H sat there and freely spilled secrets that pierce
I lived those moments in her soft pastel arms, my one true thing:
the rosebud tree.

Last winter, her strongest branch was broken by ice
By spring, frail, gritty offshoots bloomed so fully; she seemed a
complete rosebud tree.

He wants Out South, the promise land of big closets
But what manner of verse comes from a single-trunked, perfectly
pruned rosebud tree?

I tried to plant pink bleeding hearts in her lost stumps
Perhaps not enough sun, no pale petals sprouted in the dying
rosebud tree.

This space is small: I feel like I can touch its sides
Yet, it seems expansive—enough—with Wendy, her poems, and
a rosebud tree.

—Wendy

The last couplet—as is so often the case—was the biggest insight for me. I have written, read, and experienced poetry all my life, but it wasn't until this book that I truly began to delve into unknown forms and push myself beyond what was comfortable and *live* it, inviting poetry to influence the way I look at every single day. The end of that poem was a lightbulb moment. The days I've written poetry are always brighter than those when I haven't.

Poetry truly did expand my world without me taking a single, solid step. I spend a lot of time wanting things (too much time, actually) and comparing what I have—or don't have—to what others have. Logically, I know that this line of thinking is counterproductive and a defeating waste of time, but it's a trap that easily ensnares me. I need to be reminded quite often that I, in fact, have a lot. I can sit down and write a poem; I have that ability. That is no small thing to me. Before, I might have called this type of insight common sense—more like a *duh!* moment—but now I feel much better calling it an epiphany.

Soundtrack

Here are five songs that sound to me as if the voice is benefiting from some new insight or learning a much-needed lesson. I think they are good examples of how everyday life and its happenings—good and bad—can show us things we didn't know before, if we are open to seeing them. They are also good examples of how to put these special, sometimes-hard-to-explain experiences into the appropriate words.

1. "All Night Party" by Anne Clark
2. "Spark" by Tori Amos
3. "Everyday Is a Winding Road" by Sheryl Crow
4. "Suddenly I See" by KT Tunstall
5. "Breathe (2 a.m.)" by Anna Nalick

Tips on Subject
- Don't think your subject must be something of enormous scope. An epiphany is enormous simply because it occurs, not because of its contents. You know what they say: the smallest presents are usually the best. The same might be true for your epiphany poem.
- Consider everything and attempt to pay attention at all times. Who knows what will occur to you, and where? Attempt every thought. Not everything will turn into a poem, but something certainly will.
- If you are wishing and asking for an epiphany, you must be open for what the universe unveils. It's not always exactly what you ask for, but it is always what you need.
- Color is one of the easiest, simplest ways to describe a scene—sometimes in a single word—without getting lost in details. Does your epiphany have a color? It is a consideration that could supply a coherent theme to your poem.

Give It a Try

I can't put you in a frame of mind, location, or mood that will snare an epiphany as it flits and flutters by. However, here are three questions that just *might* get you thinking enough to settle down long enough for an epiphany to occur. To be sure, these are questions you'll have to ponder over the course of days—maybe even weeks—to learn something new about yourself. In any case, even if this specific meditation doesn't spark an epiphany, one of them might at least get you writing, which can serve as the flint for epiphany's spark.

1. What *is* it to be a mother, wife, or friend? (Choose the one you are having the most difficulty with.)
2. Why weren't you completely happy yesterday?
3. What do you see in the mirror?

The way to have something to write about, to attract epiphanies, is to simply to keep living, trying, learning, and striving to be better. Epiphanies teach us something about our lives that we need to learn; therefore, these lessons can only happen when you're living. And when you are lucky and aware enough to receive the lesson given you and transfer these rare happenings to a poem, you will not only remember it more clearly and effectively but you will also be encouraged to delve deeply enough to get all you can out of it. The epiphany poem can help you make sure you are paying attention to your own life.

A Poetic Pause: Quotes on Poetry

In my "real" job, I often compile quotation collections: inspirational quotes by women, sassy quotes about getting older, winning quotes that appeal to the business-type, quotes on anything from friendship to cooking to dealing with change to a love of cats; I can find an appropriate quote for just about anything. It's something I enjoy doing. Though there is some validity to Marguerite Gardiner's words, "Borrowed thoughts, like borrowed money, only show the poverty of the borrower," it is not about passing off the ideas as my own or using someone else's words to replace my own but more a matter of gaining inspiration, encouragement, and a different perspective. And sometimes someone else's thoughts get me thinking deeply enough to form a thought of my own—even a poem of my own.

Here are some quotes by women writers about writing and about poetry. Perhaps they will give you inspiration to write, encouragement to keep writing, or a different perspective to ponder when writing. You might even be blessed with words of your own.

My ideas usually come not at my desk writing but in the midst
of living.

—Anaïs Nin

Inspiration does not come like a bolt, nor is it kinetic energy
striving, but it comes to us slowly and quietly and all the time.

—Brenda Ueland

I would venture to guess that Anon, who wrote so many poems
without signing them, was often a woman.

—Virginia Woolf

Our poems will have failed if our readers are not brought by
them beyond the poems.

—Muriel Rukeyser

People wish to be poets more than they wish to write poetry, and
that's a mistake. One should wish to celebrate more than one
wishes to be celebrated.

—Lucille Clifton

To live is so startling it leaves little time for anything else.

—Emily Dickinson

. . . the houses built of words belong to no one. We have to take
them back from those who think they own them.

—Julia Alvarez

The blood jet is poetry and there is no stopping it.

—Sylvia Plath

What poetry does is put more oxygen into the atmosphere. Poetry makes it easier to breathe.

—Kay Ryan

There are no little events in life, those we think of no consequence may be full of fate, and it is at our own risk if we neglect the acquaintances and opportunities that seem to be casually offered, and of small importance.

—Amelia Barr

When I see a young (or not-so-young) writer counting syllables on her fingers, or marking stresses . . . I'm pretty sure we'll have something in common, whatever our differences may be.

—Marilyn Hacker

I don't want life to imitate art. I want life to be art.

—Carrie Fisher

If there were no poetry on any day in the world, poetry would be invented that day. For there would be an intolerable hunger.

—Muriel Rukeyser

We write to taste life twice, in the moment, and in retrospection.

—Anaïs Nin

Our feelings are our most genuine paths to knowledge.

—Audre Lorde

Chapter Ten

Be Happy; Dwell on What You Like: The Ode

If I can't have too many truffles, I'll do without truffles.

—Colette

I have (finally!), after twenty-some years of keeping a journal, actually finished one. There is a thought, list, poem, sentence, or scribble on every single page. I, *for once,* did not abandon it when I didn't write for a month or more, or misplace it. I kept it with me virtually everywhere I went and filled the entire thing. It might not seem like a big deal, but I was incredibly pleased. I have kept a journal as long as I can remember, and this is the very first one I have written in from the first page all the way to the very last. I followed through; I stuck with it; I finished something. I got to that last page, took in a deep breath of accomplishment, and let out pride.

I took the time to soak in my triumph and glanced back through the pages, flipping through my life. I had accomplished a lot in those fifteen months, so I was loosening my waistband to get even fuller of myself. Then, I couldn't be*lieve* what I was reading.

I could not get to the end of a single page without reading about something that had gone wrong, was going wrong, or that probably would go wrong. Most of it was silly, irrelevant stuff like lamenting not having enough silverware for a dinner party with friends or frustration at end-of-the-month bill paying, but the sheer volume of the complaints—big and small—hit me like Red Bull on an empty stomach. It was frankly the most depressing thing I had ever read. (And I had just finished Janet Finch's *Paint in Black,* so that's *saying* something.)

I read through that entire book of me, and thought, *who is this?* Who is this self-absorbed, depressing, pathetic little person? It didn't feel like me now and I know it didn't feel like me the entire span of those fifteen months, because I had done some things I was really proud of; at times I was so full of myself that I overflowed. I had sold a book idea *and* received a huge promotion at work. My book offer warranted half a page—the latest meaningless spat with my husband filled two pages; my promotion got but five sentences—how dissatisfied I was with my job rambled on and on.

The majority of my journal was full of all the less-than-desirable stuff that was happening *to* me—not one word of what was happening *around* me. *Seriously,* people were being elected, our country was at war *and* experiencing the most devastating natural disaster of my generation; friends were getting divorced, having babies, and there was none of that in there. Know what else was missing? Anything I actually *liked,* that's what.

I bought some really great sandals last spring during a girls' weekend in Chicago—shiny orange wedges that, every time I wear them, remind me of shopping and Mojitos, girl talk and coffee. I went to Seattle for the first time. I saw at least three musicals downtown. I had to have a favorite shirt, even if I wanted five others. What was my favorite food? What was the best book I read? What really made me laugh? What was the first really unbearably hot day of summer like? I might remember now, but I won't always—because I didn't write it down.

There was quite a bit of poetry, some of it uplifting—a haiku here and there—and some of my musings were funny. But the truth of that journal is that the majority of it was negative stuff. Yes, bad things happened to me during those fifteen months, but great things happened, too. I was honestly surprised at what I had *chosen* to dwell on.

I am a happy person most of the time, and I am really quite gifted at garnering satisfaction out of life. There are a lot of things I like.

I like coffee; a cup instantly soothes and calms me. I like it creamy but not too sweet and always a bit too hot to drink carelessly. When the holiday Coffee Mate flavors magically appear in the grocery store aisle, that is when the holidays can truly begin. I love the first warm day when I find myself craving iced coffee; it means that summer has arrived.

I like Wednesday afternoon massages. That means I've skipped work without being sick. I will know that I have *made it* when I can get them twice a month.

I like candy. Most candy, to be honest. Every season, every holiday, every special event has its accompanying candy. Halloween cannot be observed without candy corn. Every year on my birthday I buy a half-pound of sourballs and eat the entire bag in one day. Conversation hearts on Valentine's Day are a necessity; I could do without the Valentine, but do *not* ask me to give up my hearts. It's York peppermint patties in the winter and Jelly Belly jellybeans in the spring.

I like the darkest purple, almost black, polish on my toes. I feel young and rebellious. And I most like someone else putting it there.

I like wearing red; it's my favorite color. I'm always surprised that I have don't have more red attire in my closet, but I will not buy something red unless it is perfect. It's held to a higher standard and cannot be diminished by it'll-do articles. The hue must be *just right,* with a blue base; an orangey base doesn't work. I like to wear red. I feel sexy and powerful—and it looks good on me.

I like Christmas. I like being a mom. I like watching college football. I like sleeping in on Saturday morning.

Yet none of those things were in my journal. And those are the things I *want* to remember about my life, not all the meaningless spats, temper tantrums, and disappointments.

Something became clear to me: Life will be about the things I like, the things that make me happy, only if I make room to write about those things. And I must write about them because someday, when I'm old (but never gray, I'll just tell you right now), sitting on my rocker on the front porch, reliving my grand and glorious pedicure adventures, I won't be able to rely entirely on my memory—I'll need some actual written evidence. And I will *not* let the experience be the same as when I flipped through that first of many finished journals.

Life happens, but there will always be things that make me happy. (It's another one of those you-find-what-you-look-for kind of things.) Just like in *Paint in Black:* Even if page after page is death, dirty vodka glasses, and downward spirals, there's the one page at the end where she rides off, clean of the past, free, into the dust.

I'm just *not* going to wait until the last page. This new journal I'm working on—it's red, shiny, and its very first poem was an ode.

But Why an Ode?

I used to think odes were boring, outdated, stodgy, and maybe even a little ridiculous—like high-waisted, pleated, tapered khakis. Yes, I read *Ode on a Grecian Urn* in college. I liked it, but—honestly—it didn't keep me up at night. I had respect for the ode and its poetic place, but it wasn't until I read Joy Harjo's "Perhaps the World Ends Here," and a few other modern odes written by women, that I began to really appreciate it. It just goes to show you: No matter your perceptions or experience, a well-placed, well-designed pleat in a modern trouser *can* make all the difference.

An ode is simply a poem about something you are passionate about. An ode is an opportunity to write yourself happy, to dwell on what you like. Mary Renault once said, "In hatred as in love, we grow like the thing we brood upon." I think the same holds true for poetry. My poems influence my life just as much as my life influences my poems. I have to make time to write about what makes me smile, even if it is as small and simple as pink jellybeans at Easter. I've found that the more I write about what makes me happy the happier I feel.

Happy and *happiness* are such big words. It seems as if they are simply translated from language to language but never really defined. What is it to be happy? What is happiness? Such questions have kept poets, thinkers, writers, and doers busy since the dawn of time. Truthfully, I don't know. I think those are terms that render a dictionary useless; you have to define them for yourself or you'll never know it. My definition changes daily. Some days, it doesn't take much: a red satin shirt on an early fall day, a knock-knock joke from my child, or a phone call from my sister. Other days I need a bit more: evidence of kindness somewhere in the world; true, powerful words; solitude.

"Happiness lies in the consciousness we have of it," said George Sand. I think that sums it up pretty well. There is no happy fairy that flies around with her magic wand granting sad, cynical souls happiness. No one can give it to you for Christmas. It's not a label you can buy (or even earn, disappointingly enough) and wear around for all to see. You are happy when you say so. Writing an ode gives you the chance to sit down and say so.

For the ode, I asked the Posse to write about whatever it is that makes them happy, anything they are passionate about. It was an open invitation, but as Kris points out, it is not always the "big" things that can make us happy. She says, "It's easy to be passionate about and appreciate your kids, your husband, your job, and your hobbies. And I *am* passionate about those things. But sometimes, it's the little things that greatly enhance the quality of life on a daily basis." What a wonderful thing to discover that the more you look for the little things that make you happy, the more little things you find.

That was Kris's experience with the Ode. Thinking about what she was passionate about, thinking beyond the big, obvious things opened her eyes to the little things that surround her every day that she often takes for granted, but that do add quite a bit of comfort, humor, and, yes, happiness to her life. The more she looked around for a subject for her Ode, the more she was aware of those truly wonderful, but truly little things. As she says, "I think the world is a better place because we have simple comforts like Chapstick, worn-in sweatshirts, clean sheets, good books, and ultra soft toilet paper in it."

Kris finally decided on something she turns to every day as a stress reliever, reward, friend, and indulgence. She chose to write her Ode to her favorite small comfort: Diet Coke. As simplistic as it may seem, "It just makes my small world a happier place," she admits.

ODE TO DIET COKE

I've taken it for granted that you'll always be there for me because you always have been.
In tough times
All nighters cramming for college finals to all nighters with a newborn
In times of celebration
A splash of Captain Morgan and a lime wedge to celebrate my first job offer
A dash of cherry juice and a maraschino cherry to celebrate my second pregnancy.

But most of the time, in our daily coexistence,
I like you au natural.
You there, in the simple silver can.
You there, fizzing amidst the glass's clinking ice cubes with a lemon wedge lazily floating on top of you.
Wherever I am, you're always just a fridge, soda fountain, vending machine, or grocery store away.

I can have you whenever I want you.
I live for your touch.

I wait, patiently, until the noon hour, when I can justify our
relationship.
11:15, 11:36, not quite there yet.
12:02. Ahhhhh.

The moment I hear that ppppsssshhhhh-click! upon opening your
bountiful glory
I instantly gulp your precious contents
Enjoying the burn down my throat that brings tears to my eyes.
I am alive, I am better than alive, I am good.
Because of you
I am a better mother, wife, professional, and friend.
Because of you
I am a better person.

—Kris

"This ode was fun to write," Kris says. It may seem to some an odd subject for a poem, but an ode can be about anything that brings the writer joy. As she says, "Life is too full of sad stuff: the evening news, war, divorce, miscarriage, job losses, etc. Lighten up!" The ode is a great chance to lighten up and use poetry to concentrate on what makes you happy, especially the little things that sometimes get lost in the midst of the big things. We're all better people when we figure out what makes us happy and dwell on it.

In an article for *Harper's Bazaar*, Catherine Wilson astutely observes, "Some of us are boot girls. Others—the Goody Two-shoes of this world—are not." I am a boot girl. I look forward to fall more anxiously than a Sooner fan looks forward to college football or a six-year-old looks forward to Halloween, because it means one thing: *boots*. Boots make me feel tall (at 5' 4½"), powerful (not even my four-year-old listens to me), and sexy (I haven't worn a garter belt since 1995)—and, yeah: I feel happy when I wear them.

I was wearing boots when I met my husband. I was wearing boots when I found out I was pregnant and on my first day back to work from maternity leave. I was on my way to buy boots when I received my first book offer. I was wearing boots when I saw the Rolling Stones. I was wearing boots when the gorgeous guy from the eighth floor asked me what kind of scent I was wearing. I am hard-pressed to have an honest-to-goodness bad day when wearing my favorite red boots. This is a truth I know: Not everyone can wear red boots, but *I* can.

I have three pairs of black boots, two pairs of brown boots (not including my two pairs of cowboy boots), and a pair of pink suede boots—but there's just something about red boots.

I got my first pair of red boots when I was a sophomore in high school. They were suede, knee-high boots that had embellished straps that laced up and tied in a bow at the top of the back of the boot. They came in white, red, black, and tan, but I just had to have the *red*. I got them for $68 at the Wild Pair for my fifteenth birthday. (I couldn't believe my mom let me be so frivolous, but now I realize that my mom thought developing an individual style was along the same lines as forming an opinion.) My favorite way to wear them was tucked into acid-washed jeans with an oversized white sweatshirt. You'd think I'd be embarrassed and hide all photographic evidence, but I'm not. I really loved those red boots.

It's been a love affair ever since. I always have a pair of red boots in my armory. I feel like the best version of me when I'm wearing them. Manolo Blahnik said, "Boots can be dangerous. They make women think all kinds of things." Red boots make me think I can be me.

ODE TO MY RED BOOTS

She wouldn't. She would never wear red boots,
her legs navigating their careful way out of her Lexus—
opting for safe, flat—expensive!—brown boots.
She wouldn't want the Group to whisper, approval her nexus

the color of blood,
a beating and dying heart—
a president's tie.

Too precious, obvious—she thinks I try
too hard. (an eye roll, a scoff.) Her surplus store scuffed big
*   black boots*
add weight to her walk. Her heavy lined eye
meets mine. Too risky; they might laugh. She would never wear
*   red boots.*

racy lingerie,
never for a bride, a kiss,
the cherry on top.

Too tall for her half-walled gray cubicle
world—she wouldn't fit in, or even worse!, stand out—those
*   red boots*
are (sigh) not her, not at all practical.

For what would she wear with them? No, she could never wear
  red boots.

a ruby—diamond's
one true friend—a wine lover's
wine, a rose with thorns.

I am a beating heart in my red boots—
more intoxicating than wine, racy, lacy, surprising,
the cherry on top, a day's uprising,
a ruby, a kiss, a beautiful rose complete with sharp thorns.

A shoe is not you, you might say with scorn.
Ah, but you are probably one who would never wear red boots.
                                                    —Wendy

It felt energizing, like taking a deep breath on the first cold
day of winter, to write about something I like so much. The entire
time I was writing this poem, I certainly didn't have a single
thought about anything I *didn't* like. I intend to pair this poem
in my journal with my best picture of me in my red boots. I def-
initely think my future, not-gray-haired self will approve.

"I think we all want to be good—I mean *really* good—at
something in life," Debbie says, "and singing is that thing I believe
I'm really good at." So Debbie chose to write her ode to some-
thing that has amounted to some of her best memories because it
uses the best talent she has—singing karaoke. It's true. Debbie is
the karaoke queen of the group. It's something she simply loves.
"I have lots of favorite memories that revolve around singing
karaoke," she says, "the night of my bachelorette party when I

chose to go singing rather than to a strip club and walked away
with $100 and a kiss on the cheek from Tony Casillas; all the
times that I sang as an underage college student at the completely
divey (yet completely perfect for my nonconformist ways) bowl-
ing alley bar; all of the bizarre but incredibly friendly people I met
who gave themselves names like 'Savannah Dave,' 'Mr.
Microphone,' or the guy who claimed he was Garth Brooks's
nephew and always sang Garth's tunes completely out of tune."

Singing is a time when Debbie, the now married mother of
two, can be a star, the center of attention, belting out tunes that
shock the audience into admiration. She loves it and doesn't really
care what people think of that. "It's not particularly cool to say
that you love karaoke," she admits, "and that's just fine by me!"

ODE TO KARAOKE

Karaoke, my friend, I could find you every day of the week.
A billboard on a highway, beckoning me with promises of '$50
    Cash!' as my prize.
Your beer-infused microphone I seek.
Grab a book! Grab a pen! Where do I sign in?

You are my element, karaoke. Oh the pleasure you do bring.
I coyly begin flipping through the pages of your songs as friends
    ask
'what will you sing?'
Crazy? Bobby McGee? What song will it be?

I've got some competition in Sally, so I need to choose well.
Order me a shot of rumpleminze—and another. What the hell.
When my name is called, I flush, as any humble singer will do.

As I make my way to the stage I can feel their eyes on my back.
They don't know what I know . . . that I am no karaoke hack.
I can see them whispering in the crowds, surprised, wow, she's
     good!
Who me? Gosh, thanks. I really appreciate your praise.
I'm surprised I wasn't more rusty. I haven't sung in days!

Karaoke, my old friend, I do not visit you as often as I once
     did.
Though I long for you often and the days of before.
I know that if ever I get a babysitter, we'll meet again once more.
                                                    —Debbie

"There's nothing more energizing and uplifting to me than to sing," Debbie says, "It sounds totally cheesy, but I feel happiest when I'm singing." Writing this ode about it momentarily recreated that same happiness.

The ode was a big departure for Debbie in her poetry writing. She usually writes from a darker place, emotionally. "It was harder than I thought it would be to write about something pleasant and enjoyable," Debbie confesses, "and I was really surprised about that." It was eye-opening and uplifting to discover poetry as a way to dwell on the good things in life—even something as simple as a night out singing karaoke with her girlfriends.

Can't I just do what makes me happy and not waste time writing about it? you might ask. The answer is, quite frankly: if you don't write about it, you'll forget. When you cement the experience, the preference, the idea, in writing—and in an ode in particular—it is yours forever. In addition, you get to experience the happiness three times: once when it is actually happening, again in the composition of your ode, and actually innumerable times every time you reread it.

Writing a poem is never a waste of time. Few things in life are as absolute. Writing an ode helps you define *what it is* that makes you happy—but you won't figure it out in just one ode!—and demands that you consider everything from cashmere to wool socks, from volunteering your time to tucking in your kid at night, from holiday decorations downtown to the first warm day of spring. The more you dwell on what makes you happy, the happier you feel. The ode gives you reason to selfishly, indulgently, luxuriously, and *necessarily* dwell on what makes you happy.

The Ode Soundtrack

The ode and music go together so well because they have similar aspirations. As Kris says, "Music is a release, being so emotionally charged. It's like Christmas: It intensifies your existing emotions, be they joy, loneliness, or sadness. You feel your losses more deeply and are extra grateful for your blessings." That is exactly what an ode does. When you write about something that has enhanced your life, you feel gratitude for its presence as well as for the actual pleasure it brings. Here are five songs that make Kris happy every time she hears them. These five songs make her feel (as she says) "like I want to crank it up and sing at the top of my lungs, no matter how much my husband cringes, my daughter moans, and the neighborhood dogs howl."

1. "Goodby to You," by Patty Smyth
2. "Passionate Kisses," by Mary Chapin Carpenter
3. "This One's for the Girls," by Martina McBride
4. "Hit Me with Your Best Shot," Pat Benetar
5. "I Will Survive," Gloria Gaynor

So What Exactly Makes an Ode?

Like the sonnet, the ode is a form of poetry you've probably heard of before. You might have some preconceived notions about the ode (formal, lofty, old-fashioned, irrelevant, stiff, etc.). Michelle remembered falling asleep in English class when she first heard the term ode, and Kris was reminded of something Frasier Crane on TV's *Frasier* might spout. Well, you can toss them all out. Just like pleats will make a comeback every ten years or so in a completely new and flattering way, the ode is an appropriate, germane form of poetry for anyone to try even though it's been around since Grecian times. And, like any other historical writing that remains pertinent today (the Bible, the Constitution), the ode has evolved and morphed to fit a more modern tone, treatment of subject, and style—a testament to its validity in the world of today's poetry.

An ode is simply a poem of celebration that singles something out to exalt and praise, showing its significance for all to see. It is lyrical rather than narrative, which means that the poem expresses the writer's personal response to, or feelings about, something—anything, really. A lyrical poem does not tell a story (or it would be a narrative), but instead dwells in the realm of emotion.

There are three different kinds of odes: the Pindaric ode, the Horatian ode, and the Cowleyan ode. Because I find the Cowleyan ode the most natural to write, because I think it suits our purposes here best, and because this is *my* book (no one ever said life was fair!), we will concentrate on it.

The Cowleyan ode is often called an irregular ode because it allows a bit of freedom within its form—much more so than the other two do. It has been said that the irregular ode happened because Abraham Cowley didn't quite understand the mechanics of the Pindaric ode. Well, penicillin was discovered by mistake, too—so if that was, indeed, the case, I'm okay with that.

There are three main things to remember when writing an irregular, or Cowleyan, ode: there is structure—it usually rhymes, for example—but the writer is in charge of how it is built; the subject is presented in a celebratory, exalted, admiring tone from the writer's perspective; and it is generally a longer form of poetry.

The irregular ode is both an unstructured *and* structured form of poetry. The employment of a rhyme is traditional, and each stanza should have some consistency in meter or line length (or both); but the writer gets to determine the rhyme and consistency. A common rhyme scheme is abab, cdcd, efef—much like the sonnet—but it's open for interpretation and to experimentation. The meter and line length should be consistent but only within each stanza; each stanza can vary and each one can be different. That's what I mean by unstructured and structured: *you* get to determine the structure, and it only has to remain consistent through each stanza, not the entire poem.

In Grecian times, the ode was often employed to praise the accomplishments of Olympic athletes and was intended to be recited in public or set to music. Poets throughout the ages have recognized and immortalized leaders, soldiers, and heroes. Romantic poets spoke in their odes of immortality, the nightingale, or the west wind. The tone is reverent, exalted, and in awe of its subject.

The ode is often a longer lyrical poem. The Pindaric ode, for example, is at least three ten-line stanzas. The idea is that the subject has affected and impressed the writer so deeply that its praise requires many lines. It also stands to reason that the writer thinks so highly of her subject that it *demands* the importance of a long, stately poem.

These three elements—structure, tone, and length—are traditional and should be kept in mind when writing an ode. However, just as the sonnet evolved to tolerate more contemporary views of love, philosophy, and emotion in general, so the ode has been flexible in understanding experimentation and mutation.

The ode was almost a lost form. Today it may seem impossible and untrue to a poet's self to be in blind awe and devotion, considering our time of wavering faith when public images often represent only broken trust, violence, and convenient morals. These days we'd be hard-pressed to single out a politician worthy of an ode! It seems a poet's responsibility to expose rather than to exalt.

Although the ode might not have the same place in public speech as it once did, its place in a poet's private life has increased—indeed, become *necessary*. It calls us as people, women, and poets to remember what we believe in—what we find good in the world, what makes us *happy*.

Tips on Form
- It is always tempting in rhyming verse to end each line with a pause after the rhyme. Feel free to experiment. Each line can still end in a rhyme yet also flow into the next unbroken.
- Consider rhyme—though not necessary in modern poetry, it's an element that embraces the longstanding tradition and history of the ode. Since each stanza can employ its own scheme that you determine, it is flexible enough to limit frustration.
- Keep each stanza consistent. If a line is quite a bit longer than the others in a stanza you've composed, consider setting it aside for another stanza. You can use meter, syllable count, or visual length—but maintain consistency within each stanza. Remember, each stanza can differ—you don't have to maintain the same strict scheme throughout your entire ode.

- Your tone can be celebratory and realistic at the same time. Don't let the form determine your words; let your words shape the poem. As with any poem, aim for true words instead of expected words.
- Don't let the traditionally longer length intimidate you. An honest, straight-from-your-soul ode is better than one with added words any day. But if you find that your "ode" is less than fourteen lines, maybe the ode is not the right form for that particular subject.
- Your title does not have to have "ode" anywhere in it. Simply naming the subject in the title may be enough.

Posse Pointer

It may seem counterproductive, but consider both the good and the bad of your subject. Erin was honest enough to see her passion for what it was, and Debbie decided to toss away any thought of what others would think of her admission of her love of karaoke. Truthfully, the things we love the most are always full of good and bad.

For Further Reading

As is sometimes the case with older, more established, accepted forms of poetry, finding examples written by women is often difficult. To be sure, women were writing, but societal demands and expectations relegated these poems to becoming lost gems, as women were rarely published. In the ode's case, it is particularly challenging because it is a form that is just now finding its way back into modern favor. So please read the classics—if you don't know what they are, simply Google "ode," "ode examples," or "classic ode poetry"—for examples and inspiration.

Sappho is called by many the first woman poet. An ancient Greek lyric poet, much of her work has been lost, and what remains is fragmentary. Her one surviving complete poem is an ode: "Hymn (or Ode) to Aphrodite." Yet her reputation has persisted. Not only is she mentioned and revered by poets and writers from ancient times to the present day—she even has a place in pop culture. Wonder Woman often exclaims, "Suffering Sappho!"

Here are a few other examples of odes written by modern women poets. (Most are in free verse.)

- "The Paper Nautilus" by Marianne Moore
- "Australia 1970" by Judith Wright
- "Perhaps the World Ends Here" by Joy Harjo
- "Ode on Periods" by Bernadette Mayer
- "Ode to Jacob Lawrence" by Freda Denis Cooper

What Should I Write About?

Daphine de Maurier once said, "Happiness is not a possession to be prized, it is a quality of thought, a state of mind." The ode can bring about such a state of mind, because, to find a subject, you must mentally sort through what brings you joy. What should you write about? Whatever brings you joy—any shade, size, or sampling of joy. The ode's possibilities are as wide as your view of the world.

Historically, the ode was used to commemorate a significant event—whether to the poet or on a larger scale to her community or country—or to mark a development in the writer's philosophical growth, or to compliment rulers and warriors. Its tone was serious and dignified. As it is difficult to maintain such innocent, devouring adoration today—what, after all, stands up unwavering and untainted in the face of such praise?—modern poetry has allowed the ode to evolve and embrace our modern times.

It is now acceptable—and advisable, in order to reap the mental benefits an ode offers—to write about anything that evokes passion. Whether adoring your son, the first orange leaf to fall on fall's first perfect day, summer's unrelenting moments of heat, or the most beautiful black cashmere turtleneck ever to grace the tables of Nordstrom, anything is fair game in an ode. The only stipulation is that it is something *you* feel passionate about; the ode is a *purely* subjective poem.

There are some who might not think that red boots are an appropriate subject for a poem at all—that to write such a thing does nothing to enlighten readers or improve the world. In response to that, I'll borrow Kris's words: "Lighten up!" *I* maintain that if I write something that makes me happy—be it about brown wool socks on a cold winter night or the joy of an afternoon all to myself—that such happiness will spill over into my family, my life, and (with even more writing) into the world. The world can't be happy and good without happy and good individuals.

I am not trivializing the ode; I simply believe that for something to permeate and affect one's life it has to apply to all the areas of that life. Thus I use the ode to chronicle and detail what I like: and sometimes that deals with small, (seemingly) light and fluffy material. Yet to me that is just another way of making poetry relevant and applicable to life as we live it. It's a way that poetry allows me to add to my joy, as well as allowing my joy to add to me.

Jen chose to write about her favorite time of year: the holidays, a time that always brings her joy. However, like many a married couple, she and her husband only get to spend every other Christmas with her side of the family. As Jen says, "Christmas is my most favorite time of the year, and it's the only time that we're really all together as a family. Nothing beats being at home for Christmas with everyone that I love." While she enjoys her time with the in-laws, there's simply nothing quite like being around your own family for Christmas. She decided to write about that every other year just as Christmas was around the corner.

ODE TO WALLACE FAMILY CHRISTMAS

Coordinating flights
Kisses at baggage claim
Family together
If only once a year.

White lights on the perfect tree
Streaming ribbons, cascading bows
Childrens ornaments peek through
The envy of Martha Stewart.

Baking cookies for Santa
Searching for hidden presents
Giggling until morning
Trying to hear jingle bells.

Mom's homemade hot chocolate
Pecan pralines, pumpkin pie
Marshmallow sweet potatoes
Cranberry ham and turkey.

Stockings full of treasures
Presents under the tree
Waiting anxiously
All is Christmas PJs.

Sleeping until noon
No meetings to keep
Feeling like a kid
Only for one week.

Return trips to the airport
Memories to last the year
Back to busy schedules
Until the next Wallace Christmas.

—Jen

Jen thought that the best thing about writing this poem was taking "a trip down memory lane—it really made me stop and think about what I remember about Christmas and what means the most to me." Jen chose these unique Christmas times because they are so special to her, but there were many other ode subjects that came to mind after starting this one. She thought to write about fall (her favorite season) or the three boys in her life (her husband and her two sons). Writing this one ode opened up her mind to all the other things that bring her joy.

I was in Michelle's office one day, trying to give her ideas of what she could write an ode about. We were talking about the different things we like. I said, "You know what I really like? When my favorite song comes on the radio." It's true. And it's not the same when playing a CD or iPod, because hearing the song then is a *choice*. Hearing my favorite song on the radio is pure and simple luck. And it purely and simply makes me happy every time it happens. For those three minutes and twenty-two seconds, life is perfect.

ODE TO MY FAVORITE SONG ON THE RADIO

It's proof that luck exists, that minutes matter,
one unexplainable yet tangible incredible instance
when my favorite song comes on the radio

Lovers stay and liars go, with grace in the latter—
not treason nor reason can disrupt memory's melody
when my favorite song comes on the radio

I can have what I want, without conscience's chatter:
never why don't try; it's sex on a picnic table in a surprise
*   spring rain*
when my favorite song comes on the radio

The world moves at the right speed, even when it's still;
the spills and chills of that one summer sunburn tingle
when my favorite song comes on the radio

The attractive man in the Mercedes can't get his fill:
my loud so proud silent voice, a pretty face in sunglasses cruelly
*   cool*
when my favorite song comes on the radio

Exits missed, direction lost, and destination reduced to nil
it's here. no fear. the shedding of clothes never involves bother-
    some buttons
when my favorite song comes on the radio

—Wendy

An ode doesn't have to be about something grand and life-altering; often the little things—the simple pleasures of life—are the most satisfying . . . *and* the easiest to forget if we don't write about them.

What Michelle did write about was her grandmother. "Actually," she says, "I didn't start out to write about Grandma. I was writing about a lake, but, as I was writing, I realized it was more about family and friends getting together there. And it never fails: when we all get together, someone always brings up a funny story about grandma." Though she was "mortified" to try her hand at the ode, it was easier than she thought, especially when she realized it didn't have to be "long, rhyming, and, frankly, boring" (as the odes in her seventh-grade English class were) and could be about anything she wanted.

Because her grandma is no longer with her, writing the poem was, as Michelle says, "bittersweet." Yet she appreciated the excuse to sit down and write a tribute to her, something she wouldn't have thought to do before. "I think it is a good exercise; it made me think about all the great times I had with my grandma. And it made me thankful for the family I have."

ODE TO GRANDMA WANDA

Jet black hair, small in stature but big in heart.
White button down shirt, pressed blue jeans and sparkling white
* tennis shoes.*
Mischievous laugh and just a bit ornery.
Winston cigarettes lit off the stove, sometimes you singed your
* hair.*
Iced tea so sweet you should have been from the south.
A pot of coffee always strong and always on, in case someone
* should stop by and they often did.*
Bath times feared by all your grandchildren.
Attempts to scrub off tans that were mistaken for dirt, heads
* attacked with soap and water, please don't repeat.*
Afterwards we practically glowed.
Oh how you worried about all of us.
Wagging your crooked finger while lecturing us on possible doom
* or bodily harm.*
Oh how we teased you about both of those very things.
And as kids walking to the pond in search of the perfect rock.
As adults sitting around your kitchen table talking and laughing.
It would be hard to pick which was the best time.
There became a time when you mostly did not know us.
I hope you never forgot how much we loved you.
I hope you know how much we miss you.

—Michelle

An ode works well to write about people. It is less strict than the sestina and encourages you to remember all the great things about, and great times with, that person. And you don't have to wait until they're gone, either!

Of course, sometimes what brings us joy is not always the best thing for us, and sometimes what we are most passionate about can reveal priorities that are a little out of whack.

Erin chose to write about a passion that almost destroyed her. As she says, "My ode is about a three (or so) year love affair with chardonnay. Chardonnay seemed so safe. I relied on it to relax me, give me confidence, make things more fun, etc. I started drinking more and more and found myself spending a lot of time thinking about Chardonnay and when I could have some. I knew I had a problem for a long time but was not ready to stop. I finally did quit but it was not an easy choice. Even though I know I cannot have a drink again, I still feel a sense of melancholy when I see a beautiful bottle or glass of Chardonnay."

Why would Erin choose something so negative to write such an uplifting poem about? She's been sober for a year, so this ode isn't just to Chardonnay, but also a tribute to her sobriety.

ODE TO CHARDONNAY

My friend, how I've missed you,
Your color, your sweetness—
When the world was dark
You were my party dress.

My soul exhaled
When your grace touched my lips
I was warmed and sedated
From my toes to my tips.

Like a desperate lover
I grew clingy and weak
How soon could I get to you?
It's your compassion I'd seek.

Still you stood by me
As my secrets came out
You were the only one left
On whom I could count.

But even you grew bored
With the indulging, my friend—
You left me despairing
Or did I fail you in the end?

—Erin

"This poem," Erin says, "really helped me get out some feelings about my drinking. It's not something I talk about to many people—most people I know probably don't know I no longer drink. It was good to be open and honest about how deep my feelings about drinking were." Erin considered writing about other, lighter things—an ode to sharpies, an ode to her pregnant belly, or an ode to scrapbooking—but nothing seemed to flow. "I think it's because I was not feeling the passion about those topics," she says. "The drinking issue is in the forefront of my mind because it's the holidays and because I just completed an entire year sober." It was the poem she had to write at that time.

It was ultimately uplifting. She says, "Honestly, this is one of the poems I have written that has made me feel stronger and more powerful just by writing the words down." Passions change. This poem reminds Erin that she is now in control of hers.

Whether writing about fun times, family times, your favorite blue sweater, karaoke, Diet Coke, or all-consuming passions, the ode can help you celebrate what makes you happy, help you remember what makes you happy, and also help you reinforce the power you have over your own happiness.

Tips on Subject
- Acknowledge what makes you happy, and write about it—even if it seems silly and unimportant. If it makes you feel good, it couldn't be more important.
- It must be something you feel strongly about. Though an ode can be any length, the traditionally longer length springs from the intensity of the writer's feelings.
- An ode is a poem that could benefit from space. It is okay if you don't have time to sit down and get out everything you want to say about your subject at once. Because the meter and rhyme of the stanzas can differ, a diverging perspective won't challenge your form. Writing a little bit here and there might also help you get across how you feel about the subject more honestly because each day brings new thoughts and feelings.
- Keep in mind that it isn't the "form" that makes a poem an ode, but rather your subject and the way you write about it.
- Remember that this is *your* poem; odes are supposed to be purely subjective.

Give It a Try
An ode is one of the most enjoyable types of poetry to write. It's all about what makes you happy. "One of the secrets of a happy life is continuous small treats," said Iris Murdoch. An ode is a

small treat you can give yourself at any time. It can be as satisfying and indulgent as your favorite truffle as you consider, contemplate, dwell upon, and, therefore, place significance and importance to what it is that adds a spring to your step.

- Write an ode to yourself. Go ahead; celebrate yourself; get so full of yourself that it overflows on the page. Indulge in conceit; bathe in attitude; drip with confidence.
- Write an ode to your favorite season or holiday. Remember to write about what you like about it—not what is common or universal about it.
- What is the most indulgent thing you would do if you had the next hour all to yourself and no monetary limit? Use that as your ode subject.

Writing an ode can turn out to be much more challenging than you might think, because it is often difficult for us to give ourselves permission to block out all the things we should fix, work on, and change, instead concentrating on the things that we like *as is*. But you should—it's worth it. What makes you happy deserves the time you spend saying so. The more time you spend on it, the more happiness you find around you. You will probably start to see the possibilities for odes all around you. The great thing is that even if you don't feel particularly happy—even if you're faking it a little—it's a self-fulfilling prophecy: you are guaranteed to be a little happier when you've finished.

A Poetic Pause: Where to Find Inspiration?

In the beginning of your new poetic life, it may still be challenging to find inspiration to write. Life gets so busy with unpoetical things (Debbie is probably one of the gifted few who can find something to write about a dirty diaper). Writing poetry begins to feel too hard—shutting off what is happening is too strenuous, and then we get so caught up in the world as it's moving that it's downright impossible to slow down. That's okay, because you don't need endless time for contemplation, or any other kind of life than your own, to write poetry. This process is about you getting the most of out the life that you are living, not about you getting a new life. Here are a few places the Posse and I find inspiration for things to write about.

My purse. It was the basis for my list poem, but I often come across a receipt, a card, or some other memento I stashed away absentmindedly that will spark a poem. I recently found my concert stub for the Rolling Stones. I'm not sure whether there's a sestina or an ode there, but I'm working on it.

My closet. It may seem like I like clothes, but (while that is true) what I really like is the creativity I can express just by getting dressed. I like the opportunity to be myself and wear something most would not have thought of. Sometimes a favorite sweater or an old, forgotten pair of jeans will bring back a memory or evoke a feeling that only a poem can express.

The view from my back window. Nature inspires me. I wish I could spend the winter months in Vail and the summer months in the Bahamas, but that's just not the way it is. However, just outside my back window I can see it all: snow-covered trees in winter; budding tulips in spring; the epic adventures a boy can find in summer with only a slide, a tunnel, and a sprinkler; and changing, falling leaves in autumn.

Erin finds inspiration from the people in her life—most often her family. A subject for a poem, as she says, "has to be something I have strong feelings about." She doesn't have to look any further than her home: "It seems that I have found inspiration from my relationships—mainly with my husband and son," she says.

A stay-at-home mom, Heather is inspired by whatever is going on in her home that day. It was another way to be able to look at each day as a fresh experience—or, rather, a new poem waiting to be written. Her "ordinary, everyday life" quite easily turned into list poems and letter poems.

Kellie says, "I am inspired by events which have occurred in my life. I am also influenced by my family and our relationships with one another. I often use poetry as a means of expressing myself and capturing moments I want to remember." Whether it is the death of a loved one or a dream unfulfilled, Kellie's inspirations are drawn from her life as it happens. She also uses poetry as a means of communication. "Sometimes it is easier for me to write a poem rather than to make a phone call," Kellie admits.

Thelma doesn't look any further than her own mind for topics and inspiration. A lifetime of memories has given her a lifetime of potential poems. The best thing about using memories is that they are an endless, always replenished supply of inspiration.

Admittedly, it takes time and commitment to write a poem. But it doesn't take surroundings, people, or experiences other than those you already have.

About the Author

Wendy Nyemaster is a writer and editor living in Merriam, Kansas. On her best days, she is also a poet. She is a graduate of the University of Oklahoma. In her spare time, she enjoys home improvement projects, shoe shopping, watching college football, and playing board games. She lives with her husband Jon and her son Trenton.